THE EUROPEAN UNION SERIES

General Editors: Neill Nugent, William E. Paterson

The European Union series provides an authoritative library on the European Union, ranging from general introductory texts to definitive assessments of key institutions and actors, issues, policies and policy processes, and the role of member states.

Books in the series are written by leading scholars in their fields and reflect the most up-to-date research and debate. Particular attention is paid to accessibility and clear presentation for a wide audience of students, practitioners and interested general readers.

The series editors are **Neill Nugent**, Professor of Politics and Jean Monnet Professor of European Integration, Manchester Metropolitan University, and **William E. Paterson**, Honorary Professor in German and European Studies, University of Aston. Their co-editor until his death in July 1999, **Vincent Wright**, was a Fellow of Nuffield College, Oxford University.

Feedback on the series and book proposals are always welcome and should be sent to Steven Kennedy, Palgrave Macmillan, Houndmills, Basingstoke, Hampshire RG21 6XS, UK, or by e-mail to s.kennedy@palgrave.com

---

General textbooks

Published

Desmond Dinan **Encyclopedia of the European Union**
[Rights: Europe only]

Desmond Dinan **Europe Recast: A History of European Union**
[Rights: Europe only]

Desmond Dinan **Ever Closer Union: An Introduction to European Integration** (4th edn)
[Rights: Europe only]

Mette Eilstrup Sangiovanni (ed.) **Debates on European Integration: A Reader**

Simon Hix **The Political System of the European Union** (2nd edn)

Paul Magnette **What Is the European Union? Nature and Prospects**

John McCormick **Understanding the European Union: A Concise Introduction** (4th edn)

Brent F. Nelsen and Alexander Stubb **The European Union: Readings on the Theory and Practice of European Integration** (3rd edn)
[Rights: Europe only]

Neill Nugent (ed.) **European Union Enlargement**

Neill Nugent **The Government and Politics of the European Union** (7th edn)

John Peterson and Elizabeth Bomberg **Decision-Making In the European Union**

Ben Rosamond **Theories of European Integration**

Esther Versluis, Mendeltje van Keulen and Paul Stephenson **Analyzing the European Union Policy Process**

Forthcoming

Laurie Buonanno and Neill Nugent **Policies and Policy Processes of the European Union**

Dirk Leuffen, Berthold Rittberger and Frank Schimmelfennig **Differentiated Integration**

Sabine Saurugger **Theoretical Approaches to European Integration**

Also planned

The Political Economy of European Integration

Series Standing Order (outside North America only)
ISBN 0–333–71695–7 hardback
ISBN 0–333–69352–3 paperback
Full details from www.palgrave.com

Visit Palgrave Macmillan's
EU Resource area at
www.palgrave.com/politics/eu/

D0223626

The major institutions and actors

Published

Renaud Dehousse **The European Court of justice**

Justin Greenwood **Interest Representation in the European Union** (2nd edn)

Fiona Hayes-Renshaw and Helen Wallace **The Council of Ministers** (2nd edn)

Simon Hix and Christopher Lord **Political Parties in the European Union**

David Judge and David Earnshaw **The European Parliament** (2nd edn)

Neill Nugent **The European Commission**

Anne Stevens with Handley Stevens **Brussels Bureaucrats? The Administration of the European Union**

Forthcoming

Wolfgang Wessels **The European Council**

The main areas of policy

Published

Michelle Chang **Monetary Integration In the European Union**

Michelle Cini and Lee McGowan **Competition Policy In the European Union** (2nd edn)

Wyn Grant **The Common Agricultural Policy**

Sieglinde Gstöhl and Dirk de Bièvre **The Trade Policy of the European Union**

Martin Holland **The European Union and the Third World**

Johanna Kantola **Gender and the European Union**

Jolyon Howorth **Security and Defence Policy in the European Union**

Stephan Keukeleire and Jennifer MacNaughtan **The Foreign Policy of the European Union**

Brigid Laffan **The Finances of the European Union**

Malcolm Levitt and Christopher Lord **The Political Economy of Monetary Union**

Janne Haaland Matláry **Energy Policy in the European Union**

John McCormick **Environmental Policy In the European Union**

John Peterson and Margaret Sharp **Technology Policy In the European Union**

Handley Stevens **Transport Policy in the European Union**

Forthcoming

Karen M. Anderson **Social Policy In the European Union**

Hans Bruyninckx and Tom Deireux **Environmental Policy and Politics in the European Union**

Jörg Monar **Justice and Home Affairs In the European Union**

Also planned

Political Union

The External Policies of the European Union

The External Economic Relations of the European Union

The member states and the Union

Published

Carlos Closa and Paul Heywood **Spain and the European Union**

Alain Guyomarch, Howard Machin and Ella Ritchie **France in the European Union**

Brigid Laffan and Jane O'Mahoney **Ireland and the European Union**

Forthcoming

Simon Bulmer and William E. Paterson **Germany and the European Union**

Brigid Laffan **The European Union and Its Member States**

Baldur Thórhallsson **Small States in the European Union**

Also planned

Britain and the European Union

Issues

Published

Derek Beach **The Dynamics of European Integration: Why and When EU Institutions Matter**

Thomas Christiansen and Christine Reh **Constitutionalizing the European Union**

Robert Ladrech **Europeanization and National Politics**

Cécile Leconte **Understanding Euroscepticism**

Steven McGuire and Michael Smith **The European Union and the United States**

Forthcoming

Andrew Geddes and Christina Boswell **Migration and Mobility in the European Union**

Wyn Rees **EU/US Security Relations**

Analyzing the European Union Policy Process

Esther Versluis
Mendeltje van Keulen
and
Paul Stephenson

First published 2011 by
PALGRAVE MACMILLAN

Palgrave Macmillan in the UK is an imprint of Macmillan Publishers Limited,
registered in England, company number 785998, of Houndmills, Basingstoke,
Hampshire RG21 6XS.

Palgrave Macmillan in the US is a division of St Martin's Press LLC,
175 Fifth Avenue, New York, NY 10010.

Palgrave Macmillan is the global academic imprint of the above companies
and has companies and representatives throughout the world.

Palgrave® and Macmillan® are registered trademarks in the United States,
the United Kingdom, Europe and other countries.

ISBN 978–0–230–24599–0   hardback
ISBN 978–0–230–24600–3   paperback

This book is printed on paper suitable for recycling and made from fully
managed and sustained forest sources. Logging, pulping and manufacturing
processes are expected to conform to the environmental regulations of the
country of origin.

A catalogue record for this book is available from the British Library.

A catalog record for this book is available from the Library of Congress.

10 9 8 7 6 5 4 3 2 1
20 19 18 17 16 15 14 13 12 11

Printed and bound in Great Britain by
CPI Antony Rowe, Chippenham and Eastbourne

Contents

List of Boxes, Tables and Figures

Boxes

Tables

Figures

List of Abbreviations

BSE	Bovine Spongiform Encephalopathy (commonly known as mad-cow disease)
CAP	Common Agricultural Policy
CoR	Committee of the Regions
COREPER	Committee of Permanent Representatives
CSDP	Common Security and Defence Policy
CFSP	Common Foreign and Security Policy
DG	Directorate General
DG SANCO	Directorate General Health and Consumer Protection
ECA	European Court of Auditors
ECB	European Central Bank
ECJ	European Court of Justice
EESC	European Economic and Social Committee
EMS	European Monetary System
EMU	Economic and Monetary Union
ENISA	European Network and Information Security Agency
ENVI	Parliamentary Committee for the Environment
EP	European Parliament
EU	European Union
GDP	Gross Domestic Product
IGC	Intergovernmental Conference
IMF	International Monetary Fund
IR	International Relations
JHA	Justice and Home Affairs
MEP	Member of the European Parliament
NATO	North Atlantic Treaty Organization
NGO	Non-Governmental Organization
OECD	Organisation for Economic Co-operation and Development
OMC	Open Method of Coordination
QMV	Qualified Majority Voting
TFEU	Treaty on the Functioning of the European Union
UK	United Kingdom
UN	United Nations
UNHCR	United Nations High Commissioner for Refugees
US	United States
VAT	Value Added Tax

| WHO | World Health Organization |
| WTO | World Trade Organization |

Acknowledgements

The authors are very happy that this book is finally seeing the light of day. The idea behind it stemmed from discussions about teaching that we had in 2006 when we realized that we simply didn't have the right book for teaching European public policy and policy analysis within our bachelor and masters programmes. While there are many books out there on EU politics and institutions, we were unable to find the right one for our students that could both convey the dynamic nature of the European policy process, and offer the kind of practical insights that would enable students to conduct their own analyses of how and why European legislation comes about. There are also some excellent titles on public policy and policy analysis available, but these works are not tailored to the EU. We hope that *Analyzing the EU Policy Process* will fill this gap, not just for us, but for EU studies scholars and students everywhere.

We would like to thank many of our colleagues who have supported us in this project, beginning with all our colleagues in the Politics Department at the Faculty of Arts and Social Sciences of Maastricht University who have expressed their support and encouragement. We would also like to thank all colleagues who taught the second-year undergraduate course *Policy Domains – Analyzing the European Policy Process* in November/December 2009 – and the students who acted as guinea pigs – when we effectively piloted a draft version of the book. We are grateful to the tutors, but especially to Tessa Fox for her great job at course coordination while Esther was away on maternity leave. A debt of gratitude is also due to our cohort of about 250 students, who provided a great deal of individual feedback on an earlier draft of the book, both in class and through their evaluations of the course.

Looking back to the earlier stages of the project, we would like to thank Klaartje Peters for all her ideas and positive contributions to the book, particularly in Chapter 1, and remembering our brainstorming session very early on, at a café in Utrecht rail station. We are grateful to Sebastiaan Princen for contributing a chapter on agenda-setting and for his input during our earlier discussions. We are extremely lucky to have such an engaging and well-written chapter for the book.

During the writing process we were encouraged and assisted by colleagues and external academics who provided their own knowledge and policy-specific insights. Thanks to Patrick Bijsmans, Hylke

Dijkstra, Josine Polak, Karolina Pomorska and Jost-Henrik Morgenstern at Maastricht, Ana Juncos Garcia at Bristol University and Anne-Marie Penn Rodt at Exeter University for help with questions on foreign policy and external action. We are grateful to our former masters students Andreas Nordang Uhre and Charles Borkowski for allowing us to reflect on their own research experiences in Chapter 4.

At the later stages of the project we would like to thank our student assistant, Johan Rotomski, for help with the references, and Tod Hartman for extensive final editing and proof-reading. The Faculty of Arts and Social Sciences was kind enough to provide financial support to pay for these activities. Any content or typographical errors remain our own.

Finally, we would like to thank our publisher, Steven Kennedy, for his constant support, encouragement and meticulous reading and 'fine-toothcombing' of our various drafts, and the conversations about the project we had in person with him in Brussels, Potsdam, and Los Angeles. Thanks are due as well to Neill Nugent, the Series Editor, for his belief in our proposal and the complementary value of this title in the European Union Series. We are very grateful to our anonymous peer reviewers at the early and later stages of the project who provided valuable reflections on how to strengthen the content and usefulness of the book.

We hope that *Analyzing the EU Policy Process* will prove to be a useful textbook for students and scholars of the EU, and we certainly welcome feedback and criticism of the content and approach to policy analysis in the European Union.

ESTHER VERSLUIS
MENDELTJE VAN KEULEN
PAUL STEPHENSON

Notes on the Contributors

Mendeltje van Keulen is parliamentary EU adviser to the Netherlands House of Representatives. She regularly lectures and publishes on European Union politics and policy making in Brussels and the member states. Her publications include *Going Europe or Going Dutch. How the Dutch government shapes European Policy* (2006) as well as several EU articles and book chapters about the EU.

Sebastiaan Princen is Associate Professor at Utrecht University's School of Governance. His research focuses on issues of European and international policy making and the impact of the EU on its member states. Recent publications include *Agenda-Setting in the European Union* (2009) and *The New Eurocrats. National Civil Servants in EU Policy-Making* (co-authored with Karin Geuijen, Paul 't Hart and Kutsal Yesilkagit, 2008).

Paul Stephenson is Assistant Professor in European Studies at the Faculty of Arts and Social Sciences at Maastricht University, and Director of Studies of the MA European Studies. His research interests include Cohesion Policy and Structural Funds, the European Commission, national parliamentary EU committees, and the EU policy process – particularly as it concerns implementation and evaluation. He has published in the *Journal of Common Market Studies*, the *Journal of European Public Policy*, and *South European Society and Politics*.

Esther Versluis is Assistant Professor in European Studies at the Faculty of Arts and Social Sciences at Maastricht University, and Director of Studies of the Masters in European Public Affairs. Her research focuses on questions related to European regulatory governance, and she specializes in the implementation of European regulations on the national level, and the related role of EU agencies. She has published in *West European Politics*, the *Journal of European Public Policy*, and the *Journal of Health Politics, Policy and Law*.

Introduction

Analyzing the EU

The European Union (EU) is fundamentally different from other organizations that produce public policy. While debates about what kind of organization the EU is and what it should be could go on forever, the larger impression that the outside observers are often left with is of an entity that is remote and vague, its procedures unclear, or impossibly intricate. But at the same time, the scope and impact of EU policies are nothing if not concrete. Many different layers of government – local, regional, national, supra- and international – are involved in the organization of these policies, as are many different types of organizations representing interests ranging from animal welfare to pharmaceuticals, from defence materials to school books. In short, there is a potentially endless list of actors and interests that one might potentially take into consideration when conducting EU policy analysis, and the involvement of such interests differs from one policy area to another. Naturally, this intricacy of the EU raises many questions. How does this amalgam of member states and institutions work? How are issues formulated and phrased in a way that is relevant to policy analysis? How effective is the influence of lobbyists, multinationals or national parliaments? What explains the EU's action – or even, its failure to act – in foreign policy? And how can policies designed in Brussels be effective on the streets of Helsinki or Valetta?

Over the past few decades, the rich tradition of public policy analysis has produced piles of authoritative texts about how to conduct policy analysis and how to study public policy processes within and between governments at different levels. However, none of these text or handbooks about policy analysis concentrates specifically on the policy process of the European Union – that is, the interplay between member states, EU institutions and organized interests in the day-to-day shaping of common laws and policies. Yet this is a process that is central to the blossoming field of European integration studies. Of course, there are also a wealth of serious academic and practical textbooks, handbooks and teaching guides focusing on how the EU functions, why it functions as it does and how one can study and theorize about the EU. There are texts focusing on any one of the EU's particular institutions (such as the Commission, the Parliament, the Council,

1

member states), legal and political textbooks on policy processes and instruments, and books covering particular policy fields such as agriculture, structural funds or external policy, just as there are books presenting an overview of all of these features of the EU and their interaction.

What this book concentrates on, however, is how one can actually *analyze* the EU's policy process and the agenda-setting, formulation, decision-making, implementation and evaluation of its policies: How to analyze and understand how an issue reaches the agenda, how a proposal is formulated, why a particular decision is taken, how the resulting legislation is implemented, and how it is evaluated. EU policy analysis is all about understanding the 'whys and wherefores' of EU activity – or non-activity, as the case may be – in specific areas over time. How do we account for stagnation and progress, advance or decline, success and failure, decision and non-decision, integration and disintegration? And what are the tools with which we can effectively research, detect and analyze these phenomena?

The aim of this book is to:

• discuss the analysis of EU policy-making in relation to its institutional environment with the object of presenting a clear understanding of the actors involved;
• introduce the European policy process as a series of stages with different actors, instruments, procedures and interactions involved, suggesting a series of different questions that arise as the result of analyzing those stages;
• provide certain key issues for consideration when designing, structuring, fine-tuning and carrying out studies of a range of contrasting types of EU policy.

The philosophy behind the book

There are as many types of policy analysis as there are analysts. They work as students in universities, but also professionally as researchers, lawmakers, consultants or lobbyists in both the private and public sector, in education, civil service, business, law, media and market research. The ways in which each of them engages in policy analysis is largely determined by their personal or professional objective. First, policy analysts *aim* for different purposes with their research. It could be meant to educate, theorize, scrutinize, hold accountable or inform. The policy analysis undertaken may, for example, be a compulsory exercise financed by a consultancy firm that has won a publically tendered European Commission contract, ultimately meant to inform and give a verdict on existing policy which should be improved and refined. Policy analysis may also be a voluntary exercise conducted by a student or researcher with an intellectual interest in an area of EU policy. Secondly, the *results* of the analysis differ as a function of the analyst's identity. It follows that in some cases data collection, analysis and findings will have a commercial value. In other cases, the outcome will primarily serve as teaching or research purposes. Certain policy analysts will publish their findings openly to a wide audience – such as in an academic peer-reviewed journal. Others can produce confidential or in-house reports destined for policy makers or business strategists. Thirdly, the *value* of policy analysis will also differ. In some cases the ultimate goal will be to produce recommendations on appropriate action for the near future. In other cases policy analysis will simply be an attempt to better understand or explain the recent past.

The research trajectory of the policy researcher largely determines the perspective and, hence, the approach to the analysis. Some may proceed through a public policy lens, others through one based around comparative politics. But each analyst will bring the tools (theories, methodologies, concepts, sources for data collection) that they have acquired with them. There is no escaping the fact that all of these things are subjective and contribute to the exercise of policy analysis – indeed, as the German sociologist Max Weber famously remarked, there can be no true objectivity in the social sciences. How one approaches EU policy analysis is shaped *inter alia* by beliefs, ideas, familiarity and personal experience. Individual perceptions about what the EU is about – its rationale, purpose, direction and ultimate goals – will indelibly colour one's research findings. And as we know, the EU has no end goal, but is in itself a project in the making.

This book aims to help give the reader the research tools and analytical insight to access the 'real story' behind all the different levels of the EU policy-making process. With this in mind, we start from a critical modernist perspective on policy-making. That is, we take reality as socially constructed. Of course, not all constructions have equal claim to credulity: 'some constructions prove more durable than others' (Pollitt and Bouckaert, 2000, p.23). A policy analyst operates like an archaeologist, a physicist, a forensic scientist, or detective, piecing together clues and reconstructing evidence. Like forensics reconstructing a crime scene, analyzing the EU policy process is all about building a picture of how things happened as they did and why. By systematically structuring the analysis, with the help of concepts, theories and time-lines, one can discover if one's hypotheses, instincts, educated guesses, reasoned supposition or hunches are indeed sustained by the evidence.

With this in mind, we see policy theories primarily as *tools* for structuring research and guiding, framing or interpreting empirical data. Theories can help the analyst to stand back from the empirical data of the case and place it in the context of larger, more significant trends, or to translate it into generic terms or concepts. Theories thus offer the *framework* and *tool kit* for sorting and directing information and data, just as they can help in the interpretation and analysis of data. They offer concepts that help one to understand a given case's relevance to the wider study of politics and policy-making. Finally, theories can help to describe the phenomena witnessed in a particular academic or professional *terminology*, thereby offering a common vocabulary that can be applied to any case.

Just as the science of policy analysis has not developed a dominant theoretical tradition, there is no such thing as one single, all-encompassing EU policy theory. Due to the complexity and wide variety of processes within the EU, theoretical approaches to the EU policy process are always attempts to capture particular 'parts of the beast': stages of decision making, the behaviour of actors within the policy cycle or to explain results. Each of the five policy stages identified in Part II of this book (agenda setting, policy shaping, decision making, implementation and evaluation) is theoretically tackled from different approaches. Each chapter contains a separate section on theory, mapping out a selection of traditions and approaches to researching this particular stage of the policy cycle. We refer to certain seminal works on EU integration and its theories, and present key assumptions and perspectives underlying the analysis of actors and interactions as they relate to the particular policy landscape in question.

The framework of the book

We assume that the reader of this book is already familiar with the basics of what kind of organization the EU is. He or she knows about the structure of the EU, composed of the member states and the triad of EU institutions (European Commission, Council of Ministers and European Parliament) and their basic role in the EU policy process. The chapters offer insights into the interplay of these leading actors in each stage of the policy process. Reading suggestions and web links provided at the end of each chapter help orient the reader within the larger context of the particular issue, and provide suggestions for further exploration.

The book is divided into two parts. Part I examines *what* policy analysis in the EU is (Chapter 1), *why* researchers embark upon policy analysis (Chapter 2), *who* to look at (Chapter 3), and the means by *which* to go about it (Chapter 4). In Part II, Chapters 5 to 9 cover the five stages of the policy process. During agenda setting, policy shaping, decision making, implementation and evaluation, different groups of people and organizations are at play. Analyzing these different stages

Box I.1   Introducting the Tobacco Advertising Directive

The so-called Tobacco Advertising Directive (2003/33/EC) of the European Parliament and of the Council on the approximation of the laws, regulations and administrative provisions of the member states relating to the advertising and sponsorship of tobacco products was adopted in 2003. The directive bans the advertising of tobacco products in printed media, on the radio and over the internet. It also prohibits tobacco sponsorship of cross-border events such as Formula One races. It only applies to advertising with a cross-border dimension; local advertisement such as billboards or in cinemas does not fall under the directive.

The final directive marks the end of almost 20 years of cumbersome policy-making struggle, involving intensive political pressure, industry lobbies and media campaigns, as well as an annulled first version of the directive. The origins of the directive lie in the 1970s, when advertising bans were considered key to curbing smoking. For a long time, the tobacco industry successfully lobbied against these harmonization initiatives by the European Commission, but the issue regained strength in the 1990s, as concerns about public health came to the fore. The initial Commission proposal for the ban, championed by interventionist member states such as Italy and France, was opposed by more liberally oriented member states (particularly Germany, which appealed for the annulment of the first version of the directive). Successive drafts were legally challenged by member states, who argued that tobacco advertising was not a cross-border activity and as such should not be subject to internal market regulation. When opposing member states held the Presidency, the issue was momentarily stalled. But finally, domestic political change in the UK and the Netherlands, traditionally opposing the ban, opened a window of opportunity. Throughout the entire 'tobacco policy process', negotiations in the Council and within the European Parliament were characterized by fierce lobbying, public outcries and strategic voting.

Highlights in the tobacco policy process:

1991   First Commission proposal
1997   Agreement in the Council of Ministers after years of deadlock
1998   Adoption of Directive 1998/43
2000   Annulment of Directive 1998/43 by the ECJ after appeal by Germany
2001   New Commission proposal (based on guidelines ECJ)
2003   Adoption Directive 2003/33

The chapters in Part II will further explain how this issue ended up on the agenda, how the directive was formulated, what characterized the final decision making, how it has been implemented, and the role the Court of Justice played in evaluating the directive.

requires different tools and different sources. It is important to realize from the outset, though, that the policy cycle approach does not prescribe an ideal way to go about policy making. Nor does it imply that policy would be always shaped according to linear or chronological sequences. Doing policy analysis requires the realization that policy making, as all human activity, is often incremental and intuitive, passing back and forth between different venues and different stages.

Each chapter in Part II of the book offers a practical insight into real EU policy cases. We return throughout the entire book to one particular case: the so-called Tobacco Advertising Directive (see Box I.1). In addition, each chapter analyzes at least two other (always different) cases of EU policy making. Overall, this allows the reader insight into a wide variety of EU policy cases and policy instruments, suggesting ways for framing the set-up of one's own research design.

The chapters

Chapter 1 introduces the concept of 'policy' as a deliberate course of (in-)action, selected from available alternatives, in order to achieve certain preferred policy outcomes. Our analysis zooms in on events in the life-cycle of a given policy piece using the *stages approach*. The chapter also deals with the use of theory in structuring research.

Chapter 2 addresses the *institutional structure* of EU policy making, including financial and advisory bodies, which can be a particularly useful source of information in policy analysis. Here, we discuss the formal and informal interaction between EU institutions, member states and different organized interests. For each of the actors involved, relevant questions for policy research are identified.

Chapter 3 introduces the different types of *policy instruments* and *policy fields* within the EU. It categorizes the main regulatory instruments of the EU, identifying various different types of policy, be they deregulatory or re-regulatory, or softer instruments such as benchmarks and open coordination. Also presented is an overview of the policy fields to be analyzed, an important concern given that the actors and procedures involved are nothing if not a function of the type of policy in question – and in this sense they will determines to a large extent the type of questions to be asked by the observer carrying out policy analysis.

Chapter 4 provides insight into *how to analyze* EU policies. It reviews questions about scale and scope that one might be confronted with when embarking upon a research methodology in EU policy analysis, as well as providing a number of sample questions of possible relevance in the course of such research. It presents examples of methodology and theories potentially to be used in EU policy analysis.

After introducing the theory and methodology of doing EU policy analysis, Part II introduces the stages of the policy process in more detail. Chapter 5 reviews the main issues in policy analysis at the level of *agenda setting*. The political agenda determines what issues will be subjected to decision making, as well as the terms in which an issue will be framed. How an issue reaches the EU agenda can determine to a large extent which actors are involved and in which institutional forums decisions are taken.

Chapter 6 discusses the stage of *policy shaping* dominated by civil servants working for member state governments or European institutions. Private industry lobbyists, NGOs, universities and think tanks have an important role in shaping new EU policies. The chapter reviews the process in which agenda items are developed, drafted and re-formulated into draft-legislative texts and policy proposals for the decision makers to decide on. The instruments and strategies of different groups of policy shapers, civil servants, *fonctionnaires* and lobbyists are also discussed, as well as questions for framing research focused on this stage of the policy cycle.

Chapter 7 is about EU *decision making*: the hammering out of legislative texts by ministers and members of the European Parliament, and the subsequent processes of fine-tuning and re-negotiating that takes place in technical committees, known as 'comitology'. The chapter reviews the actors and institutions involved in EU decision making, the political and legal relevance of the legal basis of policies, as well as the potential use of expert and academic literature to get a grip on the intricacies of EU decision making.

Chapter 8 provides an overview of the *implementation* of EU policy. Traditionally, there has been more interest in the stages of policy formulation than in questions of how policy is implemented or how it has fared in action (evaluation). This, however, presents a paradox: why bother making policy when it is not actually put into effect? The practice of dealing with EU policies differs considerably across member states, but it is telling to note that many policies are not implemented at all, a fact which raises important questions about the effectiveness, legitimacy and credibility of the EU. The chapter concludes by identifying the main pitfalls of implementation research, and by providing some pointers for how to go about it.

Chapter 9 gives insight into how to conduct policy *evaluation* or impact studies. Because it is difficult to measure success and failure, policy evaluation can be a highly contentious field – and therefore one that is of particular interest to the analyst. The chapter reviews the different actors involved in the political, administrative and legal evaluation of EU policies, the instruments that they use, and the evaluation techniques and methodology, with a special focus on the question of *monitoring* and *learning*. The chapter also presents some potential ways into analyzing policy evaluation, as well as how to go about using different research techniques.

The book concludes with analyzing the constantly changing policy environment in which EU policy comes into being, and discusses the distinctiveness of the EU policy process. It evaluates the usefulness of the policy cycle and its stages and provides suggestions for how else we could visualize the EU policy process.

Part I

Theory and Methodology in EU Policy Analysis

Chapter 1

Doing EU Policy Analysis

This chapter starts with an introduction to what policy and policy analysis actually constitute. What is policy analysis, and how do we go about it? We start by addressing the question of who might be interested in analyzing policy and why one would want to carry out such an analysis in the first place. From there, we move on to a discussion of how one might use the policy-stages approach as a tool for policy analysis. We examine the use of theory in policy analysis, highlighting ways in which theory might be useful in structuring a research agenda.

What is policy?

Defining policy

'Policy' is a word or concept that is commonly bandied about and used with relative ease. Yet on closer inspection it is in fact a fairly difficult term to define with any measure of exactitude. As a former top British civil servant remarked in 1963, 'Policy is rather like the elephant – you recognize it when you see it but cannot easily define it', (Hill, 2009, p. 15). This confusion may stem to some extent from the fact that in many European languages there is no clear distinction between the words 'policy' and 'politics'. In German, for example, the word *Politik* is used for both. Likewise, in French, Italian or Spanish, the word policy does not translate easily.

There are as many definitions of the word policy as there are authors writing about the topic. Policy, in our understanding at least, refers to *a deliberate course of (in-)action selected from among available alternatives to achieve a certain outcome.* Let's identify the main elements of this definition. First of all, policy refers to a *course of action*, that is, to 'something 'bigger' than particular decisions, but 'smaller' than general social movements' (Heclo, 1972, p. 84). In other words, policy is more than a single rule or law. Policy can also refer to *in*action, such as the decision to stick with the status quo – for example, by not increasing taxes. At the same time, policy is usually meant to address a certain problem and therefore *to achieve a certain outcome*. The reference to a *deliberate* course of action also refers to 'purposiveness' of some sort. This is perhaps more a reference to what policy ought to be,

11

or is expected to be, rather than to what it often ends up being in practice. In real life, beyond the text books, policy may be largely symbolic or based on 'irrational' or 'emotional' grounds. EU policy, like national policy, is often initiated in response to high-profile incidents, such as the 1996 joint action on the sexual exploitation of children (*Official Journal of the European Union*, L 322, 12.12.1996), which was inspired by the media frenzy and public outcry after the arrest of Belgian kidnapper Marc Dutroux. A more recent example of allegedly 'symbolic' EU decision making is the much-debated title of *Constitution* that was given to the 2004 EU treaty revision. This particular wording caused much public debate and ultimately led to drawn-out ratification procedures in many countries, including public rejection via referenda in France and the Netherlands. Finally, in most policy areas choices must be made. There is usually the *availability of alternatives* but policy makers will not necessarily take up all the available alternatives because of the restrictions they encounter in terms of financial, personnel or informational resources, or because of historical, social, or institutional contexts.

Defining public policy

What, then, is 'public policy'? Generally speaking, the term 'public' is used to describe policy making *by governments*. Probably the simplest definition of public policy is the one by Dye (1972, p.2): 'Anything a government chooses to do or not to do'. While pretty straightforward, this definition might be considered too simple. As Howlett and Ramesh (2003, p.5) state, this could lead to the impression that any activity by governments could be described as public policy, including the purchase of paper clips. What we consider to be public policy in modern societies is closely linked to the societal perception of 'governmental functions' and the areas in which governmental regulation or intervention is justified – where there is a common assumption that the state should act, and therefore where it can carve out for itself a legitimate political remit. Obviously, this perception is prone to change: functions that we might perceive as governmental nowadays differs considerably from those that we might identify as such in the early nineteenth century, when government was considered best when it did least and the term 'public' referred to a 'space which did not involve the interference in economic and business activities' (Parsons, 1995, p.5). Across the party political spectrum, many right-leaning conservative politicians still favour minimalist state intervention, contrary to left-leaning opponents, who in recent years, following increases in government regulation impacting upon matters previously regulated by the individual, have been accused by some of operating a 'nanny state'. Even five years ago many would have frowned upon state regulation ('interference') in the financial markets, ultimately believing that the markets should be left to their own devices. But in the current financial climate, in the wake of the sub-prime mortgage crisis, the crash of the property markets and the drastic fall in share values, a general belief is emerging that the state should act as watchdog, policeman, caretaker, and so forth.

In the EU, the question of what we consider to be public policy is even more urgent than at the national level, particularly given the limits of an individual state to be able to tackle global issues such as terrorism, climate change, pollution, migration and so on. The EU has a particular hybrid character inbetween an international organization and a nation-state, which makes the discussion about its functions and competencies highly dynamic and intense. Over the decades, the 'tasks' of the EU have changed with successive treaty revisions from merely economic (for example coal and steel integration) to communitarian involvement in other policy domains – for example occupational safety and health, the environment and migration. The limits of the EU's functions are regulated according to a number of principles. Important in this respect is the principle of 'subsidiarity', introduced in the Maastricht Treaty, which determines that the EU should only undertake those tasks that cannot be performed effectively at a more local level. Subsidiarity is a much-debated concept and any analysis focusing on EU policies should therefore take notice of the relevant (perspectives on the) distribution of competencies between the national and the EU level.

Another principle to be taken into account in EU policy studies is that of the legal base within the Treaty upon which each EU policy rests – each new EU law must have a legal article as its foundation. The choice of the legal base determines the procedure and powers of the actors involved. This makes the decision by the Commission, in particular, as initiator of proposals, of 'which road to go down' highly debatable. In this sense, analyzing European policy should pay attention to the formal and informal rationale of governmental action at the EU level, which ultimately often largely determines the course (and success or failure) of the policy process.

Policy versus politics

In order to understand the meaning of policy, it is also necessary to differentiate the notion from 'politics' – even though in some languages this distinction does not exist. Politics refers to the process, by which a group of people determine 'who gets what, when and how' (Lasswell, 1935). Politics thus refers to the wider process in which policies are being created. The distinction is further clarified by Birkland (2005, pp. 4–5): 'The study of *politics* is the attempt to explain the various ways in which power is exercised in the everyday world and how that power is used to give resources and benefits to some people and groups, while sometimes imposing costs and burdens on other people and groups. The study of *public policy* is about examining the creation, by the government, of the rules, laws, goals, and standards that determine what government does or does not do to create resources, benefits, costs, and burdens.'

In the context of the European Union, the following example explains this differentiation between policy and politics. The REACH regulation (1907/2006), which regulates the registration, evaluation and authorization of chemicals, is an example of an individual *decision*. This decision – combined with all activities, action plans and instruments in the field of, amongst others, climate change, waste management, air pollution, biodiversity and water protection – constitutes the EU's environmental *policy*. The process by which the European Commission, European Parliament and Council of Ministers are influenced by interested parties (such as environmental NGOs, industry, consumer organizations, and so forth) is labelled *politics*. However, it is political debates that often determine how and when policy is shaped and decided. Any analysis of European policy should therefore take these political processes into account. Now that we have an idea of what is meant by 'policy', the question arises as to what exactly 'policy analysis' entails.

What is policy analysis?

The above-mentioned explanation of the difference between 'policy' and 'politics' is relevant when attempting to explain what 'policy analysis' is. Policy analysis is a multidisciplinary science, even if Bardach claims it 'is more art than science. It draws on intuition as much as method' (2005, p.xiv). Doing policy analysis is a very practical and pragmatic enterprise. Because conducting policy analysis entails uncovering real-world policy problems, using a multidisciplinary approach is necessary as '[r]eal-world problems come in complex bundles that are political, social, economic, administrative, legal, ethical, and more' (Dunn, 2004, p.3). According to Dunn (2004, pp.1–2), policy analysis is 'a problem-solving discipline that draws on theories, methods, and substantive findings of the behavioral and social sciences, social professions, and social and political philosophy. ... [P]olicy analysis is a process of multidisciplinary inquiry designed to create, critically assess, and communicate information that is useful in understanding and improving policies.'

This categorization very clearly illustrates that policy analysis embodies two main aims: to *understand* and to *improve* policies. These two aims can be summarized under two broad categories of 'policy analysis': the analysis 'for' policy (practical, focused on *improving* policies) versus the analysis 'of' policy (academic, focused on *understanding* policies and how they emerged).

Analysis 'for' policy

The more practical analysis 'for' policy departs from the main underlying desire to improve the way public policies work. If every policy had the effect it was designed to have, we would not need policy science (public policy studies). But more often than not, the effects of public policies are not what we expected, and improving public policy is the major incentive for policy analysis in this first category. Generally, this type of analysis is conducted by actors who are in one way or another involved with governments. Some of them work directly for a government, or are closely linked to it, representing a consultancy firm, think-tank or a research institute. Others are involved with parties that are affected by the policies of the government, such as schools, churches, labour unions, and so on. Both groups of actors have an interest in the way policies work, and in the outcomes of the process. The type of policy analysis conducted by this group thus tends to be rather 'prescriptive' in character: defining what went wrong, and what direction should ideally be followed. Policy analysis by such actors is functionally oriented and meant to contribute to improving future policy. By identifying what went well and what did not, policy analysis can lead to recommendations for use by public policy actors, for example when refining existing policy or considering alternative approaches to tackling an issue.

Analysis 'of' policy

The second community of policy analysts, that which conducts the more academic analysis 'of' policy, may have no direct interest in the policies themselves and may be more distanced from the policy practice being studied. Their focus is academic, rather than practical. They are concerned not so much with designing better policies, but rather on improving our understanding of the way policies work – or don't work, as the case may be. The research outcomes of this type of policy analysis are thus less prescriptive, but more 'descriptive', 'analytical' and 'explanatory'. The main aim is to come to grips with understanding 'how Brussels works' and to understand how policy is made in the European Union. In this regard the political scientist may be ultimately interested in the bigger questions linked to the policy-making process such as the implications of the way in which policy is made for the polity's own legitimacy, accountability, transparency, and ultimately, for democracy. The type of policy analysis conducted by this group has, in general, three main research objectives: studies of policy content (aimed at understanding the genesis and development of particular policies), studies of policy output (aimed at understanding variation, for example, in levels of expenditure of service provisions over time or between countries or regimes), and studies of the policy process (aimed at understanding how decisions are made) (Hill, 2009). Academic analysis does not occur in isolation, however. Although it is primary an intellectual exercise that often sees the application of theory to empirical data, its outcomes often inform the policy-making community. The work of academics, public policy actors and practitioners in the area of policy analysis can easily be mutually reinforcing. Individuals come together within *epistemic communities* (knowledge-based networks of professionals with expertise in a given area, often with policy-relevant expertise) and may pursue varied interests, engaging in academic research and teaching, as well as forming research consortia (pluralistic networks of university researchers and private consultants), which bid to win tender contracts to undertake policy analysis (particularly on evaluation). These contracts may be academically-oriented – for example, the 7th Framework Program, or the Marie Curie scheme – or they may be projects specific to individual Directorate-Generals of the European Commission. Programming runs on seven year cycles – 2000–6, 2007–13 – and much policy analysis research will be contracted out before each period begins or after it ends.

Returning to Bardach's claim that policy analysis draws on intuition as much as on method, it is worth remarking that it is extremely difficult to make a sharp differentiation between analysis 'of' and 'for' policy. It may be reasonably argued that all social science suffers to some extent – and can never escape – distortion of research results due to the subjective interpretation of the researcher. It is questionable to what extent analysis 'of' policy – the attempt to objectively describe – can take place without the researcher also embarking upon an analysis 'for' policy – in other words, without the researcher having a view on what 'ought' to happen. Some therefore claim that an objective analysis 'of' policy cannot exist: 'the view that social science is a matter of cumulative accretion of knowledge through the work of the human subject neutrally observing the action and interaction of the objects – letting the facts speak for themselves – is untenable' (Farmer, 1995, p.18).

In this book, we follow the position that Pollitt and Bouckaert describe as 'critical modernist'. They claim that '[r]eality is socially constructed, but not all constructions have equal claim to our credulity and certainly some constructions prove more durable than others' (2000, p.23). In other words, while we should never attempt to come to totally objective descriptions of the policy process as we can never uncover a single 'truth', we can attempt to reconstruct what has happened as objectively as possible. Crucially, good policy analysis rests on testing as much empirical evidence as possible and applying a theory or model that is internally clear and consistent. In this sense, one should be able to distinguish between descriptions and explanations that are more likely and plausible than others.

Who does policy analysis?

We have already discussed the different needs and approaches of real-world political analysts as compared to academic researchers. But we can also distinguish between different types of researchers analyzing the process. *Who* they are and *which discipline* they come from will hugely influence *how* they approach EU analysis and, in particular, *how* they use theory to choose between different sets of literature.

Political scientists who study the European Union tend to concentrate on the 'political factory' and the study of political relationships. In other words, they are particularly interested in questions related to the functioning of the EU as a political system, and they try to understand how the different actors involved function and interact with each other. On the other hand, public policy scholars are, as a rule, much more interested in the processes of decision making and the outputs or products that emerge from this political factory.

First, *political science theorists* are largely concerned with analyzing the policy process to gather real-life cases that help support the validity of their preferred theory, to help refine it as an explanatory tool for ordering, sorting and explaining the chaos of policy making. Second, *political science empiricists*, whether they come from the field of international relations or comparative politics, may be most interested in the 'isms' (see Table 1.2), conceptual frames, which account for the role of institutions and elites as agents in the process, and on the way in which the EU policy-making system and its structures determine outcomes. They may seek to interpret policy making through various lenses related to gender, class, business, networks, interests, power, norms, historical precedent, procedures, culture, and so on. There may be a large social and anthropological aspect to their analysis. Third, those from *public policy and administration*, while also focused on institutions, may investigate the way public (state) policy is developed, perhaps looking at the role of bureaucracies and committees, the use of information and expertise, the 'life' (behaviour, control and drift) of administrations and policy making as a process. They may favour theories and concepts related to the policy-making stages, such as those explored in Part II of this book.

What exactly do policy analysts analyze?

Let's go back to the definition of policy and to the example of EU environmental policy that was mentioned earlier. EU environmental policy constitutes a wide range of activities, action plans and instruments in the fields of climate change, air pollution, biodiversity, and so on. How do we analyze the environmental policy of the European Union for example? What is the 'deliberate course of (in-) action selected from among available alternatives to achieve a certain outcome' in this case, and is it actually possible to analyze such a course of action?

Try to imagine the thousands of people and millions of pages of information and data that come to be involved in and make up this policy. At the end of the day it seems almost impossible to study every policy intervention (decisions, programmes, projects, partnerships) within the framework of European environmental policy. *Where to start?* Doing policy analysis involves the attempt to find ways to cope with this. First of all, policy analysis is often about reconstructing and analyzing individual (or a few) policy instruments or decisions, and therefore policy process studies are often case studies using qualitative methods. Another way of dealing with this complexity is to disaggregate the process of policy making into different steps or stages, and to focus mainly on one stage. In this book, the stages analogy is used to dissect the process into steps, as will be introduced in the next section.

Academic scholars, when engaging in policy analysis, set about identifying key questions they wish to answer. They are usually intrigued by a problem, tension or perceived failure. In reality, they might start with a very open-ended, all-encompassing question such as, 'How might one explain...?', a question which in fact embraces all five question words (*how, why, who, what, when*) in some way. This question may be about why something happened or not. It may be about how one got from point A to point B. It might be about a change between two moments in time. As their research develops, and as they delve into the policy area, it may be that one question in particular becomes more fascinating, puzzling, mysterious, confusing or urgent. This might then form the basis of the guiding research question at that particular stage, at least while they embark on initial research – digging deeper may mean that the research question needs to be modified, especially if they 'strike gold', as it were, and uncover precious original documents or sources that can help explain the *how? why?* and *who?* Ultimately, doing policy analysis is not simply describing what happened, but analyzing and *understanding the reasons why.* Some questions may be solved relatively easily after a relatively superficial level of research. Other questions may demand drawn-out and detailed analysis that requires the collection, sorting and analysis of data or the close scrutiny of documents over lengthy periods. Some questions may even remain unanswered. It is important to bear in mind that within political science or the humanities more generally, any answer is merely a well-constructed and convincing argument that attempts to solve a question. No answers are set in stone – they cannot be found, only constructed as part of the process of research and analysis. Conducting policy analysis entails becoming aware of this relativity of the social – and hence political – reality. The essential is about building a convincing case or argument.

The policy process: 'stages' as an approach to analyzing policy

Why look at policy as a process?

Analyzing policy starts with conceiving of policy as following its own particular life cycle, thus with a beginning, middle and possibly end. Policy does not just appear one day out of thin air – although governments are sometimes forced into rapid decision making almost overnight in response to an external shock or crisis situation. Most often, however, policy evolves over time. Kingdon (2003), in this respect, refers to policy *emergence* (issues being secured on or climbing up the agenda to induce action) resulting from a process in which policy, problem and political streams converge. We might thus conceive of policy as an output in itself, the product of various inputs: political pressure (including lobbying), financial resources, the mobilization of various stakeholders (actors with vested interests) and information and knowledge (scientific data, media stories, lies). And then of course there is time – a key ingredient to baking any 'policy cake'. It is not simply enough to mix together the ingredients; only time allows it to rise sufficiently (Schneider, 1991).

Policy analysis is not an easy task. One will often be struck by what seems to be a puzzle or conundrum. In a sense, the policy analyst is like a biographer, trying to research the most important events in a policy's lifetime. One needs to attempt to understand and explain what factors lead to the experience of policy (the *who, when, how, why* and *what* behind its arrival, operation and possible departure). Questions such as the following are key:

- What was the rationale behind the policy under study? (Who was pushing and when for which problems to be addressed?)
- How did the policy develop over time? (Was the process smooth or bumpy? Did it happen quickly or slowly? Was there resistance or consensus?)
- How can the actual outcome or achievements be evaluated from the perspective of the study (Why has this policy been successful when for 50 years nothing happened? Was it implemented properly? Did it secure the desired results? Should it continue and, if so, in what form?)

Why conceive of stages?

By systematically structuring the analysis one can assert if hypotheses, instincts, educated guesses, reasoned supposition or merely hunch are sustained by the evidence found. In order to structure the analysis, it is important to narrow down the focus of the research as much as possible. One way is to zoom in on a specific course of events in the life cycle of the policy. A common and very useful approach is the stages approach, or the policy cycle, as shown in Figure 1.1.

At each stage of the policy cycle, there are different constellations of actors at play. Although some may be more involved at a certain stage, it is rare for any actor's involvement to be confined to a single stage as most stakeholders will monitor and perhaps seek to influence policy throughout the stages. Likewise, each stage of the policy process requires different tools and sources. Possible questions to ask when doing policy analysis are listed in Table 1.1.

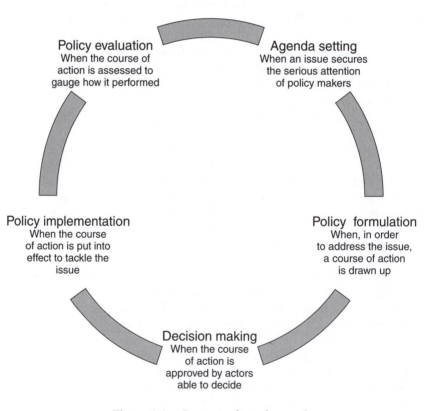

Policy evaluation
When the course of
action is assessed to
gauge how it performed

Agenda setting
When an issue secures
the serious attention
of policy makers

Policy implementation
When the course
of action is put into
effect to tackle the
issue

Policy formulation
When, in order
to address the issue,
a course of action
is drawn up

Decision making
When the course
of action is
approved by actors
able to decide

Figure 1.1   *Stages in the policy cycle*

Table 1.1   *Possible questions related to the various stages in the policy cycle*

	Who?	*When?*	*Why?*	*What?*	*How?*
Agenda setting	Who was pushing for the issue to be taken up by the Commission?	When did the issue get high up on the political agenda?	Why did politicians finally take the issue seriously?	What event or incident saw renewed commitment to the issue?	How to explain why the issue was previously ignored?
Shaping	Who was consulted in drawing up the new campaign?	How significant was the timing of the campaign?	Why was it difficult to gather relevant data?	What did the campaign hope to achieve?	How did the campaign seek to benefit all target groups?
Decision	Who needed most convincing to vote in favour? Who was most resistant?	Over what time period was/were the decision(s) taken?	Why did the Parliament and Council fail to agree?	What factors impeded the ability of the Commission to secure its desired outcome?	How was the decision taken? Was it straight-forward or complicated?
Implementation	Who transposed the directive properly?	Did they implement the directive on time?	Why did they not implement the directive at all?	What factors proved costly when implementing?	How were the challenges to implementation overcome?
Evaluation	Who are the winners and losers of the issue?	When will the lasting impacts be felt?	Why was the issue so badly received?	What is the benefit of the issue in terms of cost savings?	How successful has this issue been so far?

The advantages and disadvantages of the stages approach

Hogwood and Gunn (1984) recognize both the advantages (opportunities) and disadvantages (limitations or constraints) of the stages approach. A first advantage is that the framework breaks down policy making into a series of consecutive 'time-action capsules'. The stages approach to policy analysis suggests a linear and rational process, with one stage following on naturally from another. It suggests that there may be a specific moment in time when the policy life cycle moves from one stage to another, rather than a drawn-out transition period. It also suggests a forward trajectory or continuous logic of action in a direction that ultimately favours practical, tangible, visible, human intervention. In other words, there is an evolution from ideas in the mind, to words on paper, to action on the ground and finally reflection on what to do now and where to go next. It favours a 'continuous film approach', as opposed to the sort of representation implied in static photos of isolated moments in time. The framework allows one to look forwards or backwards from a specific moment in the policy cycle, and to situate a decision within a horizontal continuum of events. Second, the framework favours focusing on interactions between stakeholders and organizations in the policy sub-system over what is often a lengthy period of time, in which the degree of individual actor involvement may increase and decrease, and the configuration of actor groups evolve, as different interests come and go. Third, the framework offers a simple way to try to systemize existing knowledge by assuming a roughly chronological series of functional, goal-oriented stages in which multiple actors perform multiple tasks in hot pursuit of their interests, and in accordance with (though not beyond) their own capability to act. How they can act and the degree of pressure that they are able to exert may be determined explicitly by the legal, institutional and political construct of the policy-making system but also implicitly understood as flowing from the given 'rules of the game' that must be respected. In short, by breaking down a complex process into mini-processes the task of analysis is more manageable.

There are potential disadvantages, however, to the use of the stages approach. One should not assume from the framework that it pre-scribes an ideal way to go about policy making. It merely presumes a probable order of likely actions; it does not stipulate how long each one should last. Second, because of this one cannot predict the experi-ence of policy making at future stages in the cycle, even if a retrospec-tive analysis of agenda setting and decision making may be able to offer clues as to what one might expect to occur during implementa-tion. Third, the stages analogy may wrongly suggest that policy always proceeds in the neat order of the successive stages. Just as there is no precise beginning or end (or at least ones that are possible to pinpoint), there is no exact moment that policy-making activity switches from one stage to another. Stages may overlap with several activities occur-ring concurrently by different actors: a mid-term programme evalua-tion may take place during programme (policy) implementation; a series of policy decisions between EU institutions may alter the formu-lation and content of policy; policy formulation may often precede agenda setting as 'solutions seeks problems' to which they can be applied (Kingdon, 2003; Salamon and Lund 1989, in Howlett and Ramesh, 2003, p.14). In short, the process is not completely linear –

the stages can 'go back upon themselves'. It assumes that episodes of policy activity are self-contained and neat, even though in reality the process is often disjointed, a 'seamless web involving a bewildering mesh of interactions and ramifications' (Hogwood and Gunn, 1984, p.26). From this perspective, it may be more useful to think of 'aspects' of policy making, rather than 'stages'. Fourth, the use of a stages approach may lead one to over-rationalize in any explanation of past acts, based on an expectation of 'what comes next' or what should have been (based on historical examples). Fifth, it is unclear if the stages approach applies to all levels of analysis. Does all multilevel government and pluralistic stakeholder activity actually adhere to such a view of the world, or does it only apply to certain EU institutions, interest groups and bureaucracies? Much government activity is about administration in which the momentum of policy design or implementation is simply upheld without significant decisions. Finally, the policy cycle does not tell us *why*. That is, in itself it offers no indication of the reason for which policy moves from one stage to the next, or why the process speeds up or stalls. Towards the end of the cycle, policy may be re-steered to make it more responsive to the external environment – the policy landscape and challenges that policy must address will have often have altered considerably from the time when the first policy seeds were sown back at the agenda-setting stage. At any stage of the process, external events may also modify the relative importance or urgency of policy.

Given these criticisms, alternatives to the stages approach have been developed. For example, some scholars advocate paying more attention to the relationships between actors, policy styles across institutions and member states, or to the legal basis of policy-making procedures and institutions' decision-making powers (Gersick, 1991; Howlett and Ramesh, 2003, pp.16–17). This might lead to a better hypothesization about what has occurred, based on a more nuanced insight into the variables at play, but at the same time obviously complicating the analysis. However, the unique selling point of the policy-stages approach is that it offers a versatile framework. As long as it is used as a guiding tool, rather than a set of fool-proof mirrors believed to reflect perfect reality, it can act as a doorway into 'Policy Wonderland', replete with a circus of actors, interactions and procedures (and the exertion of vested interests) all performing over time.

Even with the help of stages, theories, models and concepts, any balanced analysis of the past is ultimately limited in what it can achieve. The past can never be perfectly reconstructed and even if reconstruction were possible, we would never be able to recognize it. The past is in the past and few will have realized precisely what was occurring even as it did so in what was then the present. There is only well-founded argument, built on retrospective analysis, which is itself coloured by one's own (ultimately biased) perspective in which one necessarily focuses on certain variables at the expense of others. In this sense, theory is a perspective or 'lens' to look at the process to be reconstructed. The next section goes into the role of policy theories in policy analysis.

Using theory in policy analysis

What is theory?

Theory is an integral and inescapable part of policy analysis. Students of the EU policy process often regard theories as scary, abstract and therefore potentially dull and complex – to be avoided wherever possible. Theory need not be intimidating, although it should not be used simply for the sake of doing so: invoking theory is not necessarily a guarantee of appearing serious and academic. Our emphasis on the relevance of theories as a fundamental prerequisite for any study should not be taken as an instance of academic self-indulgence. Theory can empower and strengthen. First, it provides distance, allowing one to stand well back from the empirical data of the case and place it in the context of larger, more significant trends or generic terms. Second, it allows for order by offering a framework or tool kit for sorting and directing data, which then facilitates interpretation and analysis. Third, theory can help one grasp what is going on by equipping one with concepts to help understand a case's relevance to the wider study of politics and policy making. Finally, it helps by bringing in specific language or terminology, a sort of common vocabulary that can be applied to help explain the phenomena at play, regardless of the complexity and technicalities of policy content.

   A theory is essentially a set of propositions about the way a phenomenon in real life can be explained or predicted. For example, rival theories have been formulated in order to *explain* why the European countries, at war with each other for many centuries, managed to form such a strong and successful partnership during the second part of the twentieth century. Other theories serve to *predict* the further course of this process, for instance by focusing on the potential of the European Union to act as a global 'super-power' (Leonard, 2005). Theories serve as a lens or focus to channel our observations. The type of lens we use determines the way we look at the empirical reality, and can explain why certain events are highlighted and magnified or why certain actors are ignored. For example, from an 'intergovernmentalist' perspective, one is more likely to see the courageous decisions of national politicians as the driving force behind the integration process, and to downplay the impact of the supranational actors that keep the integration process going.

Even if they are not altogether aware of it, researchers usually work with a theory from the outset of their research. Often the choice of that theory is determined by common sense and personal experience. For example, an individual who has grown up in a part of the world where political leaders and political parties tend to solve their disputes with violence instead of through cooperation and compromise might be more inclined to consider European integration as an extraordinary phenomenon. Compare such a perspective to that of a young European citizen who takes the EU for granted or considers it normal simply because it has always been there in his or her lifetime.

Making use of theories in policy analysis should thus not be regarded as a mere academic obligation, straightjacket or handcuff. Relating the analysis to existing theories can serve as a useful tool to bring order into the study and can be helpful in identifying and formulating central propositions. These hypotheses are essentially expectations about how things have proceeded or how they can be explained, the factors that are relevant and the causal relations between them. These prior assumptions may, for instance, include a hunch about the degree of rationality in the behaviour of key actors, or the extent to which key actors pursue their self-interest in the policy process. Another such perspective may focus on the extent to which the government of a member state is characterized by bureaucratic rivalry and its ability to act as a unitary actor in the EU arena. Theories may also facilitate the necessary step to operationalize central concepts of the analysis and to design a pathway to follow through in terms of one's own analysis – what is generally referred to as a methodological design.

Mapping the field of EU policy theory

In this book, when discussing theory, the focus is on those scientific approaches that are relevant for studying the EU policy process. When reviewing the '*acquis académique*' of EU policy studies, it is important to keep in mind that its roots lie both in international relations (IR) theory, and in the study of the nation-state. The focus of the first wave of European integration studies was on the grand 'why' questions: why integration, and why now? From the 1950s, the two main schools of 'neofunctionalism' and 'intergovernmentalism' constructed contrasting narratives and scenarios about the potential of cooperation between the member states of the then-European community (Haas, 1958; Hoffmann, 1966). (See Table 1.2.) The debate between the two theories was revived in the 1990s, as various authors further elaborated, differentiated, and investigated how processes of preference formation were relevant to the ways in which governments behaved at the EU level, and how the role of supranational institutions were important to understanding EU policy (Moravcsik, 1999; Sandholz and Stone

Table 1.2 *Grand theory in EU integration*

Theory	Focus of enquiry How . . . ?	Key concepts	Key proponents
Neofunctionalism Supranationalism	*How* common policy advances through the persistence/effort/ control of supranational actors	spillover (functional, political, cultivated); incremental change	Haas, 1958; Lindberg, 1963
Inter-governmentalism/ liberal intergovernmentalism	*How* the integration process is controlled by member states and decisions made at their will (opposed to above)	gate-keeping; two-level games; snapshot moments; key events	Hoffmann, 1966; Moravcsik, 1993

Sweet, 1998). However, these studies remained largely focused on the singular moments of change and crisis: the so-called 'history-making decisions', such as treaty changes and major policy turns, instead of going into the process of shaping and setting concrete European legislation and policies on a day-to-day basis (Peterson and Bomberg, 1999). Since the late 1970s, with the widening of the process of European cooperation, the domain of EU studies has grown. Academics from the political sciences and its various sub-disciplines, such as comparative politics, policy studies and public administration, became more interested in the emerging polity at the European level and the interactions between the member states and the EU. The 'theoretical new Europe' (Rosamond, 2000) further developed with successive treaty changes, which refined the balance of power between the different actors and interests in the EU policy cycle.

Although the study of European integration in many ways originated as a branch of International Relations (IR) theory, it is now approached from other disciplines such as public policy. But there are distinct and different trends *within* EU studies as well. After decades of trying to explain *what* exactly was occurring in the integration process from 1951, in the latter half of the 1980s scholars became more concerned with understanding *how* the increasingly complex policy-making system works in reality. In many ways this work continues, but lately one has seen more focus on why particular institutions matter as well as outlooks that address relationships of power, influence and interest in driving the process.

Given the observation that many studies of the way the EU formulates policies originated in the context of the study of the nation-state, it is not surprising that EU policy studies are dominated by a large residue of 'national' notions and theoretical approaches. In particular, political science and public administration studies have provided the key concepts, frameworks of analysis and tools by which the process of EU policy making on a day-to-day basis is now analyzed from an academic point of view. For example, theories on agenda setting in the European Union and the question of why some issues become prominent and are eventually translated into concrete policies, while some never are, originate in analyses of the US federal administration. The 'stages approach' as introduced in the section above developed as a framework for national policy studies, but it happened also to prove useful as a model and conceptual tool for studying the EU policy process.

Another example of concepts central to political science and applied in many EU policy studies are those of power and influence. This is not surprising, seeing as much public attention paid to how the EU works concerns the question of how power is distributed between the EU and the member states and which institutions (Council, Parliament or Commission) are influential in determining the course and outcomes of the policy process. Other academic debates centre around questions concerning the relevance of the particular institutional context in which policy is being made or the extent to which actor behaviour is driven by pre-determined will and preferences as opposed to forming during the process of social interaction with other players.

At the same time, the specificities of the EU context and actors make for a number of particularities which cannot be sufficiently described or explained using the tools of national policy analysis. The observation that what happens within the EU is not analogous to policy processes within its member states has resulted in a number of EU-specific theoretical 'schools', which direct attention to particular features of the EU policy process. One such distinct feature is the fact that EU policy making takes place at different levels: within the member states, in processes between the national and the EU level and within institutions at the EU level. The metaphor of 'multilevel governance' (see Table 1.3) has been developed in EU policy studies to describe the continuous interaction of governments, sub-national actors, EU institutions, private interests and other actors in the policy process (Marks, Hooghe and Blank, 1996). It was meant not as a theory as such but as a conceptual model for how the EU functions. It does not presume a given perspective which would highlight or downplay the role of certain factors over others in the integration process – by the 1990s

Table 1.3   *Multilevel governance and regulation*

Theory	Focus of enquiry How . . . ?	Key concepts	Key proponents
Multilevel governance	*How* the EU functions practically on a daily basis	nested government; territorial tiers; sub/supranational	Marks, Hooghe and Blank, 1996
Regulation	*How* the EU makes rules as any state-like entity would	regulatory state; harmonization	Majone, 1996

there had been 40 years of pontificating already, still trying to under-stand 'how did we get here?' by endlessly revisiting 'the story so far' in a historical context. Instead multi-level governance was more prag-matic and concerned with understanding the functional (institutional and decision-making) complexity of the EU as a *sui generis* political being by asking the fundamental: 'how does the EU actually work on a practical day-to-day basis?' Another such 'touchstone for theory' is the notion of Europeanization, which refers to the process of national adaptation to EU membership, for example by administrative coordi-nation procedures, implementation of EU policies. Many EU policy studies make use of these central concepts to order and steer their analysis of the shaping of new EU policies.

But we should also remember that theories and concepts abound in public policy and administration. They have developed independently of EU studies, often as a result of analyzing the US administration. As such, scholars of public policy have their own toolkits and conceptual frameworks for studying policy making. Indeed it is from these scholars that we get the 'stages' approach to analyzing policy processes (see Table 1.4).

One of the main challenges of this book is to reconcile the theoretical approaches to political science with those used in public policy and administration approaches in order to understand and research the EU policy process effectively. Both disciplines have much to offer and when used together can provide an enhanced theoretical and concep-tual toolkit,

On the use of theory in EU policy analysis

It follows from the preceding section that there is no such thing as a single, all-encompassing EU policy theory. As Birkland states, '[p]olicy

Table 1.4   *Theories from the 'stages approach' within public policy*

Theory	Focus of enquiry How . . . ?	Key concepts	Key proponents
Agenda setting	*How* problems become political issues and secure due attention or climb up the political agenda, how solutions search for problems	policy/politics/ political stream; windows of opportunity	Baumgartner and Jones, 1993; Kingdon, 2003
Policy shaping / decision making	*How* decisions are made or not made and the rules, procedures, and means of deciding	decision v. non-decision; rational v. incremental style	Peterson and Bomberg, 1999
Implementation	*How* legislation resulting from decisions is transposed (absorbed) and put into place politically and technically	top-down, bottom-up, instruments; principal-agent	Pressman and Wildavsky, 1973; Falkner *et al.*, 2005

studies, like many social sciences, are sometimes said to lag behind the natural sciences because we still have not developed what McCool calls a "dominant theoretical tradition", or what Thomas Kuhn would call a "paradigm"' (2005, p.12). We would like to take this one step further: due to the complexity and the wide variety of processes going on within the EU, theoretical approaches to EU policy process are always attempts to capture particular 'parts of the beast', such as stages of decision making or the behaviour of particular actors within the policy cycle. We claim it is impossible to present a common all-encompassing theory of the EU policy process. As each of the policy stages identified in this book (agenda setting, policy shaping, decision making, implementation and evaluation) is theoretically tackled from different approaches, each chapter here contains a separate section on theory. The theory sections in each of the chapters in Part II map the different traditions and the approaches to researching this particular stage of the policy cycle. In this manner, the reader is able to acquaint him or herself with the assumptions underlying the analysis of, and potential perspectives on, the key concepts, actors and relations in the policy landscape he or she will be considering.

Conclusion

This chapter has discussed the key concepts that will be highlighted in this book: policy, public policy, politics and policy analysis. It has introduced the notion of policy making as a cycle that can be conceived of as a number of stages, which, though they have a loosely temporal linear thread, do not follow precisely on from one another, as Part II suggests. Indeed, such stages may well overlap. It is preferable to consider the stages as 'centres of activity', with different types of activity re-emerging throughout the course of their application. It is difficult to identify a cycle with a clearly delineated beginning and end. Rather, policy analysis usually entails focusing on a precise piece of legislation or a bite-sized chunk of policy; it rarely takes on policy in its historical entirety. The following three chapters take a closer, more in-depth examination at what, who and how we analyze in the EU.

Suggestions for further reading

Dunn, W.N. (2008) *Public Policy Analysis. An Introduction*, 4th edn (New Jersey: Pearson).

Howlett, M., Ramesh, M. and Perl, A. (2009) *Studying Public Policy. Policy Cycles and Policy Subsystems*, 3rd edn (Oxford: Oxford University Press).

Wiener, A. and Diez, T. (2004) (eds) *European Integration Theory* (Oxford: Oxford University Press).

Chapter 2

Whom Do We Analyze?

Introduction

Whom do we analyze when we analyze the EU policy process? Conducting policy analysis is all about identifying the main actors who have a stake in the policy process at hand. What roles do those actors play? The lines of enquiry one might pursue with regard to the various actors involved in a given policy process are certainly a function of the particular approach and theoretical angle one chooses. That said, when analyzing policy we are in general less interested in the history and organization of the various actors involved and more intrigued by the role and behaviour of those actors in the aspect of the policy process we are examining. In order to concentrate on this latter question, one must first obtain some basic facts and figures regarding the actors concerned.

This book is aimed at readers who are already familiar with the basics of the different EU institutions and their place and role in the EU policy process. For anyone new to European politics, the overview of the main actors involved in the EU policy process presented here might be too short and schematic; reading suggestions are provided at the end of the chapter to enable you to update this knowledge where necessary. Conversely, for someone with a solid understanding of EU politics, this overview might appear simple and repetitive. For those familiar with the role and functions of EU institutions, but who might like a quick refresher, this chapter will be especially useful. But regardless of one's background, the aim here is to identify particular actors and how they are engaged in the EU policy process.

The institutional structure of the EU

In any political organization many actors are – either formally or informally – involved in (trying to influence) its policy-making process. The European Union is a particularly complicated political organization as it involves many different layers of government – from local to regional, national, supra- and international – as well as many different types of national, European or trans-European non-governmental organizations (NGOs) representing interests ranging from animal

31

welfare to pharmaceuticals. In this sense, the number of actors who might claim to have a say in a given policy process is enormous, and varies with regards to the type of process under consideration. For example, analyzing the genesis of EU monetary policy leads to a completely different list of relevant actors than, say, an analysis that evaluates the effectiveness of a particular EU mission in Kosovo.

The Treaty structure of the European Union under the latest treaty in place (the Lisbon Treaty, which will be referred to as the Treaty on the Functioning of the European Union – TFEU) influences the sort of actors who might be relevant to any analysis of a given policy process. Policies made under the 'ordinary' legislative procedure will require a different type of analysis in contrast to policies made under the 'special' legislative procedures. Doing policy analysis in the EU thus requires one to take into consideration the unique legal basis of the policy process under scrutiny.

The first part of this chapter provides a schematic overview of the main actors involved in the EU policy process (see Figure 2.1). Knowing the types of actors that potentially play a role in the EU policy process – and being able to understand the relations and interactions between those actors in the context of various decision-making modes, the topic of the second part of this chapter – is necessary for any policy analysis. One should note, however, that the list presented here is not exhaustive and that there will always be developments in

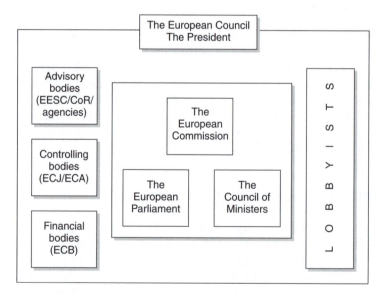

Figure 2.1   *A schematic overview of the main EU actors*

the EU policy machinery that will invoke other types of actors not identified here. In this sense, it is helpful to maintain an open-minded stance when conducting policy analysis. This chapter will not identify '*the* member states' as a separate category as, in our analysis, the member states are everywhere – one might say they are 'omnipresent'. With regards to each of the categories of actors set out below, member states play a particular, different role. In the European Commission, the member states play a role via their Commissioner (although he or she is expected to be neutral), just as in the European Parliament, the members are part of a political group, at the same time remaining nationals of their home countries. In other words, doing policy analysis is also about 'discovering' the national element in each policy process via the various actors concerned – and their knowledge, ideas, power and influence at stake.

The institutions

According to the Treaties there are seven official institutions in the European Union: the European Commission, the European Parliament, the Council of the European Union, the European Council, the European Court of Justice, the European Court of Auditors and the European Central Bank.

The European Commission

Despite its claim of independence and neutrality, the Commission is known to be highly politicized and considered to act as a powerful designer and manager of EU policy (Peterson, 2006). While it is described as having little influence over the 'history-making decisions', its power and influence in terms of day-to-day decisions is widely recognized. As we noted above, analyzing the role of actors and the Commission should go hand in hand with analyzing the specific policy field under scrutiny (see Chapter 3). The Commission's powers under competition policy (which are relatively strong) contrast with its relatively weak powers under common foreign and security policy.

In some policy fields, the Commission – particularly via some of its former Presidents – has managed to play an important role in agenda setting. Hallstein (1958–67), Jenkins (1977–81) and Delors (1985–95) are often recognized as strong Presidents who guided European integration. The ability of a Commission President to influence the process is linked to external circumstances such as national receptivity to European solutions and the wider international scenery (Ross, 1995). Jenkins, for example, is said to have had considerable influence on the development of the European Monetary System. Jacques Delors is

Table 2.1   *The European Commission*

Who	European Commission
When established	1952: High Authority 1958: European Commission
Core aim	A politically independent institution (at least in theory) that represents the interests of the EU as a whole (the 'voice of the common interest')
Actors	27 Commissioners (1 from each member state) and about 24,000 civil servants
Main functions	1 Proposing new legislation 2 Implementing EU policies and the budget 3 Enforcing EU law (the Commission is, together with the European Court of Justice, the guardian of the Treaties) 4 Representing the EU on the international stage

regarded as a policy entrepreneur largely responsible for securing member state political commitment to proceed with the single market programme. An important new role to take into consideration since the entering into force of the Lisbon Treaty is the High Representative of the Union for Foreign Affairs and Security Policy (in short: High Representative). This person, coordinating the EU's foreign policy, is also Vice President of the Commission. How and to what extent he/she will place a considerable stamp on the foreign affairs policy process very much depends on how this post will be used and developed by its holder (the British Catherine Ashton for the period 2009–14).

When analyzing the role of the Commission in the day-to-day EU policy process, we rarely turn to the President of the College of Commissioners. Practical policy work is prepared and executed by the civil servants working in the policy-specialized Directorates-General (DGs). Whereas commissioners come and go, the officials in the DGs tend to remain and in this sense are seen as a main 'repository of accumulated wisdom in the Commission', people who 'inevitably influence political choices' (Hooghe and Nugent, 2006, p.151). (Chapters 5 and 6 provide an account of how the officials influence the policy process.) Also not to be overlooked is the role of the Secretariat-General. An administrative body that supports the work of the Commission, it has also been regarded as an important policy shaper, promoting ideas about cohesion, justice and home affairs, asylum and foreign policies (Hooghe and Nugent, 2006, p.154).

While most actors on the European scene might be seen as particularly influential in one or more stages of the policy process, the

Table 2.2 *The European Parliament*

Who	European Parliament (EP)
When established	1952: Common Assembly 1962: name changed into European Parliament
Core aim	A directly elected body that represents the interests of the people of Europe (the 'voice of the people')
Actors	736 Members of the European Parliament (MEPs) (the Lisbon Treaty raises this number to 751, but this will most likely not be implemented until the next elections in 2014)
Main functions	1 The power to legislate (shared with the Council of the European Union) 2 Exercising democratic supervision over all EU institutions 3 The authority (also shared with the Council) to approve the EU's budget

Commission seems to be the most 'all-round' player with a potential role in each of the stages identified. Due to its wide variety of functions, the Commission is an actor one generally needs to consider when conducting policy analysis from the agenda setting to the evaluation stage. In the Commission, we can locate agenda-setting initiatives early on with the debating of issues via Green and White Papers and other types of communications (see Chapters 3 and 5). We can see policy shaping when new legislation is proposed (see Chapter 6), decision making tasks in the Commission's work in the comitology committees (see Chapter 7), implementation strategies when it acts as guardian of the Treaties (see Chapter 8), and, last but not least, its evaluation activities when all actors with a vested interest seek to identify whether or not policy was successful (see Chapter 9).

The European Parliament

The European Parliament is one of the most fascinating EU institutions to study in the context of policy analysis at the European level because it is the institution that has changed the most over the years. It has become more and more important and its history is a transition from 'fig-leaf to co-legislature' (Corbett *et al.*, 2007, p.1). In light of this, questions about its 'true' impact on the policy process, especially under the ordinary legislative procedure (see the following section of this chapter) and in relation to the Council, are often raised in policy studies. The EP is often analyzed in terms of its role in the day-to-day decisions, for example particularly questioning its impact in the fields of foreign and security issues. Its increased powers under Lisbon Treaty (more areas in which it co-legislates, more power over the budget, more control over the 'executive' functions of the Commission) make the EP particularly interesting for a more historical analysis, analyzing its role throughout its history.

One of the major traps to avoid when conducting policy analysis is approaching the European institutions as unitary actors. While we easily speak of the role of *the* parliament in the EU policy process, it is crucial to distinguish several distinct actors within the EP in the context of policy analysis. In its function as co-legislator, the EP is an important actor in the policy formulation and decision-making stages of the policy process. When a proposal for legislation reaches the EP, it is sent to one of the twenty parliamentary committees. These policy-specialized committees are composed of MEPs, and a *rapporteur* is appointed among the members of this committee as the primary responsible person to deal with the policy proposal in question. As one might imagine, this committee – and particularly this *rapporteur* – are noteworthy actors because they can play a crucial role in suggesting amendments to the policy proposal. One has to keep in mind, however, that MEPs are not necessarily experts on the topic at hand and as a consequence, as discussed below, may actually welcome lobbyists who can 'educate' MEPs. Some campaign groups such as Corporate Europe Observatory actually lobby against the influence of business interests on policy makers.

To what extent does the EP resemble the more 'traditional' parliaments of nation-states? How does the role of the EP in the EU policy process compare to the role of national parliaments in their respective policy processes? MEPs take a seat in one of the seven political groups, not organized by nationality but by political affiliation, or are registered as non-attached members. Some have analyzed whether party allegiance is more important than nationality and what influence the mix of competition and cooperation between the different political groups has on the ability of the EP to influence the policy process (see Hix *et al.*, 2005). The Treaties require an absolute majority of the EP (369 of the 736 votes) in order to be able to reject or adopt amendments to the common position of the Council at second reading under the ordinary legislative procedure, or to approve the accession of new member states. This institutional arrangement creates a strong incentive for political groups to cooperate because none of the groups is able to reach such a majority (the largest group of the European Peoples Parties has 264 members) and as such a 'strong bargaining culture between the groups has evolved' (Shackleton, 2006, p.112).

An additional remark needs to be made about the role of national parliaments in the EU policy process. Traditionally this role was considered to be marginal – with the exception perhaps of some national parliaments with the reputation of pre-discussing EU policy proposals and giving their governments a clear mandate (for example the British and Danish parliaments). Since the Lisbon Treaty has entered into force, national parliaments might evolve into more prominent actors in the day-to-day policy process, particularly in the policy formulation stage: they gained the right to compel the Commission to review legislative proposals. Whenever one-third of the parliaments – or one-quarter, when proposals in the field of freedom, justice and security are at stake – favour a review of the proposal, the Commission can only maintain the proposal when it manages to provide a reasoned opinion for doing so. What will be interesting to analyze in the near future is whether national parliaments will indeed use this procedure. In particular, will they be able to manage to come to an agreement within the mere eight weeks that they are allowed? Will this have a lasting impact on the EU policy process?

The Council of the European Union

While in 'Eurojargon' we so easily speak of *the* Council, everyone who knows a little bit about the working and functioning of this specific actor knows that this is an over-simplification. It is impossible to analyze the role of *the* Council in the EU policy process. When trying to do so, one first needs to specify which particular Council one intends. One also needs to allow for the fact that decisions are made at different layers. While we identify the national ministers as the actors involved at Council level, we cannot analyze that section of actors without also considering the civil servants involved in the working groups and the Committee of Permanent Representatives (COREPER) into consideration. As described in more detail in Chapter 7, the national experts and officials working in the working groups and in national permanent representations play a crucial role in the policy process because most decisions seem to be reached – or are at least 'pre-cooked' – at these lower levels. Dinan stresses the role of COREPER by noting that 'the caliber and effectiveness of permanent representative officials determines to a great extent how countries fare in the EU' (2005, p.250). Thus, taking the role of the Council into consideration when doing policy analysis cannot be done without close analysis of the input at these lower levels.

Important as well when analyzing the role of the Council in the EU policy process is the special role played by the Council's Presidency. On a rotating, six-monthly, basis, the meetings of the Council are chaired by the member state that holds the Presidency. The main exception is the Foreign Affairs Council, which is chaired by the High Representative. Before the Lisbon Treaty entered into force, when the member state holding the Presidency also chaired the European

Table 2.3   *The Council of the European Union*

Who	Council of the European Union (in short: Council, also often referred to as Council of Ministers)
When established	1952
Core aim	The principal decision-making body that represents the interests of the member states (the 'voice of the member states')
Actors	The Council comes together in ten different 'configurations' for different policy fields (for example, 'economic and financial affairs', 'agriculture and fisheries'); in each configuration, the Council consists of one minister or secretary of state from each member state
Main functions	1 The power to legislate (shared with the European Parliament) 2 To conclude international agreements with other states or international organizations 3 To approve (also together with the EP) the EU's budget 4 To coordinate broad economic policies of the member states 5 To develop common foreign and security policy

Council meetings, this role was considered rather important. Research into the working and functioning of the Presidency in the 'old style' has indicated an important potential impact on the direction and content of the EU policy process. Member states were thought to play an agenda-setting role via the Presidency (Tallberg, 2003), and in particular smaller member states were known to be able to play a brokering and neutral role as 'compromisers' when holding the Presidency. An interesting question to consider in the near future will be whether the Presidency of the Council of Ministers is still likely to have an impact with the new role of President of the European Council.

Any policy analyst should also take the role of the Council Secretariat – the administrative body that assists the Council and the Presidency in their day-to-day work – into consideration. In addition to its logistical and administrative tasks, the secretariat's staff is responsible for the more substantive preparation of the Council's work. In the difficult aftermath of negotiating the Maastricht Treaty, for example, it was the secretariat that drafted the opt-outs granted to Denmark which paved the way for ratification of the Treaty (Dinan, 2005, p.232). In particular, the Secretary-General, who is responsible for the running of the secretariat, is often considered to play a crucial role in the decision making process.

Table 2.4   *The European Council*

Who	European Council
When established	1974 (legal recognition since 1986)
Core aim	To provide political guidance and impetus to the development of the EU
Actors	The Heads of State or Government of the member states, the European Council President and the President of the Commission
Main function	Setting general political guidelines

The European Council

The Council and the European Council should not be confused with the 'Council of Europe' which is not an EU institution. This international body, consisting of 47 European countries, was founded in 1949 and aims to create a common and democratic legal area within Europe, ensuring respect for human rights, democracy and the rule of law.

While it is beyond doubt that the European Council plays, and has played, a major role in determining the development of European integration, when analyzing day-to-day decision making in the EU, the role of the European Council is a different one, and one that has changed throughout the years since its formation. Whether the influence of the European Council on day-to-day decision making has indeed increased throughout the years is an intriguing question. While its main aim has been to steer the overall (political) direction of the Union, and therefore its influence is mostly likely to be visible in 'high political' decisions such as whether or not to introduce the euro, there are also more quotidian policy decisions in which the European Council has a particular interest. In a time of financial crisis, for example, the influence of the European Council on the day-to-day decisions in the economic and monetary fields will be stronger and more decisive than in more stable economic times. Here, one might assess whether there are reasons to suspect a particularly concerted effort from the Council to move policy in a certain direction, a hunch which might be based on recognizing the intensive media attention paid to a specific topic, by way of the sheer quantity of press releases, official governmental statements, and so on. In the face of such evidence, it might be tempting to identify the European Council as an important actor at the agenda-setting stage, since all this press coverage suggests strong political influence in pushing a particular item on the policy agenda.

The most topical question to ask when analyzing the European Council in the EU policy process is the question about the actual role played by the newly established President of the European Council. To what extent will this new person – appointed for two and a half years, renewable once, the first term filled by the Belgian former prime minister Herman van Rompuy – be able to stamp-mark the EU's policy process?

The Court of Justice

The Court of Justice of the European Union consists of three courts: the Court of Justice, the General Court (previously known as the Court of First Instance) and the European Union Civil Service Tribunal. The latter deals with internal EU staffing disputes and is not described here. For reasons of simplicity, the remainder of this book will speak of the Court of Justice – the TFEU also does not distinguish between the Court of Justice and the General Court and often both courts are described together (Nugent, 2010, p.218).

While the ECJ has no formal role to play in first stages of the EU policy process – it only officially steps in during the implementation stage where it can rule against member states that have not implemented Community law in a subtle manner – it has become known for having had a major impact on the development of European integration. Through several 'landmark' cases, the ECJ has steered the direction of the EU, and in this sense might also be identified as an actor with a potentially influential role to play as an agenda setter or decision maker in the day-to-day policy process.

One of the most famous and oft-quoted examples is the *Cassis de Dijon* case of 1979. Germany tried to ban the import of this French blackcurrant-based liqueur on the basis that its alcoholic content was below the minimum laid down by German law for liqueurs. The ECJ ruled that any product lawfully manufactured and on sale in one member state may be imported into all other member states without restrictions. This landmark case laid the foundation for the mutual recognition of product standards, thereby demonstrating major agenda-setting power for future harmonization of product standards, and thus further opening up the internal market within the EU.

But the ECJ can also play a role in the day-to-day decision-making process, as the tobacco advertising case, highlighted throughout the second section of this book, demonstrates. The Council and the EP adopted a directive prohibiting all forms of tobacco advertising via the qualified majority procedure. Germany, outvoted in the Council, protested against this decision, claiming that the main objective of the directive was the protection of public health, a policy field that requires unanimity (the qualified majority procedure was used based on internal market arguments). The ECJ ruled in Germany's favour

Table 2.5 *The Court of Justice*

Who	Court of Justice (ECJ)
When established	1952
Core aim	The judicial authority of the European Union, ensures that the law is observed
Actors	27 independent judges (1 from each member state)
Main functions	1 To review the legality of acts established by the European Union 2 Enforcing EU law (together with the European Commission) 3 To interpret Community law at the request of national courts

and annulled the already adopted directive in 2000. What is significant, however, is that in its ruling the ECJ gave suggestions on how to introduce such a tobacco advertising ban more legitimately, thus playing a policy-shaping role (see also Chapter 5). These guidelines resulted in a new Commission proposal and a relatively quick agreement between the Council and the EP afterwards. The final directive (2003/33) was adopted in 2003 (see Adamini *et al.*, 2010)

The role of the ECJ in the policy process is most directly visible at the implementation stage. In the case of an infringement procedure, as we shall see in Chapter 8, the ECJ can rule against a non-compliant member state, and even impose sanctions on it. When analyzing the implementation of Community law, the ECJ is revealed as a highly relevant actor in cases where infringements are invoked.

The European Court of Auditors

Together with OLAF – the European Anti-Fraud Office (1999) – the Court of Auditors is responsible for 'protecting' European taxpayers by ensuring that the public finances of the EU are in order. While the Court is said to have been particularly important in altering the institutional balance between the Commission and the Parliament (strengthening parliamentary control over the Commission with the information it provides) (Laffan, 2006), one can also observe it exercising a more direct impact on the policy process as such given that it operates primarily by producing reports of its audits (in the early 2000s, about 120 per year). In particular, in the fields of agricultural policy and external action, the Court is active in producing special reports and

Table 2.6   *The European Court of Auditors*

Who	European Court of Auditors (ECA)
When established	1977
Core aim	The EU's independent auditor that guards the financial interests of the citizens of the Union
Actors	27 independent members (1 from each member state)
Main function	Assessing the collection and spending of EU money

studies (Laffan, 2006). But it also plays a decisive role in stimulating other institutions to strengthen cooperation in a particular policy field. For example, its special report on the trans-European network for transport (no. 6/2005; *Official Journal of the European Union* C94/2, 21.4.2006) stimulated the creation of a special agency (Trans-European Transport Network Executive Agency) in 2006 to implement and better manage this policy field.

The European Central Bank

The ECB being the 'institutional expression of a process of monetary integration' (McNamara, 2006, p.171), we can safely conclude that its direct role in the day-to-day policy process is limited to that sector only. But in that sector, it plays a potentially powerful role in the policy process, as it can independently issue guidelines, decisions and regulations. The ECB plays a formal role in the formulation of EU monetary policy, but the daily execution and operation are largely controlled by national central banks under the European System of Central Banks. Thus, the role and influence of the ECB has to be evaluated in careful relation to other national economic and financial actors.

The advisory bodies

The European Union has two official advisory bodies: the European Economic and Social Committee and the Committee of the Regions. Both of them were set up – although not at the same time – to add specific expertise to the EU policy process, but neither, as stated by Jeffery, 'has made an enduring impact' (Jeffery, 2006, p.312). This section will also address the role of European agencies as important actors in the EU policy process. While not officially recognized in the

Table 2.7 *The European Central Bank*

Who	European Central Bank (ECB)
When established	1998
Core aim	The manager of the Euro and the maintainer of price stability in the Euro area
Actors	The executive board (6 members), the governing council (governors of the 16 national central banks), the general council (composed of the executive board, governors of all EU national central banks)
Main functions	1 To ensure price stability 2 To control money supply 3 To decide upon interest rates

Treaties as advisory bodies, a large part of the agencies can be considered as such, based on their tasks and functions.

The European Economic and Social Committee

Although it does so in a different fashion than the European Parliament, the EESC also tries to provide a bridge between the Union and its citizens by giving an official voice to organized civil society. By providing opinions on all policy proposals that touch upon economic and social affairs, this committee can in theory influence the EU policy process. While its potential influence seems to be 'restricted' to economic and social policy fields, one should not forget that many other policy sectors have economic or social implications – transport, the single market, agriculture, to name just a few – and in practice with regards to policy proposals in many of the EU's policy sectors the EESC must be consulted.

The EESC also has the right to initiate its own opinions (about 15 per cent of the yearly 150 opinions issued by the EESC) and can thereby promote social dialogue in a specific field. In this respect, it has a potential agenda-setting influence. It can also function as a body that provides information about the current state of affairs to a more widely organized civil society, although in practice we have witnessed that the European lobby is highly organized and not necessarily dependent on the input of the EESC.

While the Commission, EP and Council are obliged to consult the EESC on social and economic issues, they are not obliged to heed the committee's advice. Several scholars have questioned the degree to

Table 2.8   *The European Economic and Social Committee*

Who	European Economic and Social Committee (EESC)
When established	1958
Core aim	An advisory body that must be consulted on all economic and social policy (the 'voice of the civil society')
Actors	344 members, representing employers, employees and various interests (for example, farmers, consumers, professions)
Main functions	1 Issue opinions on policy proposals regarding economic and social policy (for example, employment, social spending, vocational training) 2 The right to issue own initiative opinions 3 Encourage and bolster the role of civil society in the EU

which this theoretical influence of the EESC on the policy process is visible, some even labelling it as a 'relatively insignificant' body that the Council 'politely ignores' (Dinan, 2005, pp.310–11), or an 'ineffectual body with weak powers and an unwieldy, disparate membership' (Jeffery, 2006, p.312).

The Committee of the Regions

When describing the CoR as a potential actor in EU policy analysis, the account is similar to that of the EESC. With the inclusion of the principle of subsidiarity in the Treaty of Maastricht, it appeared logical to establish a specific body that would ensure – by providing advice on policy proposals that influence local and regional levels – that EU policy actually reflected the interests of regional and local layers. In contrast to the case of the EESC, there is a difference between member states in terms of the extent to which they use and value the CoR. Generally speaking, particularly federalized states such as Austria, Germany and Spain value the CoR as a vehicle against the central government.

The fact that the mandatory opinions delivered do not necessarily have to be taken on board by the deciding institutions colours the potential influence of the CoR just as much as it influences the EESC. While the Commission does seem to take the CoR seriously, the Council is seen to treat it with 'benign indifference' (Warleigh 1999, quoted in Jeffery, 2006, p.325). The CoR might have a role to play as an actor providing information to the relevant stakeholders, the

Table 2.9 *The Committee of the Regions*

Who	Committee of the Regions (CoR)
When established	1994
Core aim	An advisory body that must be consulted on policy proposals that affect the regional or local level
Actors	344 members, representing regional or local governments
Main functions	1 Issue opinions on policy proposals that have repercussions at local or regional level (for example, cohesion, infrastructure, health, education) 2 The right to issue own initiative opinions

regions, about the state of affairs in the European policy process. But, just as with the EESC, in practice it turns out that regional and local authorities have their own 'routes' to Brussels that in many cases seem to work more effectively than the official route via the CoR.

In summary, while being the only two official advisory bodies within the European Union, it is questionable whether the ESSC and the CoR play a significant role in the EU policy process. The deciding institutions, particularly the Council, do not necessarily take their opinions seriously, and the relevant stakeholders seem to organize themselves differently and even better when trying to influence the EU policy process.

The European agencies

Since the 1990s, the EU has followed the trend already visible in nation-states of delegating specific technical or managerial tasks to agencies. Although the European agencies are known to have less 'teeth' than their American counterparts (Geradin *et al.*, 2005), in some policy fields, the member states allowed to create agencies with relatively far-reaching powers. This had a considerable impact on the EU policy process. Policy formulation and decision making in 'risk' sectors such as medicines, food safety, disease prevention, and so on, are more and more influenced by the role of agencies. For instance, the European Food Safety Authority – while officially 'only' advising the Commission – is known to have a strong impact on decisions whether or not to place certain genetically modified products on the European market (Borrás *et al.*, 2007). Other agencies are expected to start to play a more dominant role at the implementation stage. In the transport sector, for example, the European Aviation Safety Agency and the

Table 2.10   *The European agencies*

Who	European agencies • 21 Community agencies • 3 Common Foreign and Security Agencies • 3 Police and judicial cooperation in criminal matters agencies • 6 executive agencies
When established	From 1975 onwards (most since the 1990s)
Core aim	Specialized and decentralized bodies with specific technical, scientific or managerial tasks
Actors	Varies by agency, but most agencies consist of a staff of experts in the respective policy field (ranging from about 50 to about 500) and are controlled by a management board
Main functions	Varies by agency: some have primarily information-gathering functions (for example, European Environment Agency or European Institute for Security Studies), some have advisory responsibilities (for example, European Food Safety Authority), while others have far-reaching regulatory powers (for example, Office for Harmonization of the Internal Market)

European Maritime Safety Agency have recently started employing 'European inspectors' who have the right to check the extent to which national inspection bodies are doing their work properly (Groenleer *et al.*, 2010).

A fundamental part of conducting EU policy analysis is to establish whether or not there is an EU agency in the policy field in question, and what the competences and responsibilities of that particular agency are. Only then can one identify whether a given EU agency is a relevant actor that must be taken into account in the policy analysis.

Informal actors – the role of lobbying

More than with the formally recognized players, the number of informal actors potentially playing a role in the EU policy process is seemingly endless and varies quite a bit as a function of which particular decision is being made at any given time. While we can provide examples, it is impossible to provide an exhaustive list of the informal actors that might be involved in a policy process.

The process of informal influence in the EU policy process – in other words, lobbying – is one of the most researched topics at the European scene. With Brussels being the most lobbied city after Washington, it is a popular topic amongst both scholars and students and plenty of sources are available on the role and influence of these actors that do not have a formal say in the policy process, but do have a potentially huge impact on the development and outcome of the policy process (see for example Greenwood, 2007). Knowing that EU institutions and scholars differ in their assessments of how many lobbyists there actually are in Brussels – Greenwood suggests that the figure of 15,000 is often cited, but not backed up by any authoritative head count (Greenwood, 2007, p.11) – the difficulty of providing a complete list of informal actors involved in the EU policy process becomes apparent. What we do know, however, is that lobbying takes place at all stages of the policy process, and that the influence of informal actors thus needs to be taken seriously throughout the stages. Even at the evaluation stage, one witnesses a trend of lobbyist increasingly resorting to executing policy evaluations themselves in order to influence the debate in a particular policy field, or its direction and evolution. Lobbying also takes place in all policy domains regulated by the EU, but one can note a difference in the intensity of lobbying as a function of the amount of competences delegated to the European level in a particular domain. Generally speaking, it is possible to conclude that those domains that are most intensively regulated at the EU level are also the most heavily lobbied in the EU institutions. In sectors that are still largely intergovernmental – for example common foreign and security policy – access to the EU policy process is less easily arranged, as discussed later in Chapter 3.

Lobbying in the EU policy process is important because formal institutions will never have complete control over all the information and expertise that is necessary to make well-informed policy decisions. Decision makers often need lobbyists to provide them with relevant, street-level, information. This is also one of the main reasons, amongst others combined with its own relative small size, why the Commission explicitly organizes debates and hearings with stakeholders and relevant parties in the early stages of the policy process in order to learn 'what is out there', making interest representation in the EU one of the most institutionalized forms of lobbying that exists (the Commission even finances certain interest groups). In this sense, the EU institutions show a 'systemic dependence upon organized civil society' (Greenwood, 2007, p.1).

On hearing the term 'lobbying', one most often thinks of the activities of NGOs such as Greenpeace, or of private interests such as the lobby by the chemical industry. But lobbying is done by all types of organizations and governments. This chapter merely lists the types of actors involved. Chapter 6 will discuss in more detail what lobbyists do and how they influence the policy process.

National governments

While an individual actor may be heavily influenced by its strong official role in the Council or European Council, we should not overlook national governments as institutional lobbyists themselves. Alongside their formal routes to the policy process, national governments will not shy away from using informal lobbying techniques – for example, trying to persuade fellow governments, MEPS, Commission officials or private interests to push for a certain policy outcome.

Sub-national levels of governments

The regions have their official route into the EU policy process via the Committee of the Regions, but, as stated above, this is not always the most successful way to exert influence. Most regional and local governments are in some fashion organized at the European level, either directly or via an association (for example, EUROCITIES).

Other nation-states

The size and influence of the EU make it an important partner for all of the countries in the world, but some groups are particularly affected by certain policy sectors. Think of the importance of external and development policies for neighbouring countries, or for countries receiving development funds. But also think of the impact of the EU's common agricultural, internal market and trade policy for all trading partners. Via other international organizations, but also individually, these affected countries will naturally try to influence the EU policy process.

Think-tanks

The number of think-tanks in Brussels has grown throughout the years. These institutes, the core aim of which is to conduct research into topical EU affairs, also heavily influence the policy process – either intentionally or unintentionally. Examples are the Centre for European Policy Studies or the European Policy Centre.

Private and public companies

Many multinational corporations (around 250 according to Nugent, 2010) have their own office in Brussels where they try to influence the

EU policy process. While often strategies and activities are combined in 'Eurogroups' (see below), some policy initiatives call for an independent lobbying strategy as competition can be involved.

EU-level interest organizations or 'Eurogroups'

Eurogroups are composed of members of several countries that join to 'fight' for the same cause. Most of them are associations of national organizations, but there are also groups that allow direct, individual membership. Greenwood estimates there are about 1,450 EU level groups, of whom a little more than half represent business interests (for example, the Union of Industrial and Employers' Confederations of Europe) and around one-third represent citizen interests (for example, World Wide Fund for Nature or the European Consumers' Organization). Compared to earlier counts, this reflects a growth of citizen interest representation at the EU level (Greenwood, 2007: pp.11–13). The main reason for the large number of 'Eurogroups' is the Commission's preference for talking to such federations rather than dealing with individual interests.

Different modes of interaction

When we analyze these different actors at work, we have to take into consideration the fact that the way they function, and thus the potential role they play in the policy process, varies in different circumstances. The EU policy process may seem difficult to analyze because there is not one single way in which the different institutions and actors described above interact. One of the main factors that influence the mode of interaction between the formal actors at stake – and the potential influence of the informal actors – is the type of legislative procedure that they use. This is determined by the Treaties, and varies across the different policy domains. This next section will briefly describe the different modes of interaction between the actors involved in the EU policy process.

The mode of interaction under the ordinary legislative procedure

For the majority of the policy domains, the policy process starts with a policy proposal initiated by the European Commission. While the right of initiative lies with the Commission, ideas for policy proposals can come from a wide variety of sources – more detailed information about this can be found in Chapter 5 on agenda setting. Here, it suffices to say that ideas can spring from different EU institutions, member states or certain (interest) groups in society. Generally speaking, the Commission will establish an expert group with relevant stakeholders (member-state civil servants and the representatives of the interest groups concerned) in order to gain sufficient insight into the expertise available and the most up-to-date ideas regarding the topic in question. Once the proposal leaves the Commission, it is sent to the advisory bodies for advice (when required) and to the European Parliament and the Council of Ministers for decision.

Introduced in the Treaty of Maastricht, updated in Amsterdam, and now extended to most policy areas, the co-decision procedure was 'promoted' to 'ordinary legislative procedure' in the Lisbon Treaty (Article 294, TFEU). It places the Council and EP on equal footing since agreement from both parties is required before a positive decision can be made. The Commission sends its proposal to both the Council and the EP, who both discuss the proposal in two 'readings'. In the first reading, the EP gives its advice about the Commission proposal (usually in the form of amendments) to the Council. When the Council agrees (by qualified majority) with the EP's advice, the proposal can be adopted by the first reading. However, when the Council does not agree, or only partially agrees, it adopts (by qualified majority) its 'common position' in which it expresses which EP amendments it accepts and which it does not. The Council can only propose its own amendments to the Commission proposal by unanimity. At this point, the second reading commences, during which the EP examines the Council's common position. When the EP agrees to the common position, a decision is reached. The EP can, however, again suggest amendments to the Council's common position (including reinserting its own amendments from the first reading that the Council did not accept). Together with the advice of the Commission on which of the EP's amendments are acceptable and which are not, the Council again examines the proposal. When the Council agrees with the EP's amendments (by qualified majority; only the amendments the Commission does not approve of need to be agreed upon by unanimity), the proposal is accepted. When Council and EP do not agree, however, in this second reading, the final possible stage of the procedure begins – what is termed the 'conciliation' stage. A conciliation committee, consisting of representatives of the EP, the Council and supported by the Commission, tries to come to a compromise. This final text again needs to be approved by EP and Council (without the possibility to suggest amendments). When both parties agree, the decision is finally adopted. If not, the proposal is rejected.

There are two main voting procedures within the Council that influence the policy process: unanimity and qualified majority voting (QMV). Voting by unanimity is easily explained: all 27 member states have to agree, and thus each member state has a veto. Member states can decide to withhold their vote, thereby still allowing a decision to be reached 'unanimously'. This procedure is mostly used for the so-called 'high' political decisions such as foreign and defence policy. The Treaty specifies each type of situation under which unanimity voting applies. When not specified, QMV applies as the 'default' voting method. Voting by QMV is a much more complicated process. Each member state has a certain amount of votes, related to the size of its population and economic weight. In this procedure, member states can again withhold from voting, and those withheld votes do not count in determining the qualified majority. A decision is adopted by qualified majority when three conditions are met: (1) 255 of the total 345 votes (73.9 per cent) have to be in favour, (2) a majority of the member states (14 of the 27) have to be in favour, and (3) this majority needs to represent at least 62 per cent of the total population of the EU. The Lisbon Treaty changed this complex procedure into a system of 'double majority voting'. This new procedure, which will be adopted from 2014 onwards, requires 55 per cent of the member states, representing 65 per cent of the Union's population and a blocking minority must include at least four member states.

With every Treaty change, the number of policy areas for which QMV is used has increased – with Lisbon finally making it the default voting procedure – thus making it relatively easier to reach decisions at the EU level. This obviously influences the way member states behave during Council negotiations, but it also influences the potential role of the other actors involved in the policy process. Using QMV, as opposed to unanimity, makes it more important for the actors involved to negotiate, reach compromises and form coalitions. In day-to-day practice in 'Brussels' voting hardly ever takes place; the Council actually only votes for one out of six decisions. The EU policy process is characterized by a tendency to reach agreements via consensus. Research into Council voting records since 1993 (Hayes-Renshaw and Wallace, 2006) shows that there are no all-time winners or losers in terms of EU decision making. Coalitions change with each issue, and there is no tendency for large, small, old, new, southern, or eastern member states to always form the same coalitions. Each policy process thus requires its own fresh analysis of the role of the various member states during Council negotiations. Past records do not provide an accurate prediction of the way that future policy processes will go.

The mode of interaction under the special legislative procedures

Special legislative procedures are in place to allow further European cooperation in highly sensitive areas, where member states are afraid

Table 2.11   *Three modes of interaction*

Type of legislative procedure	Possibility for the EP to suggest amendments	Veto by the EP
Ordinary legislative procedure	Yes	Yes
Consent procedure	No	Yes
Consultation procedure	Yes	No

to lose control, something that might happen under the ordinary legislative procedure. There are two procedures worth mentioning: consent and consultation (see Table 2.11).

The consent procedure (formerly the 'assent' procedure) requires the 'consent' of the EP before a decision can be adopted. In other words, if the EP does not agree, the decision cannot be adopted by the Council – the EP thus has a veto, although it cannot suggest amendments to the proposal. It can merely say 'yes' or 'no'. This procedure is mostly used for the accession of new member states and policy combating discrimination.

The consultation procedure, very simply put, gives the EP the right to submit a non-binding opinion (and suggest amendments) on a proposal. Here, the EP can only delay a proposal from being adopted, but it cannot block it. The Commission sends its draft to both the Council and the EP, and the Council decides – either via unanimity or via QMV, depending on the topic at hand – after hearing the EP's opinion. As with the advice by both advisory bodies (EESC and CoR), the Council is not obliged to take this advice into consideration. The EP's influence under this procedure is not 'reduced' to that of the two advisory bodies: the Council can ignore the EP's opinion, agree to it, or reject it, while it can only make amendments to it by unanimity. With the Lisbon Treaty extending the number of areas to which the ordinary legislative procedure applies, the consultation procedure is used less and less. It still applies to internal market exemptions and competition law.

Conclusion

When conducting policy analysis – and particularly when deciding which actors to take into consideration – it is crucial to identify the type of legislative procedure and mode of interaction in force, as not all actors play the same role in all circumstances. The types of questions potentially asked in EU policy analysis vary for each individual actor. One might analyze the role of one particular actor over time – think, for example, of the changing role of the European Parliament in the history of European integration. Alternatively, one might compare the role of an individual actor at various stages of the policy process – for example, analyzing the extent to which advisory bodies manage to influence the various stages of the policy process. But one can also analyze the relationship between several actors and weigh up their respective roles, or consider the overlapping roles of the three main institutions – the Commission, Parliament and Council. Another line of enquiry relates to the relative power of formal, as opposed to informal, actors in the policy process, or the different types of informal actors in terms of their relations to each other – for example, the role of the industry lobby versus the environmental lobby when negotiating regulation on the registration and evaluation of chemicals (REACH). Clearly, the list of potential actors to take into consideration when conducting EU policy analysis is, to say the least, extensive and it is difficult to consistently predict the types of actors that one will need to pay attention to in an analysis of a policy process. Each new policy process asks for a fresh analysis of who the primary formal and informal actors are, and, by extension, the issues of most pressing interest.

Suggestions for further reading

A more general guide to all institutions

Nugent, N. (2010) *The Government and Politics of the European Union*, 7th edn (Basingstoke and New York: Palgrave Macmillan).
Peterson, J. and Shackleton, M. (2006) (eds) *The Institutions of the European Union*, 2nd edn (Oxford: Oxford University Press).

On individual institutions or actors

Arnull, A. (2006) *The European Union and its Court of Justice*, 2nd edn (Oxford: Oxford University Press).
Corbett, R., Jacobs, F. and Shackleton, M. (2007) *The European Parliament*, 7th edn (London: John Harper).
Greenwood, J. (2007) *Interest Representation in the European Union*, 2nd edn (Basingstoke and New York: Palgrave Macmillan).
Hayes-Renshaw, F. and Wallace, H. (2006) *The Council of Ministers*, 2nd edn (Basingstoke and New York: Palgrave Macmillan).
Spence, D. (2006) (ed.) *The European Commission*, 3rd edn (London: John Harper).
Werts, J. (2008) *The European Council* (London: John Harper).

Relevant websites

On the individual institutions: http://europa.eu/about-eu/institutions-bodies/
index_en.htm.
On EU think-tanks: http://www.eu.thinktankdirectory.org/ .
On decision-making procedures in the EU: http://europa.eu/institutions/
decision-making/index_en.htm.

Chapter 3

What Do We Analyze?

Introduction

Following on from the previous chapter's description of *whom* we analyze when we conduct policy analysis in the European Union, this chapter outlines *what* we analyze at the EU level. The *what* in this chapter does not so much refer to the policy process as such – as we explained in Chapter 1, this book uses the policy process, or rather the various stages of the policy process, as tools of analysis – but more to the output or outcome of the policy process. In other words, the *what* in conducting policy analysis at the EU level here refers to the policy instruments and the various policy fields. What specific level of analysis one refers to is left open. We can research the parameters of one or several specific policy instruments, just as we can investigate (or compare) the policy process in specific policy fields. The message this chapter attempts to convey is that each analysis of every new policy instrument or policy field will be different. The EU draws upon so many different instruments, and has such a wide array of competences in different policy fields, that every new policy analysis is a unique exercise. Analyzing an agricultural regulation is completely different from researching a decision in the field of foreign policy.

Categorizing policy

There are many different categories of policy. The main reason for trying to categorize them is to provide insight into specific characteristics of policy and how and why policies are made the way they are, something that is a prerequisite of performing a solid policy analysis. Categorizing different policies shows not only that different forms of policy create different 'winners' and 'losers' (relatively speaking, that is), but that 'policy determines politics'. That is, politics is influenced by the choices that are made when not only selecting what to regulate, but also by how and via what instruments to issue policies. Choosing a particular policy type or instrument *is* a conscious political activity.

Many authors have attempted to distinguish specific policy *instruments*. Policy instruments are the 'actual means or devices governments have at their disposal for implementing policies, and among which they must select in formulating policy' (Howlett and Ramesh, 2003, p.87). The choice of a particular policy instrument can be as significant as the choice to issue policy in a certain field in the first place. It is, for example, very telling whether a government opts for subsidies or for regulation. The potential range of policy instruments is enormous at all levels of government and the EU is no exception. One of the first attempts by Kirschen in 1964 to list policy instruments led to the identification of 64 separate instruments in the field of economic policies alone (in Howlett and Ramesh, 2003, p.90).

In the 1980s, Christopher Hood (1986; see also Hood and Margetts, 2007) categorized four types of policy instruments (leading to the abbreviation NATO), a categorization still widely adhered to:

1. *Nodality instruments.* Governments confront public problems via the use of information (for example, public information campaigns, research inquiries, advertising).
2. *Authority instruments.* Governments confront public problems via the use of legal powers (for example, command and control regulation, self-regulation).
3. *Treasure instruments.* Governments confront public problems via the use of money (for example, loans, subsidies, taxes).
4. *Organization instruments.* Governments confront public problems via the use of their formal organizations (for example, delivering goods via (semi-)governmental organizations, such as defence, education, water supply).

Such a classification is not without problems, however. As this chapter will demonstrate, it is very difficult to arrive at neatly delineated categories in which policies are clearly assigned to a specific box or cell. Some policies have different characteristics that place them in different boxes at the same time – and in this sense, Hood's NATO classification is difficult to directly apply to the EU context. When scrutinizing the instruments the EU uses most, we will see that the category of 'authority instruments' is most commonly used in the EU.

In 1994, Majone labelled the EU a 'regulatory state', and this description is still widely followed. He argued that the EU could be seen as a regulatory state because it tended to regulate society largely via legal authority or regulations rather than, say, via macroeconomic stabilization or redistribution instruments. In other words, the EU resorts to the use of authority rather than to the use of the 'cheque book'.

Treasure instruments, policy tools that use money, are less common in the European Union than they are in nation-states. This is because, compared to the combined gross domestic product (GDP) of the member states, the EU's budget is relatively limited (between 1.05 and

1.10 per cent of total EU GNP). Typical treasure instruments such as subsidies and funds do exist in the European Union, but are certainly not used to as great an extent as they are by national administrations. Moran (2002, p.402) summarizes the use of authoritative instruments from a negative or 'forced' perspective: 'At the level of the EU the rise of regulation is due to weakness of means of command. The EU has neither the budget-raising capacity nor the bureaucratic muscle to impose policies on either national members or private interests. Promulgating regulations potentially solves this problem.' In other words, the EU is obliged to resort to regulations because the member states do not transfer policy fields traditionally governed via treasure instruments – for example, welfare policies – to the European level. Such areas are still largely seen as a national responsibility. Majone (1996, p.66) characterizes the regulatory state by its emphasis on the expansionist role of the European Commission through the use of influence in the policy process: 'regulatory policy-making puts a good deal of power into the hands of the Brussels authorities while, at the same time, giving the possibility of avoiding tight budgetary constraints imposed by the members'.

The applicability of the term 'regulatory state' can be demonstrated when analyzing the way the EU organizes its typical 'expenditure policies'. In regional policy (structural and cohesion funds) and in the Common Agricultural Policy (CAP), the distribution of money plays an important role. The way the EU proceeds, however, is via the use of traditional regulatory instruments, and thus regional policy and the CAP are largely governed via regulations and decisions. Another useful example concerns the way that the EU organizes its social policy. While social policy at the nation-state level might be categorized by attempts to redistribute resources between employers and workers or between rich and poor, the EU is mainly engaged in social 'regulation' that aims to address market failures (Hix, 2005, p.258).

Overview of EU policy instruments

Using Hood's classification we might presume that the EU mostly resorts to the second type, namely, authority (regulatory) instruments. Yet this on its own does not yield very much insight since the types of regulatory instruments that the EU can use are in fact quite diverse:

- Treaties
- Case law of the European Court of Justice
- International agreements
- Binding acts adopted by the institutions
- Soft law

In the European Union, the actors involved in the policy process do not have complete freedom to select any type of instrument they please. Treaty provisions guide this selection process and determine in many cases what instruments are available to choose from. These Treaty provisions are to some degree incomplete, however, and it is possible to observe many more instruments being used in practice than those which are officially described. While in the pre-Lisbon era there were many more policy instruments at the EU's disposal, the Lisbon Treaty provided for a simplification. When analyzing older EU policy, one can thus find policy instruments not described here – especially in the fields of foreign and security policy and justice and home affairs, as these former 'pillars' used to have their own policy instruments such as 'joint actions', 'common strategies', or 'framework decisions'. This raises an interesting new question in EU policy analysis: will the abolishment of special instruments in foreign and security cooperation – and the resultant switch to 'common' instruments – influence the ease with which policy is initiated in these sectors?

Legal acts

Articles 288-292 (TFEU) describe the legal acts of the Union. They specify that the EU can use regulations, directives, decisions, recommendations and opinions, of which the first three are binding:

1. Regulations are binding in their entirety and directly applicable in all member states. They can be adopted in several forms, by several actors: by the Council of Ministers on its own, by the Council and the European Parliament jointly, and by the European Commission. The moment regulations come into force, they override all national laws of the member states dealing with the same subject matter.
2. Directives bind member states to the results to be achieved, while the means of achieving that result, that is, the choice of form and method, are left open. While regulations are directly applicable, directives first need to be transposed into national legislation. Directives can be addressed to a specific group of member states only, although reality shows that they are always, with the exception of the agricultural policy field, applied to all member states. As with regulations, directives can be adopted by the Council, Council and Parliament together, or by the Commission.
3. Decisions are binding rules for those to whom they are addressed. This final binding legal instrument was created in order to allow for the regulation of a specific group, be it companies, individuals, or a single member state. Again, decisions can be adopted by the Council, Council and Parliament together, and by the Commission.

Legal acts adopted under the legislative procedure (either the ordinary one or one of the special procedures, that is, by the Council and Parliament) are called 'legislative acts'. These legislative acts can delegate power to the Commission to adopt regulations, directives or decisions to supplement or amend certain elements, for example when changes need to be made to take into account scientific or technical progress, or to update quantitative values. These we call 'delegated acts'. Another specific type of 'delegated acts' is labelled 'implementing acts'. These are adopted by the Commission when there is a need for uniform conditions for implementation. We can thus distinguish a hierarchy in EU legal acts. The delegated and implementing acts are in general of a more executive nature. They are more technical than political compared to the legislative acts issued by the Council and the Council and the Parliament. With regards to the environment, for example, a field that is heavily regulated via directives, the European Parliament and the Council have together issued a directive on energy end-use efficiency and energy services (Directive 2006/32/EC). This is more of a political topic than the more technical regulation of the Commission directive on adapting a former Council directive to new technical progress (such as Directive 2005/21/EC adapting to technical progress Council Directive 72/306/EEC on the approximation of laws of the member states relating to the measures to be taken against the emission of pollutants from diesel engines). With this distinction in mind, when analyzing EU policy, it is important to know whether a regulation, directive or decision is considered a legislative, delegated or an implementing act. This is always clearly indicated in the act itself and provides a useful insight into the behaviour of the actors involved. For example, actors might behave differently when dealing with an administrative issue than they might with regards to a more political problem.

For all legal acts, the Commission and the European Court of Justice can resort to the infringement procedure if member states do not comply. As the infringement procedure can result in penalties for member states, these instruments might be seen as classic 'command and control' regulations (for more information on the infringement procedure, see Chapter 8 on implementation).

EU regulatory policies can have differing effects on the member states that are also important to consider in policy analysis. Firstly, one has to identify whether one is dealing with deregulatory or re-regulatory policy. Secondly, it is useful to establish whether one is analyzing a regulation or directive with a minimum or maximum harmonization effect.

To start with the first distinction, the EU can push deregulation via negative integration, or re-regulation via positive integration (compare Scharpf, 1996; Hix, 2005). Deregulatory policies involve the removal of barriers to trade and competition, and re-regulatory policies refer to the establishment of new EU-wide rules. The latter can be labelled *re-regulatory* because in general they replace pre-existing national policies, and the EU now issues more deregulatory than re-regulatory policies. As Hix explains in some detail (2005, pp.261ff), the creation of the single market is a deregulatory project by nature, and there is more demand for deregulation than for re-regulation from national governments and private interests – it seems easier to reach consensus at the EU level on removing barriers to trade than on establishing new EU-wide rules. In terms of analyzing the EU policy process, the difference between deregulatory and re-regulatory policy provides useful information about the type of negotiations taking place during the policy process.

Secondly, 'minimum' and 'maximum' regulation can also have a different effect on the 'regulated', causing their policy processes to develop differently. EU directives (which only occasionally apply to regulations) are labelled 'maximum directives' when they clearly determine what requirements member states need to comply with and provide a maximum ceiling that member states cannot exceed when transposing these directives. Minimum directives, on the other hand, only determine what member states need to adhere to at the very least, but allow them to establish their own national rules that may well exceed these European agreements. This last category is generally used for consumer protection or environmental legislation and, as one can imagine, it is easier to come to a minimum agreement between the different actors during the policy process, as this allows existing (higher) national standards to remain in place. The difference between the two types of directives can be easily identified: a directive is labelled a maximum directive when it is based on articles 114–18 (TFEU), which stipulates that some directives are explicitly meant for the approximation of national laws.

Soft law: voluntary and coordinative instruments

As policy making at the supranational level is often a crucial 'balancing act' between many different actors with widely varying agendas, it should come as no surprise that the EU has a wide range of more-or-less voluntary instruments, or 'soft law', at its disposal. When strong disagreements are likely to persist between various actors, or when actors are afraid of losing control when transferring power via regulatory instruments, it may sometimes be easier to resort to this category of instruments. Article 288 (TFEU) specifies two official non-binding acts: recommendations and opinions. These come into being via the same decision-making procedures as regulations, directives and decisions, but have the difference of being without legal force. They can be issued by the same actors as the binding instruments: by the Commission, the Council or the Council and the European Parliament.

In addition to these two official non-binding policy instruments, the EU draws upon several other voluntary tools. The Council (via its Presidency) can issue declarations. A declaration is the general expression of a political line, and is not legally binding. It is most commonly used in Common Foreign and Security Policy. For example, in January 2009 the EU issued a declaration on the Russia/Ukraine problem and energy security. The main aim of this declaration was to call upon both parties to accept independent monitoring of the flows of gas through the pipelines in order to stop the interruptions of gas supply from Russia via the Ukraine.

Several international organizations have taken the category of voluntary instruments one step further via 'peer review mechanisms'. Of all the existing international frameworks where publicly available reviews are conducted, the OECD has the longest history in doing so. Already by 1961 it had began to monitor national economic policies and publish annual Economic Surveys, subjecting the draft reports to a full-day discussion in what was to be the first systematic peer review process in any international institution. The idea of this annual review procedure was that 'each country submit[ted] its economic situation and policies to the examination of all its partners. Ample opportunity [was] thus provided for discussion of major problems, and each country [was] confronted with an informed view on the impact of its policies on its neighbours' (Burgess *et al.*, 1960, p.20). One of the main ideas behind this system of evaluation was the notion that the examination of one state's performance in a particular sector by other states helps states to improve their policy making, adopt best practices, and comply with established standards and principles (Thygesen, 2008, pp.137–8). While the first peer review mechanisms did not have the possibility of resorting to sanctions in case of non-compliance – and thus might be labelled as voluntary policy instruments – several scholars argue that the push for member states to cooperate is more powerful than 'mere' recommendations or opinions for two reasons: (1) the 'threat' of 'naming and shaming' – and thus the creation of 'peer pressure' via the threat of receiving a negative reputation – influences countries' participation, and (2) the feedback obtained during the peer review process stimulates policy learning.

Within the EU we also see an increased use of monitoring and evaluation mechanisms as common policy tools. In particular, in areas where member states find it difficult to transfer responsibilities to the supranational level, but where there is a shared incentive to act beyond the use of recommendations, the use of such instruments is widespread. Although experimenting with peer review activities took place already, the significance of such activities as a policy tool was most clearly recognized by the Lisbon European Council, which established the 'Open Method of Coordination' (OMC) as a new method of governance. The Council meeting of March 2000 set out the aim of making the EU 'the most dynamic and competitive knowledge-based economy in the world', recognizing the particular need for further European cooperation in economic and employment policies. As these are also politically sensitive areas, the Council foresaw the need for a different type of policy tool that would stimulate cooperation, while at the same time avoiding the 'command-and-control' type of authoritative instruments.

In its ideal–typical form, the OMC is repeated regularly and proceeds as follows: the Council of Ministers agrees on common objectives (with indicators and benchmarks, 'where appropriate'), which are drafted mainly by the European Commission. Next, the member states, using the agreed list of indicators and benchmarks, translate the guidelines into domestic policies and report on both the policies they have implemented and planned, as well as on the progress made. The Commission then assesses and compares their efforts, identifies best practices, and formulates recommendations for each member state. This evaluation process is accompanied by peer review exercises involving both the member states and the regional, municipal and non-governmental actors. The peer review process aims at providing learning opportunities that feed back into the development of national policy and stimulate the re-formulation of guidelines. The results of the evaluation process are laid down in a joint report that must be approved by the Council. Finally, in the follow-up stage, the member states are expected to implement the measures recommended to them (Kerber and Eckardt, 2007, p.231; Radaelli, 2003, pp.14–15). The most well-known examples of the use of the OMC are the 'Broad Economic Policy Guidelines' and the 'European Employment Strategy'.

A distinct type of voluntary instrument are the instruments the European Commission has at its disposal to stimulate policy: the Green Papers and the White Papers. To use the terms of Hood's classification, these are 'nodality instrument' – that is, instruments that involve the strategic use of information. Green papers are documents issued by the European Commission to stimulate discussion. They invite the relevant actors to participate in a consultation process to discuss a given issue, which may in turn give rise to White Papers, although this is not always the case. White papers are Commission documents that contain proposals for Community action in a specific area and on their basis the Council can decide on further policy action. Famous white papers are the White Paper on Completion of the Internal Market (1985), triggering the establishment of a single market, or the White Paper on European Governance (2001), stimulating the debate on principles of good governance in the EU in the early 2000s.

Box 3.1 Inter-institutional agreement on better law making

An example of an inter-institutional agreement worth mentioning is the one dealing with the issue of better law making (2003/C 321/01). In this agreement, the European Commission, the European Parliament, and the Council of Ministers agree to ensure a better process of adopting legislation. The main aim of this agreement was to improve the quality of law making by improving the coordination and transparency between the three institutions, by increasing the use of impact assessment for all legislation, and by thinking of proposals to simplify the system of EU laws and law making. It was this agreement that helped in part to trigger the debate that finally led to the European Convention. The main idea behind the initiative was that the multiplicity of instruments and procedures used in the European Union to formulate and adopt policies has been too complex for most citizens to understand. This perceived complexity has led to what many consider to be a lack of transparency, which in turn effectively reduces the credibility and legitimacy of the EU as a political system. The inter-institutional agreement stimulated the debate that led to the introduction of the proposed simplification of legal instruments and decision-making procedures in the Lisbon Treaty.

A final very 'EU-specific' instrument worth mentioning is the 'inter-institutional agreement'. This is not a typical policy instrument as it does not aim to initiate policy but it is, nonetheless, an important tool in the working and functioning of the European Union. While the Treaties define the roles and competences of the three main institutional actors in the EU, the larger part of their day-to-day interaction is left unregulated. Inter-institutional agreements are used to put developed practices onto paper and to ensure well-functioning relations – and thus to clarify the respective powers – between the three institutions. A famous example is the inter-institutional agreement on better law-making (see Box 3.1).

Overview of EU policy fields

In a speech to the European Parliament in 1988, Jacques Delors predicted that '[i]n ten years, 80 per cent of economic legislation – and perhaps tax and social legislation – will be directed from the Community' (EP, 1988, p.140). Since that moment, the magic yet unsubstantiated number of 80 per cent has taken on a life of its own. It is used extensively by both supporters and opponents of European integration to indicate the impact the European Union has on domestic policy making. However, it is difficult, if not impossible, to place a number or percentage on the amount of policy that does in fact stem from 'Brussels'. There is so much differentiation across the various policy fields that it is impossible to arrive at a single figure. The current legislation in force in the field of taxation policy is 'limited' to 173 legal acts, for example, while in the agricultural sector – the most heavily regulated EU sector – there are currently 3,077 legal acts in force.

Beyond the question of *how* the EU can issue policies and via what policy instruments lies the question of *what* policies the EU actually issues. The EU is a special, or *sui generis*, type of organization, when compared to other international organizations or when compared to nation-states. While its competences do not match the wide responsibilities of 'traditional' nation-states, they go far beyond those of any international organization in force to date. What makes policy analysis in the EU context so complicated is the fact that the competences of the EU differ very much between different policy fields. While the EU has extensive competence in areas such as trade and agriculture, issues such as housing or domestic crime are virtually untouched by 'Brussels'. Before delving into the different categories of policy fields that the EU is engaged in, this next section will consider the important but difficult question of what determines whether policies are regulated at the EU level or not.

Why issue policy at the EU level?

Why is it that certain policy areas are heavily regulated at the European level while others are not? Indeed, why issue European legislation at all? Political debate about which competences should be delegated to the EU level and which responsibilities should remain with the nation-state or local level is heavily influenced by the principle of subsidiarity introduced in the Maastricht Treaty. This principle holds that decisions should be taken as close to the citizen as possible, and thus that policies should be issued at the lowest feasible level. That is, the EU is only to be involved when it is the most suitable level for policy action – when it can better regulate a given topic than individuals or member state governments alone could do. For each particular policy problem, the EU must consider whether or not 'Brussels' is the most appropriate level from which to impose regulation. In some policy fields it would seem to be a more suitable, and thus a more capable actor than individual member states. Few would disagree that environmental problems such as acid rain transcend national borders and call for international solutions, and that the EU level is the 'appropriate' level at which to impose regulation. In other fields it is easy to agree that the subsidiarity principle should be adhered to and that regulation is more appropriately carried out at the national, regional or local level. For most policy problems, however, this question reflects a grey zone, for cases can be made that both levels of regulation are necessary. This makes the principle sometimes difficult to apply, or can generate controversy among the actors involved. What in practice determines whether policies are adopted at the EU level?

Most importantly, the contextual factors of the international system increasingly stimulate international cooperation. Trends such as globalization render individual nation-states less competent to deal with complex policy problems such as the financial crisis of 2008/2009. Nation-states become more and more interdependent, which often persuades countries to transfer policy responsibilities to the EU level. Some sectors are obviously more influenced by globalization than others, which, in turn, can partly explain why we see more EU cooperation in some sectors than in others. However, this factor alone does not account for the EU's different degrees of involvement in various policy fields. Indeed, the degree of interdependence cannot alone account for the EU's political involvement, nor can it be entirely explained by Treaty provisions – an otherwise logical source of information when determining the amount of EU involvement in a particular policy field. There are many examples of contradictory developments: in some cases Treaty provisions allow for EU regulation in a certain sphere, while only limited progress is being made (for example Common Transport Policy), whereas in other contexts EU policy involvement occurs despite Treaty provisions (the start of environmental policy for example). Often, the degree of EU involvement in a particular field – between the application of the principle of subsidiarity or the push for growing interdependence – is influenced by varying circumstances. Sometimes we see influence exerted by certain institutional actors. Some Commission Presidents are known to have been very influential in initiating a new policy field, or further developing an existing one. The most prominent example is Jacques Delors (1985–95) who pushed for the Single European Market programme. Sometimes we see a push initiated by events or crises. The BSE crisis (mad cow disease), for example, triggered a debate about the EU's effectiveness in regulating food safety and helped to lead to the establishment of the European Food Safety Authority and further EU regulation in that field. Sometimes there is a functional logic deployed to solve problems collectively at the EU level. Policy problems can call for EU activity because they are generated by spillover from other EU activities, thereby creating pressure on member states to further cooperate. One such example might be cooperation in the field of coal and steel, which led to the need for a better established transport policy.

Each policy field, and even each individual policy initiative, has its own story to tell as to why the particular policy problem at hand was regulated at the EU level. An integral part of policy analysis is 'rewinding' that chain of events or journeying backwards in order to bring those moments into focus.

From coal and steel to justice and security

While European integration started as a rather limited 'project' regulating coal and steel in particular, over the last few decades the EU has developed into an international organization that is involved in a wide variety of policy fields. On its website, the EU lists 32 categories of activities it is involved in, which we can group into six broader categories (see Table 3.1).

It is not the aim of this section to describe the many different policy fields in detail. Rather, we will suggest that there are different categories of policies, each of which contains its own logic, and each of which entails its own particular set of issues to be considered in the context of a policy analysis. For example, as the EU initially started as a project of economic cooperation, the logic of creating a single market is much less debated than the possible need for a common foreign and security policy. By extension, Single European Market policies are much less controversial than the potential shape of the external policies of the EU. This section aims to illustrate some issues in the different sub-categories of policy fields, and, more importantly, to provide pointers as to where to find further information about each specific policy field.

Single European Market policies

Students of European integration will know that the years 1985 and 1992 were crucial for the development of a Single European Market. Although progress towards the single market certainly had its roots in the period before 1985 (the Treaties of Rome already initiated the free movement of goods, persons, services and capital), that year is crucial as it announced the adoption of the White Paper entitled 'Completing the Internal Market', which set out nearly 300 tasks, in a clear action plan with a concrete timetable, that would be necessary for completing the single market. Along with the decision to allow majority voting for about two-thirds of the White Paper proposals in the Single European Act that was adopted in 1986, it ushered in the internal market as a reality in 1992. It thus can be seen as a grand deregulatory project, removing the physical, technical, and fiscal barriers to trade, and opening national markets, mostly through the use of directives (internal market), decisions (competition and taxation) and regulations and agreements (customs).

Table 3.1 *Overview of EU policies*

Category	Commonality	Policy fields
Single Market policies	All policies established to create a Single European Market	• Competition • Customs • Internal market • Taxation
Macroeconomic and financial policies	A very specific category of policies related to macroeconomic cooperation	• Economic and monetary affairs
Functional policies	All policies with a clear, and very specific, functional purpose	• Consumers • Culture • Education, training, youth • Employment and social affairs • Environment • Fight against fraud • Food safety • Institutional affairs • Justice, freedom and security • Public health • Regional policy • Research and innovation
Sectoral policies	All policies targeted towards specific economic sectors	• Agriculture • Audiovisual and media • Energy • Enterprise • Fisheries and maritime affairs • Information society • Transport
External policies	All policies directed to activities outside the area of the Union	• Development • Enlargement • External relations • External trade • Foreign and security policy • Human rights • Humanitarian aid
Budget policies	A very specific category of policies related to arranging the budget of the EU	• Budget

Box 3.2   An example of Single European Market policies: competition policy

According to the Treaty, the EU has as its aim to ensure that 'competition in the internal market is not distorted'. One of the most powerful actors in this specific policy field is the European Commission. It has the tools to prevent anti-competitive practices; it can even directly inspect member states and can impose fines when it observes infringements. The three main branches of EU competition policy are antitrust, state aid and merger control regulations. Setting up EU competition policy has occurred in close cooperation with experts from the United States. The reason for this is simple: the US had a major stake in a solid European competition policy as the establishment of European cartels would potentially distort competition with US companies. The post of Commissioner for competition is a highly sought-after post, and those who have occupied it have not been afraid of actually using their powers in a wide-ranging manner. One of the most famous cases was the fining of Microsoft for its practice of bundling various types of software together in a single package. The Commission ordered Microsoft to pay €497 million in 2004. Microsoft appealed the decision in a drawn-out legal battle, but the Commission eventually won the case and in 2008 even imposed an additional fine of €899 million for failure to comply with antitrust decisions. In 2009 the Commission set a new 'record' by imposing a fine of around €1 billion on chip-producer Intel, arguing that the company was distorting the competition by allowing discounts to stores only selling computers with Intel chips.

Single European Market policies are heavily influenced by competition and market forces, and one can observe forces pushing for further integration not only from business groups, but also from member state governments and Commission President Delors himself, who served as 'policy entrepreneur' by initiating the White Paper in question. In this sense, the Single European Market might be seen as a policy field where agreement amongst the many actors involved around a common goal has been attained with little difficulty. This partly explains the relative ease with which the single market came into being, at least compared to other, more heavily disputed policy fields. This is not so say that cooperation in this range of policies has been completely free of impediments. One of the most important issues around Single European Market policies concerns implementation difficulties (see Box 3.2). While policy formulation and decision making might remain relatively uncomplicated, the sting is in the tail, as it were – the process of implementation after the actual decision making occurs is one of the most intriguing policy stages here. It is a policy field where uneven implementation immediately 'bites' – that is, it leads to a distortion of the proper functioning of the internal market. With this in mind, the Commission set up a 'single market scoreboard' in 1997 to demonstrate how member states performed in their implementation (a naming and shaming tool and used for starting infringement procedures).

Macroeconomic and financial policies

The main aim of macroeconomic and financial policies is economic in nature – such as the Single European Market policies – and is concerned with the coordination of national economic policies. The first plans to achieve an Economic and Monetary Union (EMU) were in place from 1970 when the Prime Minister of Luxemburg, Pierre Werner, introduced a plan to establish a EMU in ten years, although the economic recession of the 1970s quietly stalled these plans. Only in 1979, Commission President Roy Jenkins, supported by France and Germany, managed to launch a European Monetary System (EMS) to establish a zone of relative monetary stability. The positive experiences with the EMS laid the groundwork for further cooperation, and – again initiated by a Commission President – the report of the Delors committee in 1989 emphasized the need for macroeconomic policy coordination based on the principles of fixing of exchange rates, which would eventually set the stage for a single currency and a single monetary and exchange-rate policy. At the European Council meeting in Madrid that year, the member states agreed on a three-stage approach to EMU, with the first stage beginning on 1 July 1990. In 1999 the third and final stage began, with the European Central Bank coming into operation. The main event in that policy field was the introduction of the euro on 1 January 2002, currently used in 16 of the 27 member states.

While Single European Market policies and macroeconomic and financial policies both stem from economic incentives to push the EU's competitiveness, the difference between the micro and macro approach of both fields leads to different types of policy processes and thus to different types of issues to consider in terms of policy analysis. Macroeconomic policies are considered to be at the core of national sovereignty. Thus control over the national currency and key issues such as employment and finances are important for member states. While agreement is generally reached on removing trade barriers with relative ease, coordinating macroeconomic policies leads to much more contention between the different member states, as well as within them. Historically, France has been a strong defender of common European cooperation in the macroeconomic policy field, while the British have been seen to remain more reluctant. Germany has experienced internal struggles, with the German governments showing indifference, while the 'Bundesbank' has supported the idea of cooperation. All in all, it is a policy field that has been marked by periodic intense struggle between the actors concerned, and its development has been heavily influenced by external circumstances such as global economic and financial conditions. In this vein, a pressing topic for further analysis will no doubt be how the EU manages – or does not manage, for opinions are still divided – to tackle the financial crisis of 2008–2009.

Functional policies

The list of functional policies the EU regulates is long, involving as it does twelve separate policy fields. It is also not easy to make generalizations about the nature of all of these functional policies. In some cases, the EU is intensively involved in regulating a field, while in others its involvement is marginal. Some of the functional policies can be grouped together under a consistent logic, but others cannot be. Regional policy – aiming to undo internal disparities in income and opportunities between regions within the EU, using the Structural and Cohesion Funds – and institutional affairs – all policies related to the functioning of the EU institutions – are very specific and have their own logic that makes it impossible to put them into coherent groups.

A first sub-category is cooperation in the field of police and criminal matters, with the two policy fields of justice, freedom and security policy, and anti-fraud activity. Cooperation is this sphere is relatively new – it dates from the Maastricht Treaty – and has been stimulated by the combination of the removal of internal borders and the collapse of communism that triggered fear about a huge influx of immigrants to the West. Here one sees more and more extensive cooperation in the fields of asylum, immigration and visa policies, while there has been only marginal policy cooperation in the fields of organized crime and judicial cooperation in civil and criminal matters. With this distinction in mind, it is worth asking why member states are more willing to transfer competences in some specific fields of police and criminal affairs, while in other specific fields they remain reluctant to do so. Another important question concerns the influence of events such as the '9/11' terrorist attacks on policy development within the EU.

A second distinct category of functional policies are the broad range of policies grouped under the designation of 'social', in the widest sense of the word, that the EU initiates. Here, it is possible to group together five policy fields that have as their common feature the protection of a particular group or element in society: consumer protection policy, public health policy, food safety policy, employment and social affairs, and environmental policy. Treaty provisions for all of these policies were only established after the first directives (the most commonly used tool for this sub-category) were already established. In other words, it seems circumstances somehow led to extending EU competences in this field. Sometimes cooperation in the internal market pushed for the need to regulate, for example, the environment, but sometimes other external circumstances triggered cooperation.

This group of policy fields has been extensively researched. The large use of directives within it has stimulated much interest. That quite particular type of instrument, whereby one specifies only the required results leaving the form and method to achieve them open to the member states, presents both analytical difficulties and intriguing questions and challenges throughout the policy process, and at the implementation stage in particular. Equally worthy of attention are issues of the relative strength and power of the actors involved in the first stages of the policy process. In fact, this is a sub-category of policies that triggers great attention, not only from the European Parliament, but also from lobby-groups of all sorts (for example, consumer, environment, or animal rights NGOs). Analyzing the influence of crises and disasters within it is also a growing area of research. For example, how and to what extent did the BSE crisis influence food safety policy (see Box 3.3)?

A final sub-category of functional policies are those policies for which the EU does see the need to stimulate further activity or cooperation, and where member states remain reluctant to transfer autonomy to the supranational level: research and innovation, education, and cultural policy. What these policies have in common is the desire of national governments to maintain their sovereignty. Cooperation is largely arranged through voluntary instruments such as agreements, Council resolutions and recommendations, and an occasional decision. Issues typically raised in these fields relate to the subsidiarity principle and to sovereignty: what determines the need for European cooperation? Why are member states so reluctant to cooperate in these fields?

Sectoral policies

European integration began by regulating the coal and steel sectors and in the early years of integration those sectoral policies remained the dominant ones on the European agenda, with agricultural policy forming one of the most important policy fields. Over the last few decades, as a result of societal changes, the EU's sectoral policies have come to concentrate largely on new sectors, as the information society has entered the policy agenda and agriculture has slowly but surely begun to lose its initial dominant position. Over the course of these changes, however, sectoral policies have remained high in the European arena. We can identify six different sectors that the EU regu-

Box 3.3   An example of functional policies: food safety policy

European food safety policy initially started off as an integrated part of the CAP and later of consumer policy. Under pressure from the United States and the World Trade Organization – but also with the threat of transmissible diseases such as BSE and the foot-and-mouth disease in mind – food safety is now an explicit activity of the EU that not only covers food safety for consumers, but also animal and plant health and animal welfare. While the CAP was mainly concerned with ensuring an adequate food supply in Europe, this cooperation later started to raise questions about the quality of mass-produced food with the use of pesticides, food supplements, colourings, antibiotics, or hormones. The current aim is to ensure that food is traceable from 'farm to fork' and to provide consumers with more information about the ingredients of products through detailed and accurate labelling. Because of the uncertainty that dominates this field – often we know too little about potential risks and dangers at hand – it is one of the policy fields where scientific advice is crucial and plays a strategic role. In this sense, the precautionary principle also plays an important role here: in the case of a possible danger to health or the environment, and where scientific data do not allow a complete risk evaluation, this principle can be used to prevent products from entering the market, or to stop their production. In particular, the potential risks of genetically modified crops and foods have stimulated involved debates. There has, for example, been a significant debate between the European Food Safety Authority, the Commission, several member states and the US biotech company Monsanto, as to whether or not a genetically modified type of corn should be allowed on the European market. While the Commission favoured it entering the market, several member states blocked an agreement in the environmental Council.

lates, in most cases by using decisions and regulations: agriculture, energy, enterprise, fisheries and maritime affairs, information society, and transport.

The most important reason why the EU regulates certain sectors is to increase their competitiveness. Although the initial reason for starting to transfer competences to the European level for the actors involved was triggered by those economic motivations, an increasing effect of sectoral policies has been to enhance sustainability and to protect actors involved in, or affected by them. For example, while the EU's fisheries policy initially started as economically oriented deregulatory legislation in the early 1970s (removing barriers to allow member states in each other's fishing waters), over the years it came to include more re-regulatory, protectionist elements, inspired by the EU's enlargement to include fishing nations Denmark, Ireland and the UK. It now attempts to strike a difficult balance between ensuring the competitiveness of the sector, while at the same time enhancing sustainable fish stocks (it specifies a 'total allowable catch'), and promoting a sustainable marine eco-system. In this way, enterprise policy is not only concerned with creating the right environment for stimulating competitiveness and innovation, but it also attempts to achieve a workable balance between protecting consumers and ensuring environmental protection. Sectoral policies are in this sense linked to some of the functional policies listed above.

This difficult balancing act between economically driven motivations and social aims of sustainability and protection that characterizes the policy process for sectoral policies makes them a compelling object of enquiry. How does the policy process account for these different, and often diverging, interests and preferences? What does this tell us about the 'winners' and 'losers' of the policy process? Does this balancing act make the policy process typically a battle? Particularly interesting is the potential clash between the different types of actors involved. Each of the sectoral policies will have some natural opponents and proponents. In agricultural policy, we witness the dividing line between farmers and environmentalists, just as in fisheries policy the argument is between scientists and the fishing community. While scientists argue that the EU policy does not protect the fish stocks sufficiently, the fishing community complains of threats to their business.

Second, the different member states might advance competing positions as a function of the size and relative strength of a particular sector in a country. Agricultural policy, in particular, has seen sharp differences of opinion between those countries with a large agricultural sector and those who have a smaller agricultural sector: divisions that have at times even threatened the integration process (Box 3.4). Today, we witness competing points of view as to whether or not to pursue a common energy policy in light of the EU's external geo-political relations with important energy providers such as Russia.

External policies

The external policies of the EU differ enormously, not only when it comes to the degree of EU involvement, but also with regards to the very logic behind cooperation in the first place, factors that will determine to a large extent the particular questions raised in policy analysis of this area. We can divide the external policies of the EU into four broad categories: trade-oriented, development-oriented, security-oriented, and mixed policies.

Box 3.4   An example of sectoral policies: Common Agricultural Policy

With the deficit in food production in Europe at the end of the 1950s, policies were introduced to increase agricultural productivity and to ensure fair internal prices and incomes. The first regulations were introduced in 1962, and by the end of the 1960s, there was a fully fledged European agricultural policy in operation, the Common Agricultural Policy (CAP). The operation of the CAP rests on providing subsidies for crops to farmers, setting import tariffs on certain goods imported into the EU, and establishing an intervention price – that is, if prices drop below a desired level, the EU intervenes by buying those goods to ensure an increase in prices. This policy has been subject to considerable criticism over the years. Many have argued that it distorts competition in the larger world market, and that the 'safety net' that this system accords to farmers has not encouraged them to produce efficiently, leading to the so-called 'wine lakes' and 'butter mountains'. Apart from the negative effects of this policy on the relations with the EU's trading partners, the CAP has also generated internal conflict as some member states have larger agricultural sectors and consequently receive more money. The CAP is one of the EU policy fields that has changed most significantly over the course of the last several decades. While in the 1970s it accounted for nearly 70 per cent of the EU budget, this has been reduced to about 34 per cent in the period 2007–2013. Many attempts to reform the CAP have led to struggles and debates, and what the future will hold for it is very much an open question. What has been achieved, however, is that during the Doha Round of international trade liberalization talks, the EU proposed to eliminate export subsidies altogether by 2013.

External trade policies condition the position that the EU as a whole takes with regards to the larger global market. This policy field gives the European Commission an important role as the main player in negotiations with the World Trade Organization, as it negotiates on behalf of the EU member states. The external trade policy field is characterized by bilateral agreements with individual countries and regions all over the world. It is strongly linked with the EU's agricultural and development policies. The way that the EU organizes its import of products also has a direct effect on the possibility of fair trade, an issue that is gaining particular importance in the development of poorer regions in the world.

The EU's security-oriented policies can be divided into foreign and security policies and defence policies. Discussions about common security cooperation had already begun in the early years of European integration. In the early 1950s the 'Pleven Plan' or 'European Defence Community' plan for a European army was rejected by the French national assembly. Partly as a result of external circumstances such as the collapse of communism, German unification, the break-up of the Soviet Union and the war in Yugoslavia, several actors started to argue for increased political cooperation at the beginning of the 1990s. Having foreign and security policy, as well as justice and home affairs, in a separate, intergovernmental pillar seemed to be a way to convince hesitant member states to agree to further political cooperation during negotiations for the Maastricht Treaty. Since then, security policies have continued to develop in the EU. While trade and development-oriented policies are marked by the strong influence of the European Commission, its role is more limited with regards to security-oriented policies. Here, it is worth pointing out that there are often strong dividing lines between the various different member states. The inability of the EU to speak with one voice during the Iraq crisis in 2003 serves as a case in point.

The EU's enlargement and external relations policies are typically a mix of different logics. They contain elements of both security and development. Enlargement policy, for example, aims on the one hand to encourage development in candidate countries, but on the other hand strives to strengthen security. The different logics inherent to these different types of external policies lend themselves to different lines of enquiry, from the more economical, such as a trade-related perspective, to the more geo-political, such as a security-related per-spective.

Budget policies

Compared to the combined GDP of the member states, the budget of the EU is fairly limited. The way in which budgetary policies have been issued throughout the history of European integration has changed greatly over time. The EU started as an organization that was entirely dependent on the contributions of its member states. The cost of the CAP eventually rendered this situation unworkable, but attempts by Commission President Hallstein in the early 1960s to provide the Community with its own budget generated considerable friction between the member states. France, a major agricultural producer and a fierce proponent of a strong CAP, resisted these budgetary reforms, a state of affairs that led to the 'empty chair crisis', when French minis-ters refused to take part in Council meetings and the French permanent representatives were withdrawn from Brussels. Only in 1970 did the member states manage to agree, via an amendment to the Treaty of Rome, to change the budgetary system to a system of independent resources. The new system consisted of three main pillars: agricultural

levies charged on import products from third countries, customs duties
levied on industrial products imported, and VAT resources. This
reform also handed modest budgetary power to the European
Parliament. A second reform in 1975 created the European Court of
Auditors, again extending the powers of the EP. Both had as their aim
to enhance the legitimacy and accountability of the budgetary process.

A significant source of problems in the context of budget negotiations was the fact that the countries applying to join the EU at the end
of the 1960s were not consulted on the process that led to the first of
these reforms in 1970. Traditionally, the largest proportion of the
budget had been dedicated to the CAP, a fact which sparked many
conflicts and necessitated repeated negotiations between member
states. The large sums of money dedicated to both agriculture and
regional aid effectively meant that a great deal of money went to
poorer member states with large agricultural sectors. As Margaret
Thatcher assumed the role of Prime Minister in the United Kingdom in
1979, a long and intense debate over the budget began. In a movement
initiated by Wilson, Thatcher began to contest the size and composition of the EU budget, raising what came to be known as the 'British
Budgetary Question'. Given that the UK had a relatively small agricultural sector and that it imported many agricultural products and both
paid more levies and received less funds from the CAP, Thatcher
argued that the UK was paying too much and receiving too little.
Finally, at the 1984 Fontainebleau European Council, the member
states agreed to curtail CAP spending and to increase the EU's own
resources.

Since 1988, with the introduction of the system of multi-annual
packages, budgetary policy making has entered relatively easier waters,
The Delors I package (1988–92) set out to increase the budget to allow
for all policy initiatives needed to create a single market. The most
recent package was agreed in the 2005 agreement on the budget for
2007–13. This is not to say that difficulties no longer exist. It is certainly still true that attempts to drastically reform the budget –
according to some, a need engendered by the remaining difficulties
with the CAP and the costs of the latest enlargements – continue to be
blocked by several member states. A more detailed analysis of the
budget is contained in Chapter 7.

There are many important lines of enquiry related to analyzing budgetary policy processes. Money is certainly at the core of member
states' politics and who gets what, when and how remains a sensitive
issue. At the heart of budgetary politics are political choices about how
to allocate resources. In this policy process, one can observe several
distinctly different camps: (1) net contributors versus net beneficiaries,
and (2) old versus new beneficiaries of regional policy (particularly
since the latest enlargements). Questions about budgetary reform touch

upon other interests such as agriculture, regional policy, and enlargements. Some member states use the EU's budget to fight electoral battles back home. Budgetary policy making rests to a large extent on big 'history-making' decisions about multi-annual packages, but simultaneously on many smaller management decisions within each policy field.

Conclusion

When conducting policy analysis at the EU level, identifying the relevant type of policy field and policy instrument is a crucial exercise. One might say that 'policy determines politics', for different types of policy fields and different types of policy instruments have a huge impact on the dynamics of – and the politics behind – the policy process, as well as on the way in which all the actors involved in the issue behave throughout the process. As one can well imagine, policies that rest on the distribution of new resources will trigger different responses from those actors: responses that would probably be quite different were one dealing with policies resting mostly on providing information. It should come as no surprise that governments in general attempt to obtain more control over this first type of policy process, and are more willing to delegate responsibilities to the supranational level with regards to the second. Being able to concretely identify the different sub-elements of the policy one is analyzing can in turn provide quite incisive information about both the power relations and the existing political conflict between the different actors involved.

In this sense, when analyzing the policy process at the EU level, it is crucial to ensure that one gains a clear understanding of the specificities of the policy field and the policy instrument in question. This starts with the 'history' of the given policy field. When does a certain issue start to be regulated at the European level, what triggers its existence as such, and what is the formal (institutional) context in terms of procedures and competences, and so on? And what is the *impact* of the main policy instruments used in this field?

The topic of policy instruments as such triggers relatively little attention in policy analysis. But even if one might prefer to analyze the policy process or its outcomes, the question of *why* a particular policy instrument was chosen in the first place is no less intriguing. How relevant have the policy instruments selected in the EU been in terms of achieving their policy goals? To what extent is the EU using new policy instruments? Should it be more active in trying to find new types of policy tools to accommodate the intrinsically complicated nature of negotiations at the supranational level, or do the existing policy instruments suffice? When analyzing a specific policy instrument, it is valuable to know whether this specific instrument is a common feature of the larger set of instruments used in the particular policy field. Did deciding upon the form of the instruments trigger intensive debate? In any case, what is clear is that the type of policy instruments used – that is, those that are chosen not only during the policy formulation stage, but also those that are determined by the nature of the debate during the agenda-setting stage and through treaty provisions – has an almost limitless influence on how actors behave in the decision-making stage and, perhaps even more importantly, determines the effectiveness of actually putting the policy into practice at the implementation stage. One cannot stress this multi-faceted nature of policy processes enough: a voluntary instrument will trigger different behaviour from the actors across the entire spectrum when it comes to the decision-making stage.

Suggestions for further reading

Books that provide a general introduction into several policy fields

Cini, M. and Perez-Solorzano Borragan, N. (2009) (eds) *European Union Politics*, 3rd edn (Oxford: Oxford University Press).

Hix, S. (2005) *The Political System of the European Union*, 2nd edn (Basingstoke and New York: Palgrave Macmillan).

Nugent, N. (2010) *The Government and Politics of the European Union*, 7th edn (Basingstoke and New York: Palgrave Macmillan).

Wallace, H., Pollack, M.A. and Young, A.R. (2010) (eds) *Policy-Making in the European Union*, 6th edn (Oxford: Oxford University Press).

Books about a specific policy field

Ansell, C. and Vogel, D. (2006) (eds) *What's the Beef? The Contested Governance of European Food Safety* (Cambridge: MIT Press).

Bache, I. (2008) *Europeanization and Multi-level Governance: Cohesion Policy in the European Union and Britain* (Lanham: Rowman & Littlefield).

Evans, A. (2005) *EU Regional Policy* (Richmond: Richmond Law and Tax).

Goodman, J. (2006) *Telecommunications Policy-Making in the European Union* (Northampton: Edward Elgar).

Greer, A. (2009) *Agricultural Policy in Europe* (Manchester: Manchester University Press).

Hantrais, L. (2007) *Social Policy in the European Union*, 3rd edn (Basingstoke and New York: Palgrave Macmillan).

Holland, M. (2002) *The European Union and the Third World* (Basingstoke and New York: Palgrave Macmillan).

Howorth, J. (2007) *Security and Defence Policy in the European Union* (Basingstoke and New York: Palgrave Macmillan).

Keukeleire, S. and MacNaughtan, J. (2008) *The Foreign Policy of the European Union* (Basingstoke and New York: Palgrave Macmillan).

McCormick, J. (2001) *Environmental Policy in the European Union* (Basingstoke and New York: Palgrave Macmillan).

McLean, C. (2008) *The Common Fisheries Policy of the European Union; Diverging Responses in Germany and the United Kingdom* (Ceredigion: Edwin Mellen Press).

Stevens, H. (2003) *Transport Policy in the European Union* (Basingstoke and New York: Palgrave Macmillan).

Weber, K., Smith, M. and Braun, M. (eds) (2008) *Governing Europe's Neighbourhood: Partners or Periphery?* (Manchester: Manchester University Press).

Relevant website

http://europa.eu/pol/index_en.htm. On the general overview page of the EU website one can find an overview of all policy fields. Each field provides further information on other key sites, documentation, summaries of legislation and legal texts.

Chapter 4

How Do We Analyze?

Introduction

This chapter builds on the description in Chapters 1 through 3 of who is involved in policy making and what types of policy one might analyze, by offering some specific insights into research methodologies and the different types of theory that are often employed in EU policy analysis. How do academic scholars *go about* the exercise of analyzing the policy process? Which *different features* of the process do they tend to focus on – and why? In what way might *alternative approaches and perspectives* on the same policy – or specifically, individual pieces of legislation – produce different outcomes and conclusions? In fact, *how* to analyze depends to a large degree on which aspects of policy making one wishes to focus on beyond the actual choice of the policy area itself. The aspects, features and phenomena of the process to be analyzed will largely influence the choice of research design and use of theory.

Focus, phenomena and approach

Most importantly, *how* to analyze EU policy implies a series of choices regarding scale and scope. Much academic analysis seeks to account for the emergence and development, or success/failure of a single piece or type of legislation, rather than the hundreds of distinct laws that may constitute a policy area over time – and it is already difficult enough to determine where a single policy area begins and ends. A useful analytical approach is to consider pieces of EU legislation as 'stepping stones', defining moments in policy development that can be used to structure policy analysis. Some non-academic analysts are primarily interested in the technicalities and substantive features of policy content, while political scientists are usually more interested in the 'before, during and after' of the process, in pinpointing the elements of the process, trying to uncover which key factors influenced and ultimately determined how policy emerged, and why it ended up looking like it did (Box 4.1).

Scholars are interested not only in new legislation, but also in the other characteristic features of the system and the related phenomena

---

Box 4.1   How does the EU ...? Potential starting points for analysis

Administer, agree, bargain, bridge, build, clean up, consult, co-decide, co-finance, connect, coordinate, cooperate, debate, decide, develop, discuss, enact, encourage, fine, foster, guarantee, guard, harmonize, implement, innovate, inspect, interpret, intervene, legislate, level out, liaise, measure, mediate, monitor, negotiate, oversee, persuade, police, prioritize, promote, propose, protect, reach a compromise, redistribute, regulate, remove, restrict, sanction, set the agenda, share, sponsor, tender, translate, vote?

---

that can be identified within the policy-making environment, many of which may be unique and newly emerging. They key question in this sense is the way in which policy is arrived at, that is, *how it emerges*. Here, many scholars have addressed the *dynamic* configuration of actors involved, the *evolving* institutional architecture, the *transformative* language, terminology and ideas, and the *emerging* forces at play. But beyond policy outputs, academics analyze the various ingredients that make up the larger recipe of the system. New legislation is often merely a continuation of what came before with relatively insignificant incremental change. It is more the trends and patterns that can be seen in the institutional and human behaviour of those engaged in policy making that intrigue scholars – that is, the behavioural dynamics of the *process* itself. To put it another way, EU policy analysts attempt to interpret a political circus of different players who 'perform' policy making, as it were. And while there may be no human flying cannon-balls in the meeting rooms of the EU institutions, a large amount of juggling of agendas and delicate tight-rope walking occurs as the consensus necessary to arrive at decisions is made.

When doing policy analysis, it is important to keep the scale of the analysis realistic, given one's resource constraints – time, money, access to informants, and so on. This inevitably means that the analysis will be to some degree limited – one chooses what to include or exclude, whom to focus on and whom to ignore. Importantly, this implies that one will make an explicit decision as to *how to see* and *what to look for*. Embarking upon EU policy analysis without having first set these parameters is like groping in the dark – one's path quickly becomes obstructed by irrelevant information; one stumbles across upon all sorts of *seemingly* interesting information and data, but material that will nonetheless ultimately impede the analysis. And, as there are multiple perspectives on policy making, each of which will influence both

Box 4.2   Initial questions: deciding how and where to begin the analysis

1. What is intriguing or puzzling about this policy area?
2. Which particular aspects are of most interest to academics or practitioners?
3. Why is this piece of legislation in particular so crucial?
4. Has something significant changed, or evolved in a new way?
5. What is it about the policy-making process that warrants further investigation?
6. Has there been a recent policy development or political crisis that needs explanation?
7. What is the urgency, importance, or the potential added-value of this analysis – why bother?
8. What initial assumptions might one have, particularly in light of previous developments?
9. What is the historical/political context – how has the policy area developed over time?
10. Are existing accounts plausible or correct – are they convincing, thorough, rigorous?

one's research trajectory (methodology) and the tools that one will use (theories, typologies, frameworks). It is crucial to decide from the outset the angle from which one will approach the policy. That this approach is clear and transparent is vital if one's later findings are to retain validity and legitimacy. Just like policy making itself, policy analysis should be viewed as a *process* with its own identifiable stages and parameters (Box 4.2).

When conducting policy analysis, it is important to narrow the research focus down, perhaps to a policy-cycle stage and even a piece of specific legislation. This means pinpointing the specific aspects of the process that one will examine – and accounting for their existence in the first place. This delineation will then determine *how* one will go about collecting data and framing the analysis, as well as the theory that one will use to inform and explain the process. In short, before putting together a plan (methodology) one needs to determine the *aspects* or *phenomena* that one will be addressing – this, in turn, relates to the perspective that one choose or one's *way of seeing*.

Table 4.1 is by no means exhaustive, but it indicatives eight 'I's – possible avenues of enquiry when embarking upon analysis in an area of EU policy. After one formulates some general questions about the research enquiry and how it relates to a particular policy domain, it is then useful to step back and consider which broader political

Table 4.1 *Possible topics for policy analysis in the EU*

Aspects influencing policy making	Questions regarding the EU policy process	Possible focus for research and analysis
1. Ideas/ideology	Where did the policy ideas come from? Whose ideology (which member states) is reflected in the legislation? Was there conflict? Which narratives dominated?	The social construction of ideas; ideology and persuasion
2. Issues	How controversial was the issue? Was it always a problem or was it constructed as such by a particular group?	The construction of issues as problems warranting solutions
3. Initiative	Who initiated policy development? Where did it all begin? Who made the first proposals? Why now?	The importance of timing and windows of opportunity
4. Influence	Who/what has been most influential in steering the process and how did they manage to exert influence?	Channels of influence, access and actor socialization
5. Interests	Which interests (political, commercial, societal) were key in steering the agenda? How did they access decision makers?	The role of interest groups in influencing the agenda
6. Information	Who possessed the most relevant/ valuable information? Who are the experts? How was information used/ abused?	Information and expertise as power
7. Institutions	Which institutions have been most important – supranational or national; Commission or Parliament? What resistance was there and who was most active when?	The role of institutions and political leadership; scrutiny and control
8. Instruments	What type of instrument emerged and why this type and not another? Has it been effective and if not, why? Did policy develop through regulation, coercion or voluntarily? Why was legislation needed?	How the shape of an instrument may determine success; transposition and implementation

science topics the enquiry might relate to, and consequently, how an empirical analysis might contribute to the wider debate in those research areas. Scholars are often interested not so much in what the policy analysis tells us about the policy *content* itself, but rather in the ways in which an analysis of the policy area can lead to a deeper understanding of the policy *process*. The readership of academic policy analysis – for example, of articles published in academic journals – may have little knowledge of the policy area, and may not necessarily be seeking to acquire one. Readers may want to glean new insights into the use, or the applicability or limits of a certain theory, or they might be concerned with policy analysis as an exercise of intellectual enquiry: how did the analyst go about analyzing? Why did he/she choose this approach? What tools prove most useful – perhaps he/she developed their own? Was the analysis innovative, valuable or conducive to gaining new insights into the dynamics of EU policy making? As the list of eight 'I's suggests, EU policy analysts may be interested in the role of expertise, the choice of policy instruments, or the use of ideas to influence policy outcomes across a broad range of policy areas.

Mapping methodologies and research design

Conducting policy analysis entails deciding upon the scale and scope of the research, making it essential to elaborate a methodology and to design an approach. As Bechhofer and Paterson (2000, p. vii) write, 'if you want to plan a piece of empirical social research, you have to make decisions about how the research is to be carried out. You have to choose a set of procedures which enable your aims and objectives to be realized in practice'. But as we suggested above, there is no real single 'set recipe'. Analyzing the EU policy process implies engaging in a research design process that is both creative and open-ended.

What is research design?

As Burnham *et al.* (2008, p.38) note, '[t]he research design will set out the priorities of the research: for example, describing the hypotheses to be tested, listing the research questions and, most important of all, specifying the evidence needed to provide a convincing test for the research hypotheses and to provide the data needed to answer the research questions ... These priorities will determine whether the evidence should be predominantly qualitative or quantitative and how it should be collected and analyzed.' In this sense, research design might be seen as the 'logical structure of the research enquiry'. It has two functions: 'to develop or conceptualize an operational plan; and second, to ensure that the procedures adopted within the plan are adequate to provide valid, objective and accurate solutions to the research problems' (ibid., p.42). As Hakim (2000, p.6) elaborates, research design involves converting questions raised in theoretical or policy debates into feasible research projects or programmes in order to provide answers to academic questions.

When it comes to methodology there are no strictly defined or opposing camps in European studies or political science. That said, certain scholars favour quantitative methods, collecting numerical data and often using computer programs to generate statistics and profiles through which they can deduce behavioural patterns. Such 'number-crunching' can be done using a range of methods from simple counting to feeding data into elaborate computer programs. Other EU scholars, however, use qualitative methods such as textual analysis of documents and interviews to acquire new information. During the process of data collection, certain issues and opinions may emerge, confirming or contradicting a researcher's hypothesis. What is said or not said must itself be interpreted in light of the interests and the particular agenda of the actors involved. Many EU scholars conduct a kind of analysis that combines both the quantitative and the qualitative, so producing 'mixed methods' studies that do not rely solely on words or just on numbers.

Qualitative research involves collecting in-depth information from what is often a limited number of cases. The focus may be on specific policies or innovations, but this type of research does not usually allow for the making of sweeping generalizations. Most political scientists who employ qualitative methods to research the EU rely on four ways of gathering information: participation in the setting, direct observation, in-depth interviews, and the use of documents and materials. As such, they may take themselves off to Brussels, Luxembourg or Strasbourg, or to national capitals, where they have direct access to policy makers or to primary source material in archives. Their methodologies for analysis may involve discourse analysis, analysis of speech acts or media reporting, the use of case studies, content analysis, archival research, or interviewing. This type of research is published in journals such as *Journal of Common Market Studies (JCMS), Journal of European Public Policy (JEPP), Journal of Contemporary European Research (JCER), Journal of Contemporary European Studies (JCES) and Journal of European Integration (JEI).* Quantitative researchers, by comparison, engage in data modelling, predictive or retrospective numerical analysis, and forecasting. This may require a lengthy process of collecting and collating budgetary expenditure, or interpreting voter turnout numbers. Examples of such work are published in *Journal of European Politics (JEP), European Union Politics (EUP)* and *European Political Research (EPR).*

How might one go about analyzing voter turnout in the EU Elections 2009? Quantitative research is not only useful when analyzing election results, voting patterns and political preferences. It is true that these are areas on which much of the quantitative output in EU studies is focused. This can be easily explained by research designs that use surveys and polls to count votes classified by demography, region, beliefs, and so on. Many qualitative analysts might see such 'scientific' approaches as crude or clinical, unable to provide the insight into the complex, nuanced realities that qualitative research offers. Qualitative approaches stem from disciplines such as anthropology and sociology and are characterized by a more intimate attempt to get to grips with human behaviour. For example, Kousser (2004) mixes qualitative and quantitative research in order to test four theories using aggregate election returns from every EP contest, looking at survey data from the 1994 elections, to provide an insight into retrospective voting and strategic behaviour. Franklin (2001) draws on existing quantitative data but engages in reflective analysis of the structural factors explaining the decline in voter turnout since the first EP elections in 1979, noting that the new member states do not have compulsory voting, which may largely account for the appearance of decline.

The aspects of the process one is most interested in will shape and structure the research design (Box 4.3).

- If interested in the way political issues are framed and ideas communicated through political language, one might choose to analyze official communications, newspapers such as *European Voice* and official EU policy documents.
- If fascinated by the role of institutions or public leadership, one might examine speeches by Commissioners (and communications from their *cabinets*), MEPs, heads of state or even set up interviews oneself.
- If seeking to study the evolution of policy priorities over time, one might compare and contrast EU regulations and directives from different programming periods to find out what happened in between to influence new directions or priorities, or to account for any U-turns that occurred.
- If wanting to understand why one piece of legislation was transposed quickly but another met with resistance, it may be helpful to start looking back over the decision-making process by consulting official websites and databases. These often show who objected to proposals and draft legislation, when, and on what grounds they did so. Using the *PreLex* database to see the 'ping-pong' of opinions back and forth between EP and Commission can reveal much about institutional power and the battle to secure consensus.

> ## Box 4.3 Witness account 1: research focus on policy formulation and decision
>
> 'In order to investigate my hypothesis, I wanted to conduct a case study of the proposals made by the Commission of three measures contained in the 2001 White Paper: the road charging directive (also known as the "eurovignette" directive), the Marco Polo program regulation and the ILU directive (European Commission, 2001). Why these three specific policy instruments? First of all, they all came from the same White Paper, which means that they were initiated by the same body (Directorate-General of Transport) at the same time (2002 for the Marco Polo program, 2003 for the ILU and the road charging directives) and in the same policy area (transport). Consequently, these three factors were controlled and cannot have had an impact on the policy process. I wanted to see what happened to these three very different proposed policy instruments at the decision-making stage – and how to explain their fate.' *(Charles, MA researcher and analyst)*

Research methods

Table 4.2 introduces some of the methods by which one might embark upon research. Of course, one will be looking to collect data that, after interpretation, may prove or disprove one's hypothesis. Very little evidence is actually explicitly stated in black and white on paper.

Data collection may mean putting the legislation or policy document aside, going out into the policy world and contacting or meeting those responsible for influencing, pushing, promoting, debating, negotiating, objecting to, vetoing, waving through, giving the green light to, reforming or scrapping policy. This might be at the local, regional, national or supranational level. It may concern those in the private or public sector. Those involved may be the agenda setters, the decision makers or the implementers, at home or abroad.

Analysis will only be possible after having sorted the data. Starting with an effectively designed method of data collection will allow one to save a great deal of time in the long run, as being able to cross-reference samples can ease data correlation and interpretation. There is usually a reason why some data is easy to locate and other sorts of data less easily accessible – political sensitivity. This problem may be reflected in interviews, when seemingly cooperative informants may be evasive about particular aspects of the issue – when they may not in fact be telling the whole story. As politics is nothing if not a constant power struggle, it naturally follows that there will be a multitude of competing narratives and answers, from those provided by ostensible winners and

Table 4.2   *Research methods*

Types of qualitative research	Definition (after Payne and Payne, 2004)	Possible questions around this type of research
Case study	A very detailed enquiry into a single example of a political process, organization or collectivity seen as a political unit in its own right.	What influence did the Spanish government have on the recent reform of the Structural Funds, reflected in the new regulation?
Content analysis	Seeks to demonstrate the meaning of written or visual sources (such as newspapers) by systematically allocating their content to pre-determined, detailed categories, then quantifying and/or interpreting outcomes.	How did different member states report on the 1999 EP elections, and did reporting style and the issues covered influence variations in support for the EU and voter turnout?
Discourse analysis	The analysis of language and rhetoric; how political concepts, ideas, terminology, behaviour and institutional arrangements are loaded with assumptions, perceptions and understanding.	To what extent did the European Commission become 'rhetorically trapped' through its own discourse, into accepting Romania and Bulgaria as EU members in 2004?
Fieldwork	Undertaken during the data collection stage, allows for the gathering of relevant information in countries and institutional settings.	Which key factors are most responsible for transforming civil society in the new accession states of the EU, and what is the evidence?
Interviewing / key informants	Data collection in face-to-face settings or over the telephone, using an oral question-and-answer format, in a (semi-) structured, systemic way; can be recorded with permission.	What role did the CEOs of key European firms have in pushing the Commission and shaping the content of the Single Market Programme? ➤

losers in any process, from those who may be triumphant and those who may be disgruntled. As any research enquiry gets underway, a story begins to emerge. And as the researcher becomes more immersed in the particular story of this policy area, his/her knowledge of policy developments becomes more nuanced, taking the various surprises and obstacles encountered on board. The practical experience of researching – including cooperation or resistance from stakeholders, the ease or difficulty of accessing data and sources – will largely determine what one

→ **Table 4.2**   (continued)

Types of qualitative research	Definition (after Payne and Payne, 2004)	Possible questions around this type of research
Longitudinal studies/cross-sectional studies	Data collected and analyzed from the same sample (country, policy area, institution) on many occasions, over a long period of time; compare with cross-sectional studies where data is collected once only in a short period but from different samples.	Why did the trans-European networks emerge in the early 1990s to promote ambitious large-scale transport infrastructure projects in high-speed rail after 40 years of failed EC transport policy?
Participant observation	Data collection over a sustained period by watching, listening, asking questions of those going about their routine and day-to-day activities; researcher becomes a member of group.	How does the day-to-day working of the Commission, its rules, procedures, norms and organizational culture, influence policy outcomes?
Questionnaire/ social survey	Printed sets of questions to be answered by respondents, through interview or self-completion; must be tested, structured, systematic and clearly presented.	Do young people understand the Lisbon Treaty and if not, why not? What does it mean to them?
Sampling	Selecting a sub-set of people or political phenomena to be studied as representative of the 'larger universe'; sample is determined by resources (time, techniques, access, cost).	What variation is there in the active engagement by urban communities in the implementation of the Water Framework Directive, and why?

is able to analyze, and consequently colour the overall claim or argument that emerges from the analysis. Textual analysis can involve reading between the lines, interpreting euphemisms, identifying what was not said or left out, or recognizing which answers were not given and why they were omitted. Who was particularly opinionated, and who was particularly indifferent – and why?

Initial research questions are usually sorted into principal questions and a series of sub-questions. The main question is often transformed into a hypothesis, a claim that the researcher advances at the outset, based on certain assumptions and hunches about what has occurred and why. Developing a workable hypothesis means being both creative and willing to go out on a limb, to take a risk. It does not mean setting anything in stone. The hypothesis is simply meant as a loose starting point to anchor the research that allows one to then investigate related factors that might back it up. As research proceeds, it may become clear that the hypothesis does not hold, or that it might be more relevant to different cases encountered later on in the process. But as the research and writing develops, the hypothesis will serve as a central claim around which one can build up a convincing quantity of data to support. The sub-questions can be used to structure different avenues of enquiry during this process.

Deductive approaches depart from initial theoretical assumptions whereby researchers seek to derive or deduce testable propositions or hypotheses, which are then exposed to rigorous empirical scrutiny. In other words, this is the process in which the hypothesis is either confirmed or rejected. Here, one proceeds by engaging in educated guesswork and hunches. Of course, some scholars may use *inductive* approaches, simply taking the 'neutral' empirical evidence – what they see around them – as a starting point from which they then try to draw out specific observations (based on patterns, regularity, generalization, and so on) and then induce or construct theoretical propositions – an attempt to try and order the world, as it were. One might say that 'deductivists' start with the abstract and journey towards the concrete in their quest for right or wrong, while 'inductivists' start from experience and reality and try to step back from those things to see if they can then be categorized to produce a framework or model.

Mapping theories, tools and models

Theories are useful building blocks, resources that can help one to structure, solidify, and support an argument. In this sense, when engaging in EU policy analysis, it is often the policy itself rather than any particular theoretical concern that drives the initial enquiry – even if, as we noted above, some academics might not always accord an overwhelming importance to the empirical world. Theories are essentially lenses, or ways of seeing, and in that sense they are tools that should above all else offer clarity. A theory should not be a restrictive straightjacket. Theories often compete with each other, their respective enthusiasts advocating their own superior explanatory power compared with all others. However, when they are most useful, they work by complementing and supplementing each other, employed in tandem, perhaps to account for different parts of a single process. Individual

Table 4.3   *Main theories in political science*

Theory	Focus of enquiry. How . . . ?	Key concepts	Key texts
Rational choice	*How* policy actors act rationally to further their own political interests	rationality free riding rent seeking	Hindmoor, 2006; Koremenos *et al.*, 2003; Snidal, 2002
Behaviouralism	*How* political behaviour exhibits regularities over time which allow for the induction of generalizations	causation correlation statistical significance	Eulau, 1963; King, Keohane and Verba, 1994
Constructivism	*How* politics is socially constructed, perceived and interpreted	social construction intersubjectivity identity	Checkel, 1998; Wendt, 1992
Pluralism	*How* a wealth of different interests and stakeholders influence policy outcomes	power distribution elite coalitions	Dahl, 1961 Lipset, 1960
Comparative politics	*How* we can identify and explain similarities and differences between polities	comparative method or government	Lijphart, 1971; Peters, 2010

Source: draws on and further develops Hay (2002, pp.1–58).

theories cannot explain everything, but they can offer valuable perspectives on particular parts of policy making.

Table 4.3 provides a very brief overview of some of the main theories that political scientists and public administration scholars might use when choosing to research and analyze the EU and its policy process. It gives a flavour of the types of research enquiry one may wish to pursue and, depending on *how one wishes to approach the study of the process*, the type of theoretical tools that might – to continue with our optical metaphor of theory working as a lens – provide a pair of academic glasses to see through and a language with which to speak when analyzing.

Theory in political science and EU studies

Mainstream political science is characterized by three distinctive perspectives: rational choice theory, behaviouralism, and (new) institutionalism. Rational choice theory is based on the assumption that political actors are themselves 'instrumental, self-serving utility-maximizers', that is to say that they always act to increase their own material benefits, regardless of the consequences. Modelled on neoclassical economics, rational choice is meant as a predictive theory, by which one deduces how actors will behave (Hay, 2002, pp.8–9). Behaviouralism is also meant to be predictive, although it is not based on testing hypotheses about forms of behaviour, but focuses instead on extrapolating and generalizing from what has been observed, looking at empirical evidence and the frequency of events, allow for the quantification as well as the description of data (Hay, 2002, p.10).

But it is perhaps (new) institutionalism that is now most prominent in contemporary EU studies. This perspective is clearly the most useful for policy analysis, placing, as suggested in Chapter 1, great emphasis on the role of the supranational institutions vis-à-vis the member states. It emerged as a conscious response to both the 'behavioural revolution' of the 1960s and the 'ascendancy' of rational choice theory, effectively marking a return to the more traditional forms of institutional analysis of the early twentieth century. It rejects the simplified assumptions of rationale and motive influencing political behaviour implicit in rational choice theory. It also challenges the assumptions of the regularity of human behaviour on which behaviouralism theory rests. Instead, it sees the world as more complex and open-ended in terms of social and political change, placing great importance on the institutional context in which events occur and policy is made, such as history, timing, sequence, culture, rules, norms, expectations, and (often) irreversible consequences (Hay, 2002, pp.10–12).

Constructivism and pluralism can also be applied in analyses of the EU policy process. For example, it may be useful to see how certain ideas from political science – for example, how politics is socially constructed by those actors closely involved in the process itself (Table 4.3) – have a parallel in theories in EU studies based around social constructivism (Table 4.4). Moreover, pluralism is often adopted by scholars to analyze the huge variety of actors engaged in EU policy making – lobbyists, NGOs, think-tanks and civil society – as discussed in Chapter 1. Finally, it is important to point out that comparative politics is not really a theory as such, but more of an approach to analyzing political constructs. In the context of EU studies, it is generally concerned with comparing the organization of political systems across EU member states. Analysts from different schools of academic thought have their own sets of vocabulary and concepts with which

Table 4.4   *Different strands of new institutionalism*

Theory	Focus of enquiry. How . . . ?	Key concepts	Key texts
Historical institutionalism	*How* an institution's behaviour may be explained by how it behaved in the past	path dependency points of critical juncture punctuated equilibrium	Pierson, 1996
Rational choice institutionalism	*How* an institution's behaviour may be due to the pursuit of vested interests by it or other institutions	principals and agents, stable preferences	Farrell and Héritier, 2005; Scully, 2005
Social constructivist institutionalism	*How* an institution's behaviour may be determined by own rules and norms	organizational norms, culture, rules, procedures	Checkel and Moravcsik, 2001; Zürn and Checkel, 2005
Actor-centred institutionalism	*How* key elites within institutions control or steer the process, shape outcomes	games real actors play, institutional rational choice	Scharpf, 1997a

they try to describe political phenomena, in effect personal and subjective lexicons that they and their peers defend. In fact, what often occurs is that specialists soon develop their own way of speaking amongst themselves.

Rational choice, constructivist and other approaches have influenced the study of *institutions*, and present-day EU scholars now analyze these institutions from several perspectives. The particular way in which one approaches these institutions is to some degree a function of the type of research being carried out. For example, an analysis of why member states delegate tasks to the Commission, or why there has been a growth in new EU agencies, has tended to favour rational choice institutionalism because such a perspective seemed most suited to that sort of issue, characterized as it is by motives, costs and benefits, principals and agents. Yet archival research may allow one to take a historical institutionalist perspective, approaching the issue through longitudinal studies, seeing how it has changed over time and 'unravelling' the conditions, precedents and expectations that caused things to evolve into their present form. Social constructivists interviewing officials in the Council Secretariat or following business as it is conducted inside the building may be able to draw insight from the ways that the rules, norms, traditions and culture of the institution itself influence the political outcomes that it produces.

As we noted in Chapter 1, the late 1980s saw what is termed the 'governance turn' in EU studies. After several decades of almost exclusive concern with European integration *tout court*, scholars began to be interested in the day-to-day details of EU governance. Some of the theoretical approaches that we list brought *metaphors* to the idea of the configurations of actors in the policy process and how they came together, hence the idea of *networks*, a metaphor used to describe interactions between stakeholders, suggestive of the hubs and spokes on a bicycle wheel or a spider's web; *garbage cans*, where much is just thrown in and emptied out randomly; and *fusion*, with its connotations of nuclear science experiments, with actors and institutions moving together and apart in different directions and at different speeds over time, but essentially in an evolving, changing, dynamic way, like the atoms in a molecule. What these three metaphors have in common is that they indicate processes that are dynamic, organic, or in flux, rather than being fixed or static (see Table 4.5).

Choosing between theories and applying more than one

One may choose to analyze policy making in one domain with certain pre-conceived ideas about the relevance or applicability of a particular theory, but this is not necessarily always the case – often the choice of theory comes later and may involve exploring and testing more than one. In a PhD defence (viva) one question is nearly always guaranteed to be asked of the candidate: 'Why did you choose this particular theoretical approach over others?' The researcher must defend and justify his or her choice, but also demonstrate that due consideration was given to alternative approaches. The implication is that an alternative approach or theoretical application may very well have led to different findings, and, as such, different conclusions. Therefore, while political analysis may *allow for* a convincing, well-researched and argued case, it is important to keep in mind that in social and political science the veracity of this 'reconstructed account' of the past is open to alternative (conflicting and refuting) versions of the 'truth'. Much may depend on *how convincingly* one argues. Alternative research designs or similar methodologies with different theories may well lead to entirely different findings and outcomes.

An excellent example of how very different theories of policy making can be applied to analyze a case is a 2008 journal article by Chih-Mei Luo, 'Interpreting the Blair Government's Policy-making on European Monetary Union: An Examination of Public Policy Theories'. Luo attempts to analyze one member state's attitude, behaviour and

Table 4.5   *Theories for analyzing EU governance and decision making*

Theory	Focus of enquiry. How . . . ?	Key concepts	Key texts
Policy networks	*How* actors configure and collaborate (as a metaphor)	actor clusters interests/stakes	Compston, 2009; Peterson, 2005
Fusion	*How* the process is about the changing relations between government– administration	administrative interaction, politics fuses bureaucracy	Wessels, 1997
Garbage-can model	*How* the policy process is completely random and chaotic in its workings	decisions irrational, chaotic, disorderly, unstructured	Cohen, March and Olsen, 1972

national position on the question of joining the single currency. The author draws on pluralism, Marxism, rational choice, and a core executive model to depict the UK government's position, arguing that in fact all four are relevant to the issue – even if one is finally shown to be the most appropriate overall. But the author goes further still by providing an in-depth discussion of the strengths and weaknesses of each theory's applicability, confirming that no single one is able to adequately capture the whole dynamics of the particular reality. The core executive model and rational choice could best help explain and describe the dynamics of the EMU policy process, whereas pluralism could explain the accidental emergence of the five economic tests invented and placed at the centre of government policy in its attempt to depoliticize the debate. Finally, Marxism best accounted for the form and arrangements put in place. While most academics may *deduce* or *induce* using one theory, Luo's article is rare in its ambitious attempt to use and apply multiple theoretical approaches.

Mapping issues in the EU policy process

Why do scholars choose to analyze policy by focusing on certain aspects or related issues rather than others? As we will show in the following chapter on agenda setting, policy issues rise up and down the agenda, each of which makes claims on the attention of policy makers. So it is logical that certain incidents, accidents, deadlines and crises might mean that for political reasons certain issues take precedence, whereas others are virtually ignored. The ascendancy of an issue on the political agenda will be of great interest to scholars – what is this new issue, and why does it receive high-profile treatment? How has it risen up the agenda? It is often during important meetings such as European summits that new priorities are discussed or signed up to, just as with the beginning of a new EU presidency, when member states bring their own particular issues to the political table. Negotiations for Treaty reform are also a process through which new institutional and decision-making arrangements are laid down. In this sense, looking back on the last 20 years of EU studies, one often notes a great outpouring of analytical interest in issues that follow on from key moments in EU policy making. For example, following the Single European Act, which entered into force in 1987 and set '1992' as the deadline for the completion of the single market, there was great academic analysis of the role of business interests and lobby groups in pushing their market agenda.

In recent years, we have seen these kinds of studies focus on issues of transparency and regulation, with particular efforts devoted to analyzing the Commission's lobby register, launched in June 2008, in which associations and firms can sign up on a voluntary basis. One could also mention the 'ingredients' of the Treaty on the European Union signed at Maastricht, which introduced not only the Cohesion Fund, but the notion of EU citizenship, insisting on the principle of 'subsidiarity'. Thereafter, there was significant analysis of what citizenship would mean in practice and of the use of the Cohesion Funds by the 'Poor Four' (Spain, Portugal, Ireland, Greece). Who spent their money best and what was the experience of implementing projects on the ground? How was subsidiarity legally interpreted across the member states?

In the case of internal crisis, the mass resignation of the Santer Commission in March 1999 due to allegations of corruption gave way to a process of institutional reform that was studied by scholars. In the case of external crisis, such as civil war in the Balkans (1991–1995) or the Russia-Georgia conflict (2008), the large group of scholars working on Common Foreign and Security Policy (CFSP) have sought to analyze the EU's (in)capability as a military force, as opposed to a normative power promoting its values.

In some cases scholars have been analyzing policy making that has proceeded based on mutual agreement and 'shadowing' without legislation. An example of this might be the Open Method of Coordination in areas such as the Bologna Process to promote the mutual recognition of university education and degrees, encouraging worker/researcher mobility and ensuring the completion of a single market in education. Many people engaging in analysis will be seeking to focus on issues that are timely, urgent, innovative and – importantly – under-researched.

Some claim that there are more female scholars analyzing 'soft' EU policies such as education, health and social policy, while men research foreign affairs and defence, but the idea of a gender divide is very much a myth. What is paradoxical perhaps is that it is in the areas where the EU is arguably least successful, such as in carving a Common Foreign and Security Policy or acting effectively as a united voice on the world stage, that there appears to be a great concentration of academic interest, while in its most successful areas such as internal market or competition policy there are relatively fewer analysts. Perhaps this is indicative of a larger interest in why things go wrong, rather than why they go right.

Table 4.6 provides a brief glance at the 'menu' of EU studies in term of the different areas that scholars research and analyze. Here, we introduce some key concepts in the study of EU governance, political science and, in particular, institutionalism. Together, these areas constitute the essential research focus of much EU policy analysis today. Clearly, that focus has come a long way since its original shape in the form of US scholars, looking on from afar and trying to fathom how to conceptualize what was going on during the early days of the integration process (Haas, 1958; Lindberg, 1963).

The ways in which scholars analyze the policy process depends on their chosen focus – the subject of their analysis may not necessarily be a policy area in its broadest sense but rather one feature of an issue, of a political force, or of a larger political–philosophical question related to policy making. Factors such as structure, agency, institutions and ideas, all of which 'contain, comprise and constitute' the political system, are key concerns for most researchers. The systemic features, the phenomena that occur throughout the policy process, and the bigger political questions surrounding it all, offer different levels of focus for policy analysis. Browsing recent back issues of the key EU journals mentioned above and noting the article titles and their focus can in fact be time well spent, providing as it does a quick insight into the 'state of the art' of the field, and a list of the particular issues with which EU scholars are concerned at any given moment.

Key issues for consideration

Research as a linear process?

Textbooks generally present policy research and analysis as a linear process – just as public policy experts might try to claim the policy process to be a linear process, as we suggested in Chapter 1. Burnham *et al.* show how research can be seen as a 5-step chain of consecutive processes: theory specification and the development of hypotheses;

Table 4.6 *How scholars might analyze the EU policy process*

Issue/feature	How scholars examine the EU policy process. By looking at . . .	Key texts
Political leadership	Strong or effective political leadership by individuals, institutions, and member states and its role in determining outcomes	Cini, 1996; Tallberg, 2003
Europe and the world	The EU as a 'hard' (military) power or 'soft' (norms and values) power; what the EU actually stands for, promotes, 'exports'	Smith, 2004; Krotz, 2009
Decision making and treaty reform	How decisions are made by institutions; the distribution of power and competences held by each as enshrined in treaties (see Nice)	Christiansen, 2002; Beach, 2004
Lobbying and interest groups	Influence of business, industrial, public health and civil society groups; their access to policy makers ultimately shaping the agenda	Greenwood, 2007; Schendelen, 2006
National parliaments	National parliaments' efforts and capacity to scrutinize the executive and exert influence on formulation and decision (Lisbon Treaty)	Duina and Oliver, 2005; Kiiver, 2006
EU committees and 'comitology'; expert groups; high-level groups	How hundreds of committee-like structures in the EU institutions shape policy formulation and secondary, 'street-level' legislation in implementation, trend in committee growth	Christiansen and Kirchner, 2010; Gornitzka and Sverdrup, 2008
Coordination mechanisms/ open method	Formal and informal ways of steering and monitoring policy to secure intended goals; voluntary convergence without legislation	Borrás and Jacobsson, 2004; De la Rosa, 2005
Phenomenon/force		
Socialization and formal/informal influence	How political influence may be exerted not only via formal channels, but informally in corridors and through social interaction	Crum, 2006; Lewis, 2003

→

→

Table 4.6   (continued)

Issue/feature	How scholars examine the EU policy process. By looking at . . .	Key texts
Europeanization	'Top-down' and 'bottom-up' impact on the shape of policy between supranational institutions and member states; 'goodness of fit'; minimizing costs of adapting to policy	Featherstone and Radaelli, 2003; Graziano and Vink, 2008
Institutional architecture and new agencies	The emergence of new regulatory and executive agencies engaged in activities to support the main institutions; the continuum from loose networks to formal institutions	Geradin *et al.*, 2005

Some big questions

Democracy/ democratic deficit	Accounting for whether the EU is democratic and accounting for why it might not be so	Follesdal and Hix, 2006
Expertise/ideas/ information	How information and ideas circulate and are used by policy makers, reliance on 'experts'	Sverdrup, 2006
Legitimacy/ institutional reform	The legitimacy of EU institutions as agents; steps to improve internal working mechanism	Arnull and Wincott, 2002
Transparency/ accountability	Pressure to make the policy-making process clear, understandable and accountable	Bovens, 2007; Fischer, 2004
Media and the EU public sphere	The role of media in reporting and 'constructing' the EU and 'spaces for debate'	Bijsmans and Altides, 2007; Fossum and Schlesinger, 2007
Citizenship/ civil society/	Promoting the idea of EU citizenship and the rights it confers; active citizen participation	Jenson, 2007; Vink and De Groot, 2010
Risk/security/ external relations	Internal and external security; coping with crisis; EU as a single legal entity, 'actorness'	Duke and Ojanen, 2006; Lavenex, 2004

data specification; data collection; data analysis; publication. This sort of linear model has the advantage of clarity, with each stage conceived as a step in a logical sequence, one following after the other. Yet, as the authors also observe, '[r]esearch rarely goes according to plan, although this is not an argument against having a plan' (Burnham *et al.*, 2008, p.52). Social science can involve some guesswork, as well as some fortuitous 'lucky breaks'. In this sense, thinking about EU policy analysis research as a 'labyrinth' is a useful analogy – the researcher loosely follows a linear model, at the same time being able at any point to 'loop back' and repeat some of the steps in the light of new data, or refining or even refuting an original hypothesis to develop more nuanced or targeted questions (ibid., p.53). In some cases, the research process might instigate the development of an entirely new conceptual framework, while some further stages of analysis might be postponed, such as those based around generalizing or theorizing, as more data is collected. Many people might find both the characterization of research as a linear sequence and the metaphor of the labyrinth misleading, given that research and analysis can often be far more messy, and far more uncertain, than one might initially imagine when embarking upon it. Encountering contingencies such as the unplanned-for need to negotiate with gatekeepers about one's own ethical dilemmas means that one's methods will often be redefined during the course of the research.

Data collection and analysis

Before embarking on targeted research into a particular piece of legislation or policy development, it is a good idea to browse the European Union institutions' webpages, particularly those of the Commission and its relevant Directorate-Generals and EP working groups. This will help one to contextualize recent policy developments, not only historically, but with regards to where policy fits into the larger scheme of EU policy priorities. The websites contain press releases and downloadable media, provide access to recent proposals, and signpost key legislation. It is also worth bringing up the 'organigram' or map of the organizational structure of the DG to see how the institution allocates staff according to thematic areas and policy-making tasks. Here, one will often be able to see the names of heads of unit, people who one might contact with questions, or an eventual request for an interview. Most DGs also have a library and information resources centre that one may be able to access.

Existing academic literature and analysis will in most cases provide an adequate introduction to the key questions, as well as conveying a sense of the most contemporary debates in the field in question and the general balance of what has been done and what has not, and what researchers (think they) know and what remains to be investigated. Analyzing a considerable amount of secondary and even primary data is practically a prerequisite for embarking on any kind of interview, or spending precious time developing questionnaires. This is particularly important as the answers to many of the questions that one might initially have can be found in the documents with relative ease. What contact is made with EU officials and other stakeholders, whether by email, phone or face-to-face, should be used to acquire additional information based on participant observation and direct involvement in policy making. Questions should be carefully constructed to shed light on issues that require particular exploration. Interviews are opportunities to explore hunches and suppositions, and seek out personal, experience-based opinion.

Some scholars decide at the outset that they will only analyze certain data, such as speech acts of official legislation, but even with this criterion in mind, they will have to decide the specific parameters of their enquiry. A media analyst might do a cross-national analysis of reporting on the Lisbon Treaty across the EU by deciding upon three keywords ('Lisbon', 'constitution', 'draft treaty') and only a sample of countries (UK, DE, FR), addressing certain titles (two broadsheets per member state, one left-wing, one right-wing), on a specific day (Monday), across a defined period of time (Jan 2005–Dec 2008), and where the words appear in the titles only. Such boundaries allow the researcher to lay down rules to avoid interference and guard against bias or distortion in the collection and thereafter the analysis of data. Setting out these delineations also makes the research feasible given constraints of time and resources (Box 4.4).

Objective analysis, not subjective recommendations

The aim of academic policy analysis is *not* to make recommendations or to help inform the European Commission or member states as to what they should and should not do better – that is the domain of the desk officers and civil servants. The aim is to analyze objectively and try to fit the pieces of the puzzle together – to explain *why* things turned out as they did, or uncover the dynamics and forces at work in the EU policy process.

Quite a bit has been written over the 60 years of EU policy integration and the comparable length of time that its analysis as an academic discipline has existed. If an initial literature review shows that there has already been extensive analysis of the policy area, one needs to be certain that there will be added-value derived from further analysis – added-value, not in the sense of monetary recompense, but in terms of the intellectual rewards that further analysis will bring. The researcher often has a hunch about why analysis will be valuable, but such an

> ### Box 4.4   Witness account 2: interviews and content analysis
>
> 'Because I was essentially interested in examining the role of citizen par-
> ticipation in policy implementation at grass roots level, I felt the best
> approach was to conduct a series of interviews. I would of course have
> to engage in some in-depth content analysis first, to contextualize recent
> events on this small island in the wider policy context of both EU and
> Danish environmental policy. I was struck by the fact that nowhere was
> citizen participation included as a criterion for success in any of the
> public policy literature on implementation. Thus, not only was I inter-
> ested to investigate if the project's success could really be accredited to
> citizen participation – and if so, how transferable such a model would
> be – but if I could then (if I wished) contribute something to the imple-
> mentation literature, to help refine the tools for analysis. I contacted
> potential interviewees in advance but I had not quite expected such ter-
> rible weather. In fact, the heavy rain and lack of local transport impeded
> my access to some local residents but to my surprise there was actually a
> visiting delegation from the US so I was able to make comparisons with
> similar such initiatives and experiences elsewhere. I got great interviews
> though not from those I had expected. Luckily the weather improved,
> and I managed to interview the local residents as well.' (*Andreas, MA
> researcher and analyst*)

intuition still needs to be argued in a convincing and systemic way in
an extended research proposal. All policy analysis needs justifying at
the outset – Why bother? Why now? Who cares? In short, why are
policy developments in a particular domain of interest to an academic?
What is so puzzling and urgent to merit scholarly attention? What can
the analysis possibly hope to explain? Before embarking on any data
collection, these questions should be carefully considered in order to
narrow down the research question.

Conclusion

This chapter has attempted to illustrate that *how* one goes about policy
analysis of the EU depends on who you are, the aims of the exercise,
and the resources available. The aim has been to explain *how* one
makes choices regarding theory and methodology/research design,
choices which will initially depend to a large degree on personal
interest and curiosity. *How* one chooses to pursue analysis of a policy
issue depends on the particular issues at hand, and on aspects

regarding the emergence, development and impact of policy that the analyst him or herself deems most worthy of investigation. This, in turn, will be conditioned by the interests, influence, actors, institutions, or phenomena that one identifies as being of particular interest as they interact in the policy process. The process usually starts with a puzzle felt to be worthy of further investigation, and hence a question that can be turned into a hypothesis. This chapter has sought to illustrate the reality of EU policy analysis. Here we conclude the first part of the book, following Chapters 1, 2 and 3, which discussed why one might want to analyze the EU policy process, who is involved in terms of the interactions between elites and institutions, and a clarification what precisely we mean by EU policies.

Part II will embark upon the five stages of the policy process, and unravel what happens during – and how the policy process could be analyzed in – the stages of agenda setting, policy shaping, decision making, implementation and evaluation.

Suggestions for further reading

Burnham, P., Gilland Lutz, K., Grant, W. and Layton-Henry, Z. (2008) *Research Methods in Politics*, 2nd edn (Basingstoke and New York: Palgrave Macmillan).

Marsh, D. and Stoker, G. (2010) *Theory and Methods in Political Science*, 3rd edn (Basingstoke and New York: Palgrave Macmillan).

Sabatier, P.A. (2007) (ed.) *Theories of the Policy Process*, 2nd edn (Cambridge: Westview Press).

Part II

EU Policy Analysis in Practice

Chapter 5

Agenda Setting

Sebastiaan Princen

Introduction

Imagine you were called upon to be the next President of the European Commission. What kind of issues would you wish the Commission to work on? Once you start thinking of all the issues you could take up, the sheer number can easily become overwhelming. Would you focus on unemployment, or terrorism, or environment? And if you were interested in environmental issues, what issues would you take up – maybe global warming? Protecting endangered species of animals? These are just the things that *you* might deem most important. However, interest groups, MEPs, and member state governments would doubtless also be urging you to take up certain issues and leave other issues by the wayside. And since you and your fellow Commissioners would only have 24 hours in each day, you could not possibly deal with every issue at once. This would mean making choices. In short, as the new Commission President you would be facing a familiar problem – setting priorities, that is, having to focus on some issues and ignore others, at least for the time being.

The list of a government's priorities is known as its agenda, and there are two reasons why the agenda is crucial for understanding policy-making processes. First, the agenda determines what issues will be subjected to decision making. If an issue does not gain sufficient attention from policy makers (that is, if it does not reach the agenda), then it will never come up for decision making. Therefore, politicians and interest groups eager for a decision to be taken first need to place the issue on the agenda. Conversely, politicians and groups that are happy with the way things are going will likely try to keep the issue off the agenda. After all, if one wants the status quo to be maintained, the most effective way to avoid unwanted change is to prevent the issue from being discussed in the first place.

A second reason why agendas are so important is that they determine the *terms* by which an issue will be discussed. Any issue can be defined in different ways. For example, the issue around using coal-fuelled power plants to produce electricity might be seen as an environmental issue (the use of coal leads to air pollution), as an economic issue (coal as a cheap alternative to oil), as a social issue (coal mining is an important source of employment in some economically weak regions), or even as a foreign policy issue (the use of coal may reduce the dependence on Russian oil and gas imports). Whichever definition dominates the agenda will determine to a large extent the options that will then be considered. If the use of coal is predominantly seen as an environmental issue, the logical option is to close down coal-fuelled power plants and look for alternative sources of energy. If, by contrast, the economic, social, or foreign policy perspective becomes dominant, the focus is more likely to be on expanding, or at least retaining, the use of coal. This is why a great deal of politics and policy making revolves around attempts to define and re-define issues. In so doing, some issues and policy options will come to the fore, while others will remain in the background, hardly considered. In this sense, apart from determining *which* issues are discussed, agenda-setting processes also determine *the terms in which* they are discussed.

Agenda setting in the EU: who is involved and what do we analyze?

What are agendas?

In the literature on agenda setting, different types of agenda have been studied. We can discern three main types. The *public agenda* includes the issues that citizens ('the public') find – or at least are seen as – important. It is the set of issues that receives the most attention in 'public opinion'. When researchers want to find out what is on the public agenda, they do so by asking people in opinion polls what they think are the most important problems facing them or their country.

The *media agenda* consists of the issues that receive attention in the media, in newspapers, magazines, and television. The media cannot report on every newsworthy item that comes along. Hence, they also make a selection, highlighting some issues and stories and ignoring others. One has only to compare a left-leaning newspaper and a right-leaning one, or a tabloid and a 'quality' newspaper, to see how the media select news rather than simply 'reporting' it neutrally. Because the media are an important source of information for many people (including politicians), its agenda is an important topic for research.

Finally, the *political agenda* includes the issues that policy makers are working on. In more formal terms, it can be defined as 'the set of issues that receive serious consideration in a political system' (compare Cobb and Elder, 1972, p.86; Kingdon, 2003, p.3). Within the political agenda, one can make a further distinction between the 'governmental agenda' and the 'decision agenda' (Kingdon, 2003, p.4). The govern-

Table 5.1   *Types of agenda*

Type of agenda	Definition	Example
Public agenda	The set of issues that receive attention from citizens	The autumn 2008 Eurobarometer poll indicated that EU citizens saw 'rising prices' and 'the economic situation' as the two most important problems facing their country (European Commission, 2008a, p.21)
Media agenda	The set of issues that receive attention in the media	The news items that make it to the evening news or the front pages of the newspapers
Political agenda		
• Governmental agenda	The set of issues that are being discussed by policy makers	The issues that are being discussed during 'question time' in the plenary sittings of the European Parliament
• Decision agenda	The set of issues that are subject to decision making	The Commission proposals that are submitted to the Council of Ministers and the European Parliament

mental agenda includes the issues that are being discussed in policy-making institutions, such as parliaments and government departments. These issues are being considered but not (yet) in terms of concrete decisions to be taken. The decision agenda goes one step further: it includes the issues on which a decision is set to be taken. Table 5.1 summarizes these various types of agenda.

In this chapter, we are interested in the EU's political agenda; that is, in the issues that receive serious consideration in the EU's policy-making institutions (in particular, the Council, the Commission, and the EP). This account will not focus on the public agenda or the media agenda regarding the EU. However, it is important to keep in mind that these three types of agenda do not develop in isolation from each other. It may well be that the content of the public agenda and the media agenda influences the political agenda, and vice versa.

So far, we have spoken of the EU's political agenda as if there is one single agenda for 'the EU' as a whole. In reality, we can identify different agendas for different EU institutions. The European Parliament has an agenda (that is, a set of issues it pays attention to), as do the Commission and the Council. These agendas may overlap but they are hardly ever identical. For instance, the EP may stress human rights issues in the EU's foreign policy, while the Council may give priority to establishing diplomatic ties with foreign governments. Within these institutions, we can discern even more specialized agendas. Within the Commission, for example, the agenda of DG Enterprise is not the same as that of DG Environment. Each DG has its own priorities and its own 'pet issues'. Therefore, an issue might well be on the agenda of one institution but not another. Nevertheless, we can speak of an overall 'EU agenda' insofar as some issues appear on the agendas of the Commission, the EP, and the Council at the same time.

Who is involved?

For an understanding of who is involved in EU agenda setting, it is useful to make a distinction between two types of issues with different associated agenda processes: those that impose themselves on the EU agenda 'from above', and those that work their way up the EU agenda 'from below' (Princen and Rhinard, 2006). This distinction runs parallel to that between 'high politics' and 'low politics' in the international relations literature. The actors involved in these two types of issue differ, as do the dynamics that lead to their admission onto the EU agenda.

Let's start with an example of an issue that has come 'from below'. Box 5.1 tells the story of the EU Tobacco Advertising Directive. This was an issue that gradually rose up the EU agenda as health policy experts became convinced that smoking was bad for health and that advertisement bans were a good way to reduce the prevalence of smoking. This consensus led to recurring attempts to place this issue on the EU agenda. Characteristic of this type of agenda process is that:

- The crucial actors are policy experts, who discuss policy options among themselves and develop some kind of consensus about the issues that should receive priority in their field.
- Policy debates remain limited to one policy sector and the agenda is set within that sector.
- Issues rise up the EU agenda gradually, gaining momentum as the consensus among policy experts solidifies.

This type of issue normally develops outside of the public view. There are several places where this may happen, often simultaneously:

- Each year, the European Commission publishes a work programme for the coming year, in which it outlines the policy projects it intends to take up. DGs, and within those DGs, specific units, can suggest issues for inclusion in the work programme. As a result, many issues that are included in the work programme evolve from within the Commission's own bureaucracy.
- The European Commission often develops new ideas in what are known as 'expert groups'. Expert groups include specialists on a

Box 5.1   Placing tobacco advertising on the agenda

Since the late 1980s, smoking has become a permanent feature on the EU agenda. Yet, this did not happen overnight. Domestic policies to curb smoking in the EU member states began to appear during the mid-1970s. Advertisement bans were the main instruments considered by governments at the time. In order to coordinate these initiatives, member state health ministers met to discuss them at the EU level. Seeing the growing rise of the issue in the member states, the European Commission started working on a proposal for a directive that would have harmonized domestic legislation by banning tobacco advertisements across the EU. However, in November 1979, even before the Commission could present a formal proposal, the EU ministers of health blocked this initiative, partly fuelled by lobby efforts on the part of the tobacco industry.

The issue of smoking re-appeared when the 'Europe against Cancer' programme was adopted in 1987. Europe against Cancer was aimed at reducing the incidence of cancer in the EU. It was adopted on the insistence of Italian prime minister Bettino Craxi and French President François Mitterrand, who had been prompted to do so by their medical advisors. When the European Commission presented its first Action Plan under the Europe against Cancer programme, smoking was singled out as one of the priority areas. In subsequent years, seven tobacco-related directives were adopted. In addition, the Commission launched a proposal for an EU-wide advertisement ban. Being the most far-reaching of all tobacco-related initiatives, this proposal met with strong opposition from a number of member states, and it was shelved after the early 1990s.

In the late 1990s, the proposal re-appeared on the EU agenda after a few opponent member states had begun to change their positions. During this period, tobacco and smoking-related health risks also gained new impetus on the global health agenda through the World Health Organization's Framework Convention on Tobacco Control, which was ratified by more than 150 states and called on governments to curb tobacco use. Boosted by these changes in fortune, the proposal for an EU ban on tobacco advertisements resurfaced and a final directive was adopted in June 2003 (2003/33/EC).

Source: Princen, 2009.

given issue, either from member state governments or from interest groups. Expert groups allow the Commission to obtain information about the prevalent ideas and approaches in an area, and to test the political feasibility of various policy options.

- The European Commission has established consultative 'forums' in a number of policy areas. These forums bring together representatives from interest groups and experts in the area with a view to developing new ideas and sounding out support for Commission initiatives. Examples include the Forum of Financial Services Users (the 'FIN-USE forum') and the EU Health Forum.

- In the European Parliament, MEPs with similar areas of interest, regardless of their political group, meet in so-called 'intergroups'. Examples include the Sports Intergroup, the Intergroup on the Welfare and Conservation of Animals, and the Intergroup on Ageing. Some intergroups are set up by MEPs themselves, while others are organized by interest groups in their particular fields of interest. Intergroups hold informal meetings where MEPs, interest group representatives, and policy experts can discuss issues and recent developments. From these discussions, a consensus about new issues for the EU agenda may arise.

- Interest groups regularly meet with Commission officials, MEPs and member state officials to discuss issues and policy ideas. By systematically 'plugging' an issue with policy makers, they hope to raise it higher on the EU agenda.

- Member state officials can also approach the European Commission to gain attention for an issue. In addition, they can develop ideas among themselves, which they can then present to the EU institutions. In this way, issues and policy ideas are 'uploaded' from the member states to the EU level.

- When a member state holds the presidency of the Council of Ministers, it has additional opportunities to place an issue on the EU agenda. Each presidency usually organizes a number of conferences around issues that it feels should receive more attention. When these issues are picked up by other member states and the EU institutions, they become part of the EU agenda. An example is the Swedish presidency of 2001, which organized a large conference on young people and alcohol in order to place the issue of alcoholism on the EU agenda, perhaps because the high levels of teenage depression and suicide in Sweden may be linked to alcohol abuse (Princen, 2009, pp.94–5).

- The President of the European Council may use his position to put forward ideas and place them on the EU's agenda. For instance, in February 2010, European Council President Herman van Rompuy launched the idea of an 'economic government' that would provide closer coordination of economic policies between the EU member states. This idea was then taken up by the European Council as part of its new economic strategy for the EU.

- Issues need not be developed within the EU itself. Some issues are first developed in other international organizations, only to be 'imported into' the EU at a later stage. Dostal (2004) showed how ideas for the liberalization of labour market policies were pioneered in the Organisation for Economic Co-operation and Development (OECD). These ideas subsequently informed much of the EU policy debate on this issue. Likewise, in the case of the EU Tobacco Advertising Directive, the World Health Organization (WHO) played a role through its Framework Convention on Tobacco Control. Hence, in these cases, agenda processes in the EU can only be understood if processes in other international organizations are taken into account.

Given the variety of actors and the range of forums in which they interact, agenda setting from below does not emanate from just one source. Rather, different actors in different places may try to get an issue onto the EU agenda. Often, they do so simultaneously. It is their combined efforts that lead to success or failure. Rather than looking for the ultimate source of an issue, it is therefore more useful to try to understand the conditions that are favourable or unfavourable to an issue.

When issues come onto the agenda 'from above', a different set of actors is important. A good example can be found in the tale of the EU battle groups, which is told in Box 5.2. The concept of EU battle groups was developed by top officials in France and the UK and supported by Germany, and it only came onto the EU agenda after the top leaders of the three countries had put the idea forward and it was endorsed by the European Council.

Characteristic of this type of issue is that:

- The crucial actors are government leaders and other top politicians.
- Policy debates are part of broader strategic and political considerations.
- Issues rise on the EU agenda quickly.

Hence, these issues come onto the EU agenda from the top political level. This explains why they rise so quickly. It also implies that it is often much easier to pinpoint a limited number of actors who were instrumental in putting the issue on the agenda.

The distinction between issues that come 'from above' and those that come 'from below' is useful for recognizing different agenda-setting dynamics. However, the two dynamics seldom occur in these pure forms. Most issues show a combination of both dynamics, even if one

Box 5.2   EU battle groups

Ever since the creation of its Common Foreign and Security Policy (CFSP) in 1992, the EU has struggled with ways to give itself more teeth. Member state governments have differed widely in terms of foreign policy priorities and have been very reluctant to cede powers over foreign policy (let alone military deployments) to the EU. In addition, member states have differed widely in terms of military capability, with France and the UK having by far the strongest armies. These two European powers led different camps within the EU. Some member states, including the UK, stressed their ties with the United States and opposed EU initiatives that would weaken those ties, opting instead for cooperation through NATO. Other countries, including France, wanted to strengthen the EU's military capabilities as an alternative to the US-led NATO.

Following the failure of the EU to adequately to respond to the war in the former Yugoslavia, the French and UK governments reached a compromise in 1998: the UK supported the creation of an EU military force, while France acknowledged the importance of NATO. In 1999, at the Helsinki European Council, all EU member states agreed to the build-up of a 'rapid reaction capability' that could be deployed in crisis situations and for humanitarian and peace-keeping operations. Later, in talks between French and UK officials, a more specific response time of 5–10 days was established.

In June 2003, the EU engaged in its first military operation ('Operation Artemis') to stabilize Ituri, a province in Eastern Congo. Building on this experience and the earlier intentions to build up an EU reaction capability, France and the UK proposed the creation of EU 'battle groups'. A battle group was to consist of 1,500 soldiers. Supported by Germany, this proposal was presented to and endorsed by the other member states in early 2004. It was decided that at any given time, at least two battle groups would be on standby could be deployed within 5–10 days of a decision by the European Council to stage an intervention. EU battle groups reached their operational capacity in early 2007.

Sources: Andersson, 2006; Lindstrom, 2007; Salmon, 2005.

dynamic is more pronounced than the other. Take the example of the tobacco advertising ban. This was predominantly an issue that developed among health policy experts. Yet, an important role was played by French President Mitterrand and Italian Prime Minister Craxi, who pushed for the adoption of the Europe against Cancer programme in the mid-1980s. After that, however, the specific issue of a tobacco advertising ban was developed by health policy experts again. That is, depending on the type of dynamic that was prevalent, different sets of actors were involved in the process.

Theoretical perspectives

With a clear idea of what one wants to analyze and which actors are involved, one can then turn to the question of what determines the EU's political agenda. This section discusses a number of theoretical perspectives that can be used to understand the rise and fall of issues on the EU agenda. These perspectives have been developed in the context of domestic politics (in particular in the United States) but they can also be used to understand how agenda setting works in the EU.

The multiple streams model

A key figure in the literature on agenda setting is John Kingdon (2003). He is the father of the so-called 'multiple streams' model, which builds on a model of decision making known as the 'garbage can model' (Cohen, March and Olsen, 1972). According to Kingdon's model, policy-making processes consist of three streams that evolve separately and show distinct dynamics:

- The problem stream consists of problem perceptions among policy makers.
- The solutions (or policy) stream consists of proposals for government action.
- The politics stream consists of political activities and developments, such as elections, lobbying campaigns, and shifts in public opinion.

According to the model, these streams develop largely in isolation from each other. This notion may initially appear somewhat counter-intuitive. Most of us are probably used to thinking of solutions as a response to problems: a problem is identified and then policy makers start looking for solutions. In practice, Kingdon argues, it is often the other way around. Some people (in government but also in private industries and at universities and research institutes) spend their careers developing and refining policy options they believe in or have a vested interest in. They do so irrespective of any specific problem. Whenever a suitable problem presents itself, they then try to link their policy option to that problem in order to 'sell' it to decision makers. So, instead of problems looking for solutions, it is a question of solutions looking for problems!

This explains how one and the same policy idea may pop up over and over again as a solution to very different problems. Remember the example of coal-fuelled power plants that was discussed in the intro-duction above? Suppose you are a coal-mining company. This means you have an interest in extending your coal-mining operations, so it would be helpful if government supported coal-fuelled power plants. Now, if policy makers worry about high oil prices, you could suggest that coal might be a suitable (thus cheap) alternative for generating electricity. If oil prices are not a major concern, but politicians worry about the loss of employment in mining regions, you could claim that coal-fuelled power plants would reduce unemployment in those areas by encouraging coal mining. Finally, if the economy is going well but relations with Russia become strained, you could make the point that coal-fuelled power plants are a good way of reducing dependence on Russian gas and oil. That is, you can link your preferred solution (coal mining) to different problems, depending on what happens to be on policy makers' minds at any given time – even if your interest in the solution has nothing to do with those problems.

Although the three streams develop in isolation from each other, sometimes they come together: a problem is seen as important, a fea-sible solution is available, and political events are favourable. This is called a 'policy window' or 'window of opportunity'. When a window opens, an issue moves to the top of the political agenda. This, however, only lasts until attention fades and other issues come to prominence in turn. Then, the window closes again and advocates of a proposal have to wait for the next window to open. This is depicted graphically in Figure 5.1.

Policy windows can open for several reasons. A major crisis or shocking event (a so-called 'focusing event') can suddenly bring some problem to the fore. An example might be the case of the European arrest warrant, discussed in case Box 5.3. Until the early 2000s, there had been debates about simplifying procedures to extradite suspected

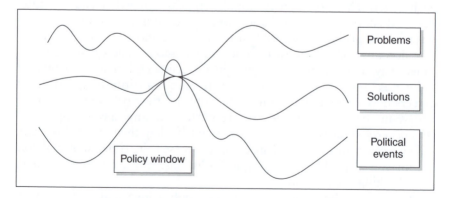

Figure 5.1   *Kingdon's multiple stream model*

Box 5.3   The European arrest warrant

The problem underlying the European arrest warrant is an old one: what to do if someone is suspected of a crime in country A but is residing in country B? The police of country A cannot simply go to country B and arrest the suspect. After all, states do not allow foreign law enforcement officers to operate on their soil. The traditional answer to this has been for country A to ask the government of country B to arrest the suspect and hand him or her to the authorities of country A. This is called 'extradition'. Simple as it sounds, extradition has always been a difficult and cumbersome procedure. Extradition does not take place directly between law enforcement authorities but between governments. As a result, it is a diplomatic process in which governments may refuse extradition for all kinds of political reasons. Moreover, many countries put strict restrictions on extradition and refuse to extradite persons of their own nationality.

In the EU, it has become increasingly easier for people to travel across borders. This holds true for criminals as well as for 'ordinary people': after committing a crime in one member state, it is easy for the perpetrator to go to another member state. Therefore, in parallel with the increasing mobility of persons, member state governments started to discuss ways of simplifying extradition procedures. In 1995 and 1996, two conventions on extradition were adopted under what was then known as the EU's 'third pillar' (justice and home affairs). These conventions needed to be ratified by the member states before they would enter into force but several years later most member states had not yet done so.

In 1997, the Schengen Agreement, which abolished border controls between member states, was incorporated into EU law through the Amsterdam Treaty. In response to this development, the European Council held a special meeting in the Finnish town of Tampere in 1999 to discuss the creation of 'an area of freedom, security and justice' in the EU. On the basis of the Tampere Council conclusions, the Commission prepared a proposal for a framework decision (the third pillar variety of what is otherwise known as a 'directive') on a European arrest warrant. The issue of a European arrest warrant received its final (and decisive) boost with the terrorist attacks of 9/11. Pressed to show that the EU could 'deliver' on anti-terrorism issues, the proposed European arrest warrant moved to the top of the EU's agenda, and the framework decision was formally adopted in June 2002.

Sources: Alegre and Leaf, 2004; Den Boer and Monar, 2002; Plachta, 2003.

criminals across borders for quite some time, but little progress had been made. When the terrorist attacks of 9/11 shook the Western world, the issue of terrorism suddenly rose to the very top of the EU agenda. Politicians in the EU wanted to show that they could respond quickly and effectively to this new challenge. The proposal for a European arrest warrant, which also covered suspects of terrorist activities, was the perfect opportunity for doing this. Thus, 9/11 opened a window of opportunity for the proposed European arrest warrant, which was able to 'sail through' on the waves of concern about terrorism. In terms of the distinction we made above, this is an example of how an issue that had developed 'from below' was pushed forward when it was joined by a dynamic 'from above'. When the two dynamics met, the issue suddenly jumped to the top of the EU agenda.

An event such as 9/11 is called a 'focusing event': a dramatic occurrence that focuses attention on a problem that formerly was not considered that pressing. Because it occurs in the problem stream, the policy window that opens is called a 'problem window'.

In addition, policy windows can also open because of developments in the political stream. These are called 'political windows'. An example of such a development in the political stream is a change in government. When in 2004 José Manuel Barroso became president of the European Commission, he announced that his Commission would above all give priority to the Lisbon Agenda, the ambition of the European Council firmly stated in 2000, and reiterated in 2005, to make the EU the most competitive economy in the world. This meant that issues relevant to this ambition – or which could at least be framed to appear to be – suddenly rose on the agenda while it was more difficult to 'sell' issues that could not be defined in competitiveness to the Commission.

In the multiple-streams model, the link between problems, solutions, and political events, is made by policy entrepreneurs: individuals who actively try to bring problems and solutions together. By bringing the right people together at the right time, they are able to take advantage of policy windows when they open.

A good example of a policy entrepreneur is Commission President Jacques Delors at the time of the Single European Act (see Sandholtz and Zysman, 1998). By the early 1980s, European integration had lost much of its dynamism. Little progress was made in harmonizing the laws and regulations of member states because European directives tended to be very detailed, giving rise to elaborate debates in the Council of Ministers and leading to bureaucratic and inflexible legislation. In the mid-1980s, the new Commission President, Jacques Delors, saw the opportunity to break the deadlock by using the concept of 'mutual recognition', which had been developed by the Court of Justice. 'Mutual recognition' implied that member states recognized each other's laws and regulations as equivalent to their own, even if the practical details differed. This principle became the core of the Single European Act and its associated programme of completing the single market by 1992. Delors operated as a policy entrepreneur by linking a problem (deadlock in EU decision making) with a solution (mutual recognition) and selling this to member state governments.

Problem definitions and frames

The multiple streams model shows how issues can reach the top of the agenda by combining problems, solutions, and political events. In this process, a crucial role is played by the way issues are defined. We outlined how this might work with the (fictitious) example of the use of coal for the production of electricity. All this suggests that, in agenda-setting processes, the definition of a problem is not a given, but something that political actors actively try to influence. Much of the political struggle at this stage revolves around exactly this: how an issue should be defined and what aspects of that problem should be deemed most important. Rochefort and Cobb (1994) have referred to this as the 'politics of problem definition'.

Another term for problem definition that is often used in the literature is 'frame'. A frame consists of the (explicit but often also implicit) concepts and assumptions that are being used to structure reality (Benford and Snow, 2000; Schön and Rein, 1994). Frames can be very simple, but more often than not they are rooted in deeper preconceptions. In Box 5.4, this is explained for the debate on genetically modified food in the EU.

Frames and venues

Frames are important in agenda-setting processes, but they are only one side of the equation. The other side is formed by what Baumgartner and Jones (1993) call 'venues'. Venues are the institutional forums in which decisions are taken on policies. The EU can be seen as a venue alongside other venues, such as each of the member states and other international organizations. However, within the EU we can also distinguish different venues, such as the EP and the Commission or, within the Commission, the various DGs. As was argued above, each EU institution, as well as each Commission DG, has its own 'pet issues' and key concerns. A new issue has the best chance of coming on a venue's agenda if it ties in with these existing pet issues and key concerns.

Consequently, institutional structures are not neutral. Because of the way they are organized, venues are more receptive to some issues, claims and concerns than to others. Elmer Schattschneider (1960, p.71)

Box 5.4   Frames and problem definitions around genetically modified food

Genetic modification is used to change the genetic make-up of plants and crops in order to increase their yield and/or insert desirable traits. In the EU, the use of genetically modified plants and crops has been a highly contentious issue, in which proponents and opponents have taken irreconcilable positions. For proponents, genetic modification is a way to increase the efficiency of agriculture and the quality of food. For opponents, it is a risk to the environment and food safety. Underlying these different definitions of problems are widely diverging views on the technology.

Proponents argue that genetic modification is simply an extension of older techniques of cross breeding and is even safer because specific genes can be inserted into organisms. Opponents, by contrast, argue that genetic modification is fundamentally different from traditional plant breeding techniques, because it involves direct changes in an organism's genome. As a result, so they argue, genetic modification may have unpredictable and potentially disastrous consequences.

On the face of it, this is a debate that pits different empirical claims against one other. Upon further reflection, however, it becomes apparent that the arguments of proponents and opponents are rooted in much deeper understandings of nature and the role of scientific knowledge. To give just one example, proponents argue that the safety of genetically modified plants and crops can be assessed by doing controlled scientific experiments. Opponents, by contrast, claim that controlled experiments cannot unveil all potential risks because in reality all kinds of unpredictable interactions between organisms may occur. Moreover, they argue that unless full certainty exists about the safety of genetic modification, the technology should not be used. These are not just disputes about empirics; they reflect deeper beliefs about the way nature works, the role of humans in nature, and the validity of scientific arguments in policy debates. Only by unravelling these assumptions underlying the two competing claims can we understand the sources of the different frames in this area.

Source: Princen, 2002, pp.193ff.

has famously said that 'organization is the mobilization of bias': by creating organizations with specific tasks, participants and decision-making procedures, some interests are 'organized in' while others are 'organized out'. This is why every political system creates its own bias in favour of some issues and against other issues. This bias greatly influences the type of issues that are likely to make it to the agenda.

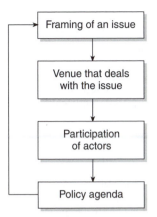

Figure 5.2 *The relationship between frames, venues and policy agendas*

In the context of the EU, it has often been claimed that the EU's institutional set-up (its remit and the way it makes policies) favours issues of economic liberalization over issues that relate to the protection of non-economic interests (see Scharpf, 1997b; 1999). After all, the EU was set up to create a single market among its member states. Even though the EU has expanded its activities greatly over the past decades, economic development still remains its core task. Thus, issues that relate to that objective find a more receptive ear in Brussels than issues that address different concerns.

Having said this, the EU is not a monolith. Within the EU, there are different venues that are receptive to different types of issues and arguments. A key task for political actors that want to place an issue on the EU agenda is therefore to frame the issue in such a way that it appeals to the venue that is targeted.

Hence, the struggle over competing frames or the definition of problems largely determines the venue that will deal with a particular issue. Going back to the example of coal-fuelled power plants, if the problem is defined mainly in terms of air pollution, then logically the European Commission's DG Environment will deal with it. If, by contrast, it is seen as an issue of cheap power production, it belongs much more logically within the remit of DG Energy. This, in turn, will strengthen the initial frame, because each DG will invest in the aspect of the issue that falls within its remit.

Thus, the frame determines the venue, which determines the type of policies that will be developed. This, in turn, tends to reinforce the initial issue frame. This relationship is summarized in Figure 5.2.

The key theoretical concepts, main points underlying them, and the main author(s) associated with them are summarized in Table 5.2. On

Table 5.2 *Key theoretical concepts in agenda-setting theory*

Concept	Main point	Key author(s)
Garbage cans/ multiple streams	Issues rise to the top of the agenda if three streams of problems, solutions and political events coincide	Kingdon
The politics of problem definition	Problem definitions are not given or objective but the outcome of political struggles	Rochefort and Cobb
Framing	Political actors define reality according to prior assumptions that structure the way phenomena are interpreted	Benford and Snow Schön and Rein
Venues	Institutional policy making units are more receptive to some issues than to others	Baumgartner and Jones
The mobilization of bias	Through institutional structures, some interests and concerns are included while others are excluded	Schattschneider

the basis of these concepts, we can now proceed to the question of what key issues one should take into consideration when analyzing agenda-setting processes in the EU.

Key issues for consideration

Based on the theoretical insights discussed above, three questions are crucial when analyzing agenda-setting processes:

- How is the issue framed?
- What venues are dealing with the issue?
- Is this a favourable time for pushing the issue?

Each question can be subdivided into a number of more specific questions. An overview of these questions is given in Table 5.3.

Answers to these questions can be found in three types of sources:

- Policy documents give information about policy frames, the venues that deal with an issue, and developments in the policy process over time.
- Interviews are a way of gaining more insight into the background to policy debates, as well as the political processes that take place 'behind' the official documents: the debates and events that are not officially recorded, but that shape agenda-setting processes.

Table 5.3 *Key questions in the analysis of agenda-setting processes in the EU*

Main question	Sub-questions
How is the issue framed?	• In what terms is the issue defined? • To which other issues is it linked? • How does the framing of the issue relate to existing EU policies? • What does the framing of the issue include? • What does the framing of the issue exclude?
What venues are dealing with the issue?	• Who decides on the issue? • Which venues are excluded from policy making? • What difference would it make if other venues dealt with the issue?
Is this a favourable time for pushing the issue?	• Can the issue be linked to events that have recently received a large deal of attention? • Have recent changes in the composition of key actors affected receptiveness to the issue?

- Secondary sources, such as existing academic studies and journalistic accounts, may already contain answers to many questions. When using this type of source, however, one should always be aware of the objectives that the author had in mind. Neither academic studies nor journalistic reports are neutral; they are always written from a certain point of view.

Below, we will take a look at each of the questions listed above and see how they can be answered in practice.

How is the issue framed?

As we saw in the theoretical overview, framing is key to understanding agenda-setting processes. Several specific questions can be asked in this regard.

In what terms is the issue defined?

We saw above that issues can be defined in various ways, and that this is an integral part of agenda-setting processes. Consider the following two issue definitions in relation to the same issue: the use of genetic modification. Here is an excerpt from the Commission's Communication 'Life Sciences and Biotechnology – A Strategy for Europe':

Life sciences and biotechnology offer opportunities to address many of the global needs relating to health, ageing, food and the environment, and to sustainable development. How can Europe best attract the human, industrial and financial resources to develop and apply these technologies to meet society's needs and increase its competitiveness? (European Commission, 2002, p.5).

Now compare this to the following statement taken from a position paper by COPA/COGECA, the group representing EU farmers:

Outside the EU, the use of gene technology in agriculture, especially genetically modified crops, has increased during the last few years. In Europe, however, the potential use of this technology in agriculture has raised many questions on the potential benefits and concerns of this technology. Recognizing society's concerns, COPA and COGECA consider that European farmers and their cooperatives cannot ignore these developments or reject them out of hand without a fully informed debate. (COPA/COGECA, 2000, p.2)

The European Commission defines the problem as how to stimulate the biotechnology industry so as to reap the benefits from the technology, whereas COPA/COGECA focuses on the societal concerns in relation to biotechnology. By defining the central problem differently, the Commission and COPA/COGECA try to place the issue on the agenda in a different way – as an issue of industry development and as an issue of consumer concerns, respectively.

Which other issues is the issue definition linked to?

Issues are seldom defined in isolation. Usually they are linked to other issues. These links can make an important difference to the way the issue is conceived and the venues that deal with it. A telling example can be observed in the area of fisheries policy. In the early 2000s, a number of environmental NGOs tried to obtain a ban on bottom trawling, a technique whereby nets are 'scraped' across the floor of the sea. This is a quote from an interview on that process with a lobbyist for Greenpeace:

The technical bottom trawling moratorium ... was presented by NGOs as a biodiversity issue. The problem is that it damages highly sensitive habitats in the deep seas ... So there the environmental ministries woke up and realized they needed to take part in the discussion. (Princen, 2009, p.144)

What Greenpeace, and other environmental groups, did was to link the issue of bottom trawling to the issue of biodiversity. In this way, it was no longer 'just' an issue of fisheries management (related to the depletion of fish stocks), but it became an environmental issue. As a result, it came onto the agenda of environmental policy makers. This is a textbook example of the sequence that we saw in Figure 5.2 above – and it started by defining one issue in terms of another issue.

How does the framing of the issue relate to existing EU policies?

Often, it is easier for an issue to reach the EU agenda, if it can be presented as the logical extension of existing EU policies. This makes it more self-evident that the EU should be involved in the issue. After all, if the issue is merely an extension of something the EU already does, then surely it falls within the EU's remit! For an example of this, read the basic argument for an EU-wide tobacco advertisement ban that was given in the 1989 Commission proposal:

> Nationals of the twelve Member States are increasingly drawn, for purposes of learning languages, or for professional reasons, to newspapers, magazines and publications from other Community countries. Similarly, advertising by means of bills and posters, which in all the Member States conforms to the same rules as those governing advertising in the press, is increasingly cross-frontier in nature, since nowadays, advertising of tobacco products is centralized at European and even at the international level. It is important therefore to ensure, in accordance with public health requirements within the meaning of the EEC Treaty, the free movement of such publications and to prevent obstacles to trade arising as a result of these publications and bills and posters failing to comply with national provisions on tobacco advertising. (European Commission, 1989, p.2)

In this way, the Commission chose to justify its proposal in terms of the restrictions on internal trade in printed media that differences in national legislation could cause. In terms of the EU's legal competences, this made sense, because the EU could adopt directives with a view to eliminating distortions of the internal market, whereas it could not adopt directives to protect health. This way, a tobacco advertisement ban could be placed more easily on the EU agenda, even if the underlying reason for proposing the ban had much more to do with the protection of health.

What does the framing of the issue include?

The way an issue is framed may already imply certain policy options. The following excerpt, from the conclusions of the 1999 Tampere European Council, suggests such a scenario:

> 33. Enhanced mutual recognition of judicial decisions and judgments and the necessary approximation of legislation would facilitate co-operation between authorities and the judicial protection of individual rights. The European Council therefore endorses the principle of mutual recognition which, in its view, should become the cornerstone of judicial co-operation in both civil and criminal matters within the Union. (European Council, 1999)

Just as we saw with the case of the European arrest warrant, this European Council meeting was an important step toward the creation of a European arrest warrant. Yet, the term 'arrest warrant' is not mentioned anywhere in the text of the Council conclusions. The European Commission is only invited to draw up proposals for a 'fast track extradition procedure'.

This could have still taken different forms. However, in point 33 of the Conclusions, the concept of 'mutual recognition' is introduced as a guiding principle in the area of judicial cooperation. When applied to the call for a 'fast track extradition procedure', this principle almost automatically implies some kind of European arrest warrant. The way the issue of judicial cooperation was framed in the Tampere European Council conclusions therefore already favoured a specific policy option.

What does the framing of the issue exclude?

Just as the way an issue is framed includes some options, it also excludes others. Again, the opposing definitions of genetic modification by the European Commission and COPA/COGECA that were reproduced above are revealing. The Commission's definition implies a number of policies to stimulate the biotechnology industry in Europe (which are in fact proposed in the same document). At the same time, it excludes policy options that are aimed at restricting the use of genetic modification or prohibiting its use – simply because they do not fit with the stated problem of how to 'attract the human, industrial and financial resources to develop and apply these technologies to meet society's needs and increase its competitiveness'.

Which venues are dealing with the issue?

Who decide(s) on the issue?

When analyzing the venues involved in an agenda-setting process, one should first determine who decides on an issue. As we saw above, the venue's characteristics will determine how likely it is that an issue reaches the EU agenda. Also, if one knows which venue or venues deal(s) with an issue, one will be able to understand better how and why the issue is framed and reframed.

Returning to the example of the EU battle groups presented in Box 5.2, key decisions on the creation of battle groups were taken by the French and UK governments, and then ratified by the European Council. Hence, an understanding of the motives of the French and UK governments is crucial for understanding why, how, and when the issue came onto the EU agenda.

In the case of the tobacco advertising ban, the decisions were taken by the Council of Health Ministers and the European Parliament. Within the EP, the responsible committee during the 1990s was the Committee on the Environment, Public Health and Consumer Protection. The 1989 proposal was drawn up by a Commission unit specifically created around the Europe against Cancer programme. All of these venues were particularly receptive to health-related issues and arguments, so that they put smoking on the agenda as a health threat. They cared less about the economic viability of the tobacco industry or the livelihood of tobacco farmers, aspects that would have received more attention in venues within the EU that dealt with economic affairs and agriculture (Boessen, 2008, p.69).

Which venues are excluded from policy making?

If one wants to understand agenda setting, it is important also to look at the venues that were *not* included in policy making. This quote comes from an article by Scott Greer, who has studied EU policy making on health services:

> Some of the most important legislation affecting health, as well as the conceptual categories used to interpret health policy, is shaped by trade, economics, and industry departments rather than health departments. Two member state officials spoke in 2004 and 2006 interviews of health ministers' irritation when they found the Court and colleagues in industry and trade ministries were 'reshaping their systems while their health ministers discussed cancer research'. (Greer, 2008, p.224)

Within the EU, the issue of health services is discussed by a range of venues. Rather than by the Council of Health Ministers, issues of the financing and organization of health services were initially put on the EU agenda by Councils and Commission DGs working in economic and financial areas. The ministers and officials in these venues were mostly preoccupied with issues such as the financial burden of health care expenditure and the free trade in (health) services between EU member states. They were less likely to stress issues such as the quality of health care or equal access to health care services for all citizens. In this sense, one might see the question of which venues are not involved in policy making as equally important for understanding agenda-setting processes as the question of which venues *are* involved.

What difference would it make if other venues dealt with the issue?

This question builds on the previous one. If one knows which venues are available, and which venues are involved and not involved in policy making, it is helpful to try to imagine how the issue would have come onto the agenda if some other venue had dealt with it. What would have happened if DG Agriculture and the Council of Agricultural Ministers had been the main venues for deciding on tobacco advertising? Answering this counter-factual question (that is, a question about what *would have* happened) allows one to see more clearly what kind of 'mobilization of bias' occurred in a given case.

Is this a favourable moment to push the issue?

Can the issue be linked to events that have recently received a large deal of attention?

As we saw above, issues can sometimes be pushed up the agenda by a focusing event. In analyzing agenda-setting processes, it is therefore important to be aware of such events and, more importantly, the way they can be used by political actors to promote their causes. For example, one can see the impact of the 9/11 attacks on the issue of a European arrest warrant in the conclusions to the European Council, available on the Council website, at the end of 2001. Not a single word is said about the European arrest warrant in the conclusions of each of the six European Council meetings held between January 2000 and September 2001. Instead, the heads of state and government were occupied with issues such as economic growth (the Lisbon Agenda) and enlargement. On 21 September 2001, there was an extraordinary European Council to discuss the terrorist attacks. This is what the conclusions to that meeting had to say about the European arrest warrant:

> In line with its conclusions at Tampere, the European Council sig-
> nifies its agreement to the introduction of a European arrest
> warrant and the adoption of a common definition of terrorism ...
> The European Council directs the Justice and Home Affairs
> Council to flesh out that agreement and to determine the relevant
> arrangements, as a matter of urgency and at the latest at its
> meeting on 6 and 7 December 2001. (European Council, 2001,
> pp.1–2)

The European arrest warrant was mentioned again in the conclusions
of the two European Council meetings following the extraordinary
meeting. Thus, the European Council conclusions show clearly how
(and why) the agenda shifted after 9/11. What is also interesting to
note is that the European arrest warrant was used for much more than
just terrorist crimes, and, terrorism was only one of a list of crimes that
was covered. Even though these other crimes were by no means related
to the 9/11 attacks, their inclusion in the then *proposed* European
arrest warrant carried them along on the wave of anti-terrorism policy
created by the attacks (see Alegre and Leaf, 2004, p.202).

Have recent changes in the composition of key actors affected receptiveness to the issue?

Changes in government or the institutional composition of venues may
cause shifts in receptiveness to issues. A good example that is relevant
to EU tobacco policy can be found in another international organization: the World Health Organization (WHO). The idea of negotiating
a global treaty on tobacco control had been put forward in the early
1990s and was supported by the World Health Assembly, the WHO's
main governing body, in 1996. Nevertheless, the issue remained relatively low on the WHO's agenda. Then Gro Harlem Brundtland took
office as the new WHO director general. According to three people
who were closely involved in WHO tobacco policy at the time, the
arrival of the new director gave a strong impetus to the issue:

> Immediately upon taking office in 1998, Brundtland announced
> her 2 priorities – tobacco control and combating malaria. Under
> Brundtland's tenure, negotiations of the WHO FCTC were under-
> taken. Resources were made available to the new Tobacco Free
> Initiative, headed by Yach, to develop a framework convention on
> tobacco control. The negotiation of the WHO FCTC gained polit-
> ical momentum and turned into a worldwide public health move-
> ment. (Roemer *et al.*, 2005, p.938)

This passage identifies an important change in the WHO agenda, brought about by a change in the organization's leadership. The fact that Brundtland designated a number of key priorities at the beginning of her tenure as director general had a number of consequences. First, it signalled to other actors that she, and thereby the WHO, would be (politically) more receptive to tobacco-related initiatives than the WHO had been before. Second, internally within the WHO, additional resources were made available to develop tobacco control policies, exemplified in the creation of a new formal programme (the Tobacco Free Initiative mentioned in the quote). This, too, meant that tobacco control policy moved to a higher position on the WHO agenda. This, in turn, had a galvanizing effect on the debate in the EU and helped to push the issue up the EU agenda as well.

Conclusion

This chapter has discussed different types of agendas, the actors involved in setting the EU's political agenda, theoretical perspectives on agenda setting, and the questions that might be asked in order to best get to grips with agenda-setting processes. By asking these questions about a policy issue, it is possible to find out how and why that issue came onto the EU agenda. Conversely, it is equally important to ask why some issues did *not* make it onto the EU agenda, or why they did not make it onto the EU agenda at an earlier time. In that way, a more systematic and well-grounded understanding of agenda dynamics in the European Union can be obtained.

Suggestions for further reading

Baumgartner, F. and Jones, B. (1993) *Agendas and Instability in American Politics* (Chicago and London: University of Chicago Press).
Kingdon, J. (2003) *Agendas, Alternatives, and Public Policies*, 2nd edn (New York: HarperCollins College Publishers).
Princen, S. (2009) *Agenda-setting in the European Union* (Basingstoke and New York: Palgrave Macmillan).

Websites

Many documents relating to the process leading up to a formal proposal can be found on the EU website.
Pre-Lex (http://ec.europa.eu/prelex/apcnet.cfm?CL=en) is a database managed by the European Commission. It gives overviews of the formal steps in decision-making procedures that take place between the Commission and the other EU institutions, with links to relevant documents. Although it omits

the process leading up to the publication of a Commission document, it is a good source of information for what subsequently happens with that document.

Documents on specific issues can be found on the websites of the responsible Commission DGs (http://ec.europa.eu/about/ds_en.htm).

Agendas and conclusions of European Council and Council of Ministers meetings are available through the Council's website (http://www.consilium.europa.eu/).

Most interest groups post position papers and other materials about the issues on which they are working on their websites.

Chapter 6

Policy Shaping

Introduction

The first image that springs to mind when one is asked to think about EU policy making may be that of national politicians coming together in a large room full of European flags and lined with translator booths to accommodate the working in 22 official languages. When the media focuses on EU policy making, it mostly departs from certain grand and by now relatively well-known contexts: European Council summits, European Parliament plenary meetings in Strasbourg, and government ministers meeting in the Council of Ministers in their various configurations: transport, health, trade, education ministers, and so forth.

At the same time, and paradoxically, a second observation many people often have is that of the supposed complexity and 'closedness' of EU policy making. For outsiders, the rules of access for European lobby groups to the corridors of the EU institutions are notoriously unclear. Access, however, is crucial in terms of analyzing EU policy formulation, or 'policy shaping', the theme of this chapter. Any analysis will be less complete without first-hand insight into what happened during the period in which the law, policy or report was put together in Brussels and in the national capitals. Such insight can shed light upon any process of policies being formulated or shaped by policy makers of different sorts: politicians, experts, interest groups, and administrators all (attempting to) chisel away at a proposal through various rounds of meetings, decisions, reviews and debates, until they end up with a 'final product'. It is actually very often the same group of people (national officials, Commission officials, lobby groups) who are involved in different stages of the process, from the 'pre-cooking' of amendments for ministerial decision making to the fine-tuning of the agreed-upon texts so that they are better adapted to existing practices. In many cases, the result of the evolution of a policy is that one ends up with a 'lowest common denominator' version of a law or policy document, a compromise that manages to satisfy all parties after a lengthy process of negotiation and consultation. This chapter introduces these people, their instruments and strategies, as well as some perspectives and tools with which to approach them. It illustrates these processes with the help of a number of specific case-studies.

EU policy shaping: who is involved and what do we analyze?

What is EU policy shaping?

EU policy making is by no means linear; it does not necessarily always follow a delineated set of formal procedures. Rather, it is incremental and intuitive, going back and forth between different venues, from policy shaping to decision making and back if need be. This is because the EU is a consensus-driven type of political system. As such, its ability to 'pre-cook' decisions in the stages 'before the hammer falls', as it were, is fundamental to the reaching of agreement between the member states, EU institutions, and other organized interests. This chapter is about the stage of policy shaping in which decisions are 'pre-cooked' before they reach the stages of negotiations and agreement. But just as there is no clear demarcation between the stages of agenda setting (Chapter 5) and policy shaping, the line between policy shaping and decision making (Chapter 7) is equally difficult to pinpoint. As we suggested in Chapter 5, some issues emerge on the EU's political agenda from below. A problem or, a potential solution to that problem, appears from 'below', before it then gradually develops and is further articulated through deliberations between policy experts in expert committees or working groups – as was the case with the Tobacco Advertising Ban Directive. Other issues are pushed from the top political level downwards. The EU arrest warrant, for example, was pushed through the policy process in record time in the aftermath of 9/11. Often, it is a combination of the two that allows for a new policy to be considered. Once a new topic or issue has made it onto the EU's agenda and has acquired the attention of policy makers, it needs to take on shape, form and content. Agenda items are developed into draft legislative texts and policy proposals for the decision makers to decide upon. Different actors attempt to get the text shaped and reshaped by means of negotiations, lobbying efforts, and the drafting and proposing of alternatives to those versions put forward by the Commission. Where policy shaping is about identifying and constructing alternatives, decision makers finally agree to choose one option and mark it into a final text. This chapter deals with this 'preparation' and 'blending' of the draft policy, while the next chapter on decision making addresses the 'cooking' of legislative texts by ministers in the Council and members of the European Parliament. But decision making also includes the 'seasoning' and 'presentation' of texts to make them palatable, edible, digestible by those who will have to implement them. In EU jargon, this is the phase of 'comitology' that sees different committees of experts fine-tuning draft legislation.

Who is involved?

The shaping phase of policy is dominated by two groups of civil servants. First, the 'national' civil servants, working for member state governments at the national level. Second, the European officials (in French: 'fonctionnaires') employed by the European institutions: the Commission, the Parliament, and the Council Secretariat. During their fine-tuning of legislative drafts and policy proposals, they are fed by technical experts and lobbyists representing interests from industry, academia, NGOs, or civil society groups. This section reviews a number of essential steps and actors in this 'multilevel union administration' (Egeberg, 2006).

The European Commission

The European Commission is the centre-piece of much of what happens at this stage. It has the right of legislative initiative for all policy issues within the first pillar. In the field of foreign policy, it shares the competence of coming up with new initiatives with the member states. The Commission eagerly exploits this 'power of the pen'. It produces a steady flow of draft policy according to five-year strategic programmes and annual working plans. In 2008, the Commission presented 420 legislative proposals, 318 communications and reports, nine Green Papers and one White Paper (European Commission, 2008). In contrast to many predictions, this was not significantly less than before the 'big bang' enlargement of the 2004, which apparently did not lead to a fall in productive output (Kurpas *et al.*, 2008).

The Commission thus functions as the hub of a spoke of different policy networks. A key person in this hub is the *chef de dossier*, a Commission *fonctionnaire* who is responsible for taking a proposal throughout the shaping stages. As the Commission is a small organization with only about 5,000 policy staff and much EU policy is relatively technical in nature (setting norms, quota and data), the *chef de dossiers* cannot draft proposals in isolation. A third reason for their intensive networking is strategic: the Commission needs to secure support for ideas by the early stages of a policy cycle. After all, the extent to which the Commission is successful in including the member states, parliamentarians and lobbyists in its shaping process, conditions to a large extent the degree of opposition that the policy will receive at the decision-making stage. Then, the Commission is dependent upon the Council and the MEPs to approve its plans (see Box 6.1).

The Commission works with expert committees of specialists from different organizations in different places – for example member state governments, citizens groups, and industry lobbies (see Box 6.2). These

Box 6.1 Politics within the Commission: the case of REACH

REACH is the name for the new European chemicals legislation (regulation 1907/2006/EC). It stands for Registration, Evaluation and Authorization of Chemicals and represents a major revision of existing chemicals legislation, placing as it does the burden on industry to prove their products are safe before entering the market.

The basic idea behind the new regulation was to ensure ecological protection against hazards stemming from certain chemical substances. Initially, DG Environment of the European Commission was strongly in the driving seat. During the writing phase, however, the contentious issues of testing and registration of chemicals on the market raised the interest of industry lobbyists. The European chemicals industry has strong interest representation both at the level of the member states as well as in Brussels. The lobby successfully pushed for more influence from the more industry-oriented DG Enterprise. This DG gained ground within the so-called 'inter-service' procedure in which text drafts circulate within the Commission, making the drafting phase highly contentious. Experts from both DGs, assisted by specialists from national ministries, worked on a draft regulation which incorporated both the original environmental concerns as well as more market-oriented regulatory instruments to implement the new EU law. When the time came for decision making on the drafts, the issue of responsibility was shifted up to the Council level. The main discussion focused on the question of which Council configuration would be appointed 'responsible' for the negotiations. Just before publication of the proposal, the Italian Presidency of the Council decided that REACH would be tabled in the Competitiveness Council. This might be seen as a victory for the chemicals industry. At the same time, however, it threatened to make the shaping of the text even more cumbersome, as government ministries from across the different member states were involved in preparation for this Council configuration. A solution was found by setting-up a special working party under the Council, the 'Ad Hoc Working Party on Chemicals', bringing together civil servants with a background in both environmental policy, and those with expertise in economic affairs. Together, this group of national experts discussed successive drafts of the proposal and prepared them for decision making by their ministers. Two years of heated negotiations followed, in which both the 'green' and the 'industry' sides, as well as lobbyist representing *inter alia* the interests of small business, consumers, and labour unions, tried to amend the texts. The Council and European Parliament reached a final agreement in 2006, with the regulation entering into force on 1 June 2007.

Box 6.2   Policy fights in shaping the Tobacco Advertising Directive

The Tobacco Advertising Directive offers multiple examples of infighting by experts, lobbyists and institutions attempting to shape the final EU law to their liking. The initial draft of the ban on tobacco advertising was largely a product of Commission civil servants, working in close collaboration with the EU's cancer expert committee as well as a separate agency, the European Bureau for Action on Smoking Prevention (BASP). This latter office was established by the Commission in 1990 and provided information and arguments in favour of the ban. The UK, Germany and the Netherlands strongly objected to BASP, claiming that the Commission had financed its own lobbying agency. But the proposal was also heavily lobbied by opponents, led by the economically powerful tobacco industry. It joined forces with the advertising companies and the Formula One industry for a massive – and hugely expensive – advertising campaign in European newspapers and magazines aiming to evoke emotional response from consumers. In one instance, the UK government demanded an exemption for the sponsorship of sports, allegedly after a large gift was made to the Labour party from the Formula One chairman Bernie Ecclestone. For its part, the public health lobby had neither that quantity of people nor the financial resources to possibly counterbalance the tobacco industry. Instead, it chose to resort, and rather successfully, to indirect strategies: letters, resolutions, position papers, press releases and conferences aimed at shifting opinions within national governments.

Once it was clear that the proposed ban would, in effect, materialize, the shaping strategies by the EU's lawmakers (Council and European Parliament) gained ground. One example was the strategic vote by the European Parliament. A majority in the plenary accepted the Council's common position in the second reading, even though the members of the parliamentary Committee for the Environment (ENVI) were not at all satisfied with the common position. The MEPs believed, however, that agreement would no longer be possible once the dossier had reached the conciliation phase. Therefore, the EP chose to proceed tactically, voting in favour of the compromise agreement of the Council, rather than risking the possibility of no decision whatsoever on a tobacco ban being reached.

Source: Adamini *et al.*, 2010.

different venues can offer much insight into the policy drafts the Commission is working on, as well as form possible points of access for primary source research. In drafting laws, the European Commission works closely with the EU's own regulatory and executive agencies. Their main function is providing technical advice in specialized areas, such as medicinal policy (the European Medical Agency in London) or the European Gender Agency in Vilnius. Some are primarily involved in regulation and implementation of policy fields, such as the Maritime Safety Agency in Lisbon. These agencies function rarely in the political spotlight, but they can prove a useful source of information and data for policy analysis.

EU policies are often shaped as much by rivalry between the Commission services, as they are by controversy between the member states and the Parliament at a later stage.

Although the notion of 'the' Commission suggests a single actor, a lot of policy shaping takes place within the walls of the different individual Commission offices, which are dispersed across Brussels. The impact of this dispersion within the Commission should not be underestimated. The Directorate-Generals (DGs) often act as quasi-ministries, rendering the Commission something of a breeding ground for internal rivalry and 'bureaucratic politics'. For the purpose of analyzing EU policies, a look within the Commission is therefore essential. When a text is drafted by the *chef the dossier* and his colleagues, proposals work their way up the chain of command. In this process of 'inter-service consultation' texts are amended and re-drafted within and between the different units of a Directorate and Directorate-General, until they meet with the approval of the Commissioner in charge.

Once it reaches the political realms of the Commission, a proposal is discussed inside and across the DGs. The procedure of inter-service consultation is meant to make sure that all DGs are consulted about new policy proposals. Other DGs that have an interest in the proposal are consulted by the DG responsible for drafting it, and may propose modifications to the draft text. This process can be very long, especially when different perspectives lead to conflicting interests or positions. For example, DG Health and Consumer Protection (known in Brussels-jargon as DG SANCO) may be more likely to look at how the interests of patients are guaranteed in a particular dossier, while DG Enterprise may champion the interests of the pharmaceutical industry. In case of internal controversy, an '*avis suspendu*' can be issued, indicating that an opinion has been withheld. Inter-service consultation also guarantees that policies in different field are coordinated – the so-called 'mainstreaming'.

A key role falls to the Cabinets: the offices of the personal aides of the Commissioners, also called 'mini-Councils within the Commission' (Peterson and Bomberg, 1999, p.39). Before the weekly Wednesday meeting of Commissioners, the Cabinet chiefs meet to prepare the regular Commission meetings. Cabinets are also an important centre of influence for the national capitals. Although the Commission is formally independent from the member states, governments actively try to co-shape EU policies, for example through fellow nationals within the Commission administration, either as an official ('administrator'), or in the form of permanent officials or seconded national experts.

How the drafting process goes forward once a proposal has left the Commission depends on the issue and the relevant procedure. In the case of a draft law (regulation, framework directive or recommendation), a negotiating process starts between, on the one hand, the governments of the member states united in the Council and, on the other hand, the European Parliament. But the tasks of the Commission are not finished the moment a proposal leaves its offices. Each DG has regular contacts with 'its' working groups in the Council and with the relevant sectoral committees in the European Parliament. In adopting the necessary technical measures, the Commission is assisted by committees made up of representatives of member states (see Chapter 7). In comitology committees, evaluations are discussed and possible reviews of legislation are prepared. This involvement from agenda setting to implementation and evaluation makes the *chef de dossier* an indispensable source for the policy analyst.

The Council of Ministers

All EU laws have to be formally sealed in meetings of the Council at ministerial level. But as is the case in domestic policy making, in the EU, government ministers have the bulk of the work prepared for them by working groups of national officials. The Council working groups at the bottom of the EU's hierarchy have no formal legal powers, but in practice they form the backbone of the policy-shaping process. It is there where many of the laws and rules receive their final shape – estimates have it that some 90 per cent of all dossiers are actually settled before they reach the level of ambassadors or ministers (Hayes-Renshaw and Wallace, 2006).

There are around 200 Council groups, chaired by the delegation of the country holding the rotating Presidency. In these meetings, in the Council's Justus Lipsius Building, civil servants go through the proposals article by article, debating them in detail and often changing the wording in continuous discussion with ever-present Commission representatives who (re-)write the proposal. Some working groups are very active, such as the one on the environment which meets about three days a week in order to deal with the large number of environmental *dossiers*. There are also 'sleeping' groups, which may not convene for months and only re-awaken when new proposals are issued by the Commission or under political pressure by a new Presidency. A number of policy areas have their own standing, high-level senior committees, a few examples being: foreign policy, debated in the Political and Security Committee; immigration and asylum legislation, discussed in the Strategic Committee for Immigration, Frontiers and Asylum; and trade policy, dealt with by the Committee on International Trade. Until the Lisbon treaty revision, this committee of senior civil servants was named the Article 133 committee, after the eponymous Treaty article.

Notwithstanding the (exaggerated) public image of the alleged size of the Brussels policy process, it is actually a small group of officials that debates the same set of issues in different venues. The national officials in working groups who debate draft proposals are very often the same people as those who have previously offered advice to the European Commission during the drafting stages. Although officials work on the basis of national instructions, these only give the framework within which negotiations should take place. In practice, national coordination systems should produce positions that are sufficiently *flexible* for government representatives to enjoy some room for manoeuvre during the negotiations. Amendments are proposed throughout the process and as such, outcomes often involve intricate compromise. Instructions for negotiators often have to be adapted on the spot to changing circumstances or the shifting positions of the other negotiators, whereas tight domestic compromises might leave their hands tied.

Those aspects that cannot be agreed upon by member state experts are referred to the EU ambassadors of the member states in the Committee of Permanent Representatives, known as COREPER, after its French acronym. This body in fact consists of two separate committees. COREPER II is composed of the permanent representatives, normally diplomats of ambassadorial rank. It is a relatively intimate group that meets once a week on an official basis, as well as informally with great frequency, to discuss the EU's political, financial and foreign policy. COREPER I brings together the deputy permanent representatives who deal with the EU policies that are related to the internal marked: transport, environment, social policy. Apart from its socialized atmosphere, the added value of COREPER lies in the fact that it is not sub-divided into policy sectors, as are the Council and the Commission (with the exception of agriculture, for which there is a 'Special Committee on Agriculture'). This makes it easier to reach package deals since experienced negotiators have a degree of oversight across multiple and different sectoral working groups.

If agreement is reached in COREPER or the working groups, the points for discussion and decision appear on the ministerial Council agenda as A-points. These are issues that have already been decided upon before the ministerial meeting, and thus have only to be formally hammered out at the start of the meeting. This leaves time for the more difficult B-points to be discussed and decided upon by the ministers during the meeting. At the same time, Council meetings are generally a good venue for discussing the content-related issues that ultimately affect a policy's shape, since national delegations bring together experts and negotiators all working in the same field or sector.

The European Parliament

While the negotiating process goes on in the Council, proposals are debated in the European Parliament. The EP is a political institution composed of 736 directly elected politicians, who represent national political parties. The absence of an in-built majority makes the EP something of a hotbed of coalitionbuilding and consensus politics, a feature which largely determines the way that the EP engages in policy shaping. For a majority to emerge, a lot of political 'horse trading' goes on behind the scenes. Such informal negotiation and bargaining may also occur regarding draft legislation (Commission proposals, Council common positions, and parliamentary amendments), budgetary politics, as well as with regards to non-legislative acts (questions, resolutions, and reports). Such loose and unpredictable 'politicking', presents a challenge for policy analysts as it may be difficult to obtain firsthand data about how influence and interests have been exerted or acted upon 'behind the scenes'.

The bulk of the parliamentary shaping work is done in the sectoral committees, which cover most areas of EU policy. Each committee assembles a number of MEPs from different political parties and nationalities. In such a setting, a Commission proposal, as amended by the Council, appears on the table as a matter for discussion. Although all MEPs can amend the legislation inside a Committee, there are some people who will lead the debate and discussions in the political groups. There are a number of key roles in the intra-parliamentary shaping work:

- The *rapporteur* is the MEP who writes the report with all the amendments. He or she produces a draft report, including suggested amendments to a proposal.
- The shadow *rapporteur* from each of the EP's political groups advises the committees on how to vote for amendments.
- The group coordinator keeps an eye on the committee work for the political party.
- The committee chair may have a strong political impact upon the group proceedings.

The draft report by the *rapporteur* is the basis for the vote in the plenary meeting in Strasbourg at the end of the month. Particularly controversial legislation will be at the centre of talks by the *rapporteurs*, political groups, Commission representatives, Council staff, and interest group lobbies. After all discussion the whole Parliament itself – and not the committee – proceeds to vote on it, generally by a normal majority.

Party politics are important for any understanding of how the EP finally votes. Studies of the voting registers of the EP since it was first directly elected in 1979 actually show that party behaviour within the EP is quite cohesive and predictable (Hix, 2007). This makes party politics an important explanatory variable in how the EP finally shapes policy proposals. But there are many informal processes going on in the background. One example is the parliamentary 'intergroups', which bring together MEPs with a particular interest or personal concern. Although informal, these groups may have an impact on the formation of coalitions and alliances across political groups (Corbett *et al.*, 2007).

If the Council and Parliament cannot agree on a piece of proposed legislation, negotiations intensify in a special conciliation committee, composed of equal numbers of Council and Parliamentary representatives, joined by European Commission representatives. Once the civil servants and parliamentary staff in this committee have managed to reach an agreement, the text is sent once again to the Parliament's plenary session, as well as to the Council, so that they can finally adopt it as law. It is extremely rare that a procedure becomes truly stalled so that no decision can ever be made. The EP plays an important role under the ordinary legislative procedure. Whether or not it chooses to use its powers depends on the circumstances.

The open nature of EU policy making means that a multiplicity of actors are drawn towards the Brussels institutions, like moths to a flame, or perhaps, with what are often large financial stakes involved in mind, like bees around a honey pot. Just as governmental actors may use the policy-shaping stage to advocate ideas that have not been taken up at home (at the national level), so interest groups, NGOs and other international organizations will lobby in an attempt to exert influence. The Commission consults the EESC and the CoR on the regional and social–economic effects of newly proposed EU legislation. Although the impact of their advice is often questioned (see also Chapter 2), their in-depth reports can be a valuable source for the views held on European policies by civil society and the media in the member states.

Another source of information is provided by the professional lobbyists who operate in Brussels. As the European Commission discovered when, for the sake of transparency, it attempted to propose a voluntary register for lobbyists active in Brussels, the definition of lobbying may be somewhat disputed: Chapter 2 introduced different types of lobbyists and the tactics they may have when attempting to influence the shape of EU policies in a way that best reflects and serves their (often business) interests. Their key way of working is to assemble information on particular areas of EU policy and to 'sell' this information to decision makers, with the goal of securing a decision in their favour. Depending on where formal competencies and informal contacts lie, lobby campaigns may use the national route or the Brussels route. The national route runs via the national capitals of the member states, though government departments, coordination authorities, working group meetings or individual contacts with civil servants, as well as in interaction with sub-national interests, national business corporations, or local NGOs. The 'Brussels' lobby route runs through the EU institutions, starting with access to the drafting stage by the Commission and then winding through the different levels of the Council, from direct contact with members and groups within the European Parliament to presence at the level of European Council summits. An example of direct business lobbying at the highest level is that of German Chancellor Gerhard Schroeder, apparently persuaded by Ferdinand Piech, board member of Volkswagen, to postpone an item from the Environment Council during the EU Council presidency.

Of course, very often lobby groups use several different routes at the same time in order to maximize their influence. For example, the social partners (trade and employers organizations) do not only have a separate advisory body, the EESC, but they also have regular access to the intergovernmental EU decision-making meetings of the 'EU troika': that is, representatives of the present and future Presidency and the European Commission. These meetings take place during the 'preliminaries' – the run-up events to the European Council summits. Representatives of the social partners are also included in the informal preparation of the Employment and Social Affairs Council by the member states.

Many interest groups or firms operating domestically are organized at the EU level in Eurogroups or federations, conglomerations that often join forces where a common interest is involved. For example, the European Banking Federation unites about 5,000 banks throughout the EU. During the financial crisis in 2008, it was very active in representing the interests of the sector in newly developed financial and economic regulation initiatives, for example through intensive contacts with the European Commission.

Although lobby organizations are usually short on staff, they compensate with expert knowledge on a particular issue, which may be useful for decision makers. The European Commission in particular, which is famously under-staffed, is certainly open to outside information. In fact, its informational deficit is eagerly exploited by lobbyists, especially those in more technical areas, whose selective presentation of information constitutes a strategic move. Lobbying is essentially a long-term activity, relying to a large extent on knowing the right people in the right building, and on personalized contacts with privileged people. Lobbyists often draft position papers that put forward a particular perspective on a draft policy. They may use the pan-European media – the *Financial Times*, the *Euronews* TV channel, or websites like *EurActiv* – to advance a particular position. Certainly, lobbyists may often constitute a good information source in terms of new initiatives, political relations. They can provide useful access to otherwise unavailable (re)sources. They are generally known to be very informed about the latest developments in the EU policy field. However, apart from being biased and loyal to the specific interests that they represent, their neutrality is also disputed in the sense that many of them receive financial support from the EU institutions themselves – something that has engendered accusations of cooptation and dependency. That said, some scholars – such as Schendelen (2006) – argue very much in their favour, asserting how they are a key resource for the EU policy process.

Member states

It is important not to forget the relevance of events that occur at the national level. What happens in Brussels accounts for only a fraction of the resources and efforts the national governments devote to EU policy making. Many member states have a large stake in obtaining access to the different stages at which EU policies are shaped in order to influence the outcomes of the policy process. When analyzing the shaping of a particular law, report or policy document, one should pay close attention to what was happening in the national capitals of the member states, and how the position of key member states came to be shaped in the first place.

Member states are very different in how they organize EU policies domestically. Political structures, cultures, or administrative traditions, as well as the size of the political apparatus and the priorities for EU policies differ per country. The UK is a prime example of a *centralized* system, with a central role for the Prime Minister's Cabinet Office and weekly interdepartmental meetings of (traditionally politically neutral) civil servants, who consider forthcoming meetings in Brussels and set for ministers' negotiating mandates. In more fragmented or *decentralized* systems, such as Germany or The Netherlands, where the civil service may be politicized, coalition politics and the relative autonomy of ministries or regions make coordination more difficult. This can potentially be damaging for the success in negotiations as different officials may take different positions with regards to the same policy in EU negotiations. A lack of coordination may also cause implementation problems, when ill-coordinated policies have to be put into effect in the member states. Size is also a variable here, as large governments have

Box 6.3　Negotiating at home and in Brussels: the EPB Directive

The Energy Performance of Buildings Directive (2002/91/EC), was adopted in 2002 to allow the EU to meet the environmental ambitions outlined in the Kyoto protocol. As many member states had problems with implementing measures, including a shortage of professionals issuing 'energy certificates', the Commission proposed a 'recast' in November 2008. The proposal soon turned out to be highly contentious both within member states and at the EU level. Parliamentary concerns, voiced by *inter alia* the German, UK and Dutch houses of representatives, largely centered around the alleged 'subsidiarity' of the proposal. Should the EU be involved in national housing policy? Interestingly, the opinions of various parliaments differed. Where Hungarian, Finnish and Swedish MPs did not consider the proposal to breach subsidiarity, the outcome of a similar 'subsidiarity check' in the German and Dutch parliament was much more critical. These parliaments also contested the 'proportionality' of the Commission proposal, pointing at the alleged overly ambitious level of detail of EU standards and the excessive administrative burden that would follow from implementing the new system. Following its critical analysis of the proposed EU law, the Bundesrat advised the German federal government to delay ratification of the directive, to gain more time to analyze concerns with the proposed text. The British House of Commons suggested a national impact assessment. In the Netherlands, the House of Representatives (Tweede Kamer) rejected the proposal upon grounds of both subsidiarity and proportionality and summoned the relevant Cabinet minister to object in the Council.

Continuing disagreement on targets, standards and responsibilities in the new energy saving scheme between national delegations and the EP, which opted for a greener stance, led to 'trilogue' meetings in which representatives of Commission, Council and EP tried to forge a compromise. The UN climate summit in Copenhagen (December 2009) acted as a deadline for reaching a political compromise in the Council, with the text signed off by Energy Ministers in November 2009 coming just before the global conference. The final deal still had to be finalized between European Parliament and the Council.

more staff at their disposal and can thus 'play a wider field', whereas smaller member states are forced to set priorities, which may, as a result, make them more focused.

Political culture is also important. National officials accustomed to a consensus-building style of negotiating are more accustomed to the need for coalition-building at the European level. Finally, although size and organization do matter, a lot ultimately depends on ambition.

Although the UK is active in EU policy making, both its image as an 'awkward partner' and its preference for intergovernmental solutions, have tended to make it something of an outsider during Council negotiations (although Poland and the Czech Republic now appear to be following a similar trend). The long held pro-European consensus in Germany, as well as that country's significant economic power, influence the nature and style of its policy-shaping activity, despite the high degree of administrative fragmentation that exists there.

Generally, there are three groups of actors at the government level involved in the preparation of EU policy making: coordinating authorities, government departments, and national parliaments. Foreign Affairs Ministries or Government Offices of the Prime Minister coordinate the process, but have seen their powers decrease with time. The increasing scale and scope of EU policies make it hard to draw up a comprehensive picture of what role national civil servants are playing in different working groups, or expert and comitology committees, at any given time. The emergence of the European Council as the strategic political forum where many political deals are struck has meant that Government or Prime Ministers' Offices have become more involved in the organization of national EU-policy making. National Permanent Representations in Brussels are like embassies of the member states to the EU. They have both 'upstream' functions (providing a Brussels contact point for national officials) and 'downstream' functions, providing information for and advising the national capital on recent EU developments (Kassim *et al.*, 2000). National parliaments have traditionally been considered the 'losers' of European integration, as the process as a whole was held to strengthen the executive level of member states governments *vis-à-vis* the legislative. But national parliaments have gradually gained more powers with each successive treaty changes since the 1990s. The representatives now receive all Commission proposals directly from the Commission so that they can perform a subsidiarity check on new EU policy proposals. The majority of parliaments also use intensified controls or 'scrutiny' in order to maintain a constant influence on the positions their national governments take in Council negotiations. To this end, parliamentary committees have special EU staff offices that produce expert advice for the benefit of MPs. The EU policy reports commissioned by the UK House of Lords, for example, are a trusted source of information on EU policy developments. In the Netherlands, members of Cabinet appear before the sectoral committees before each Council meeting to discuss the issues of the day as regards EU negotiations and the Dutch position. In so-called 'mandating' systems of parliamentary control, to which the Danish Folketing adheres, government ministers are also obliged to later explain their stance in the Council negotiations to the relevant parliamentary committees (see Box 6.3 for an example of diverging reactions of national parliaments).

Theoretical perspectives

The previous section has illustrated the plethora of organizations and individuals active in the procedurally complex field of shaping new policies, all bringing interests and preferences together, on what can sometimes seem to be something of a collision course. It is not surprising that the types and number of analyses seeking to describe, explain and at times prescribe how EU policies are shaped are as diverse as the process itself. Much of the recent theoretical work on EU policy making has emphasized the process as a complex affair, one that is difficult to capture with static models focusing on formal competencies. The theoretical section in this chapter concentrates on studies of policy networks and socialization, perspectives that are particularly relevant when looking at this stage of policy shaping.

In current thinking about how EU policies are shaped, a great deal of attention is paid to the role of the EU institutions. The notion of 'institutions' refers not only to the three policy-making organizations at the EU level (Commission, Council and Parliament), which are considered to have formed their own layer of administration, and in that sense might be seen as an autonomous force in the shaping process (Sandholz and Zysman, 1998). It also encompasses, in a more general or theoretical sense, any set of formal or informal rules, norms, or practices that are seen to influence the behaviour of actors (Aspinwall and Schneider, 2001). In this broad sense, they are considered to be important intervening variables, given that they inevitably condition the preferences of policy makers, thereby entering into politics themselves. For example, the spread of qualified majority voting (QMV) has turned out to have a profound impact on the strategic behaviour of national governments in EU policy shaping, setting in motion as it did the practice of coalition-building in early stages of policy shaping. Majority voting has thereby become one of the institutions determining how EU policy shaping works in practice.

A useful theory in terms of research around the EU policy-shaping stage is the principal–agent theory (Hawkins *et al.*, 2006), introduced earlier in Chapter 4 as a feature of rational choice institutionalism. The creation and evolution of COREPER is a case in point. In the early days of the Community, once member states had delegated the authority for the informal preparation of negotiations, they found themselves no longer able to control the outcomes of the process that they had set in motion; there was institutional 'drift'. Other examples of delegation in the EU might be the practice of comitology, or the representation of member states on the boards of the EU's new agencies to control the decision-making powers of the European Commission.

Other scholars have looked more at the importance of softer rules and informal practices in EU policy making. As we mentioned in

Chapter 4, historical institutionalists look at the way decisions tend to 'lock in' future decisions through the process of path-dependency (Pierson, 1996). In contrast to looking at individual policy sectors in isolation, this perspective on EU policy making can shed light on how competencies emerge and decisions follow up on each other.

The relevance of culture and informal practices are central to socio-logical approaches to EU policy-making, where attention is placed on how patterns of interaction and behaviour emerge between partici-pants in particular institutional settings. Recent studies suggest that the experience itself of working closely together towards shared goals around the tables of the European institutions (common decision making) has an effect on the norms, values, and even interests of the participants. An example might be the general commitment to con-sensus of Council participants when it comes to deciding on legislation, such that 'real' voting in the meetings is relatively rare. In studies, many negotiators at the EU level have expressed the idea that they assign more weight to arguments put forward by colleagues enjoying considerable *expertise* in the subject at hand, and comparatively less to those whose arguments might be reinforced by a perceived political weight – a tendency that might be good news for experts from the smaller member states. Particularly within Council working parties and COREPER, participants sometimes report feeling 'responsible' for the proceedings. In this sense, EU committees and working groups from across the spectrum might be seen as functioning as a kind of policy community (Heclo, 1978), characterized by stable networks, the recog-nition of expertise, and a common belief that cooperation is better than going it alone. This bears some resemblance to the 'cultivated spillover' that the neofunctionalists (see Chapter 1) anticipated – offi-cials ended up 'brokering' deals and negotiating to secure policy inte-gration, their commitment to the political process engendered as the result of engaging in the policy-making process itself.

National representatives enjoy a special position in the EU policy framework. They have to operate strategically on two levels: on the one hand, they serve their national ministries, where they spend the majority of their working time; on the other hand, when shaping EU policies, they function as part of the EU administration. A very impor-tant question is then to what extent the preferences they bring to EU policies are given to them beforehand (instructed or programmed), and to what extent they are socially constructed during their interaction (Checkel, 2001). Research suggests this process of 'socialization' depends on the type of venue where negotiators meet. For Commission expert committees, participants are invited because of the expertise they bring to the negotiations. National civil servants participate on the basis of personal invitations and are generally not mandated or controlled by any coordinating authorities in charge of EU affairs.

Here, the focus is on sharing independent expertise relevant to policy content, instead of negotiating between pre-fixed positions. The latter is what happens in the Council working groups and comitology committees. There, most participants are official government representatives, presenting coordinated mandates and literally sitting behind their national flag. In these Council venues, negotiating and bargaining has ceased. However, because those same people meet regularly and often discuss similar topics, the notion of reaching consensus informally – without a vote – is very important; it is one of the implicit 'rules of the game' that allows the institution to function effectively. To ensure that such a working practice (or tradition) is upheld, it is often the case that significant consideration will be given to whatever particular national demands have dictated the formal national negotiating position.

When analyzing the policy-shaping stage, insight into the political and administrative actions within member states is important. Bulmer (1983) was one of the first academics to point out the relevance of domestic processes when analyzing how member states arrive at their national positions. This area was largely neglected by traditional intergovernmentalist reasoning, which looked at member states as single actors with rational interests. But Moravscik (1993, 1999), the initiator of liberal intergovernmentalist theory (see Chapter 1), connected the interplay of dynamic domestic social and political processes determining state preferences with the strategic bargaining of state representatives at the EU level. Viewed in this way, the Single European Act was only possible because the preferences of three of the most important member states (France, UK and Germany) converged at that particular point in time. Relevant in this sense is also Kingdon's political stream, discussed in Chapter 5.

Since the mid-1990s there has been significantly more study of the impact of the EU in the member states, or Europeanization (see, for example, Cowles *et al.*, 2001; Featherstone and Radaelli, 2003). Two broad strands can be distinguished in Europeanization literature. First, there are studies focusing on (explaining) the impact of EU membership on political and administrative structures, cultures, and working practices in the member states. The impact of the EU is found to be 'differential' (Héritier *et al.*, 2001); in other words, it is incremental, irregular and, uneven over time and between locations. A second strand centres on explaining the implementation or transposition deficit: why have national governments experienced so many problems in implementing the measures that they have agreed on when shaping EU legislation (see Chapter 8)? Early explanations focused on administrative shortcomings in the implementation process. Recent studies, by contrast, have investigated the 'goodness of fit' hypothesis, linking implementation performance to activity at the shaping stage. The 'fit' between existing national arrangements and proposed new European rules and legislation is seen to be instrumental in explaining the way that member states position themselves in EU policy making. This link between shaping and implementation is central to the third strand of Europeanization research (Keulen, 2006). The assumption in much of the literature is that national governments will act as 'guardians of the status quo', protecting national traditions against intrusion from the EU level. Adjustment processes are expected to be more problematic if the degree of 'misfit' between the EU and the national level is high. Nevertheless, governments may strive to change the status quo at the domestic level, for example in response to party political pressures. In this way, governments purposefully press for new policy arrangements to be set by EU law, using 'Brussels' as a lever to achieve domestic change (Börzel, 2002).

When analyzing EU policy shaping, one will soon find out that not only the central governments of the member states are heavily involved, but so are many sub-national actors: regions (German Länder, French regions, Spanish Autonomous Communities), provinces (UK counties, French departments) and municipalities. The degree to which regions are affected by EU policies depends on the specific domestic division of policy competences. In many member states, regions and municipalities are responsible for the legal implementation of EU legislation at street level. The management and allocation of EU funds for social–economic cohesion policies – for example, the Cohesion Fund – may also be a sub-national responsibility. By sharing policy competencies at different levels, the EU's system is characterized by multilevel governance (see Chapter 1). As a result, regional representatives often attempt to shape EU policies, arguing that stakeholders should be involved in shaping policy content, rather than just having it delivered to them by central government. This representation in Brussels ranges from actively lobbying of the Commission to formal representation in permanent offices, which function as meeting places for regional interests in the EU's capital. Analyzing the activity and influence of regional governments can be an interesting angle of policy research.

Key issues for consideration

There are a number of questions to consider when analyzing EU policy shaping.

- Who has an interest in the policy proposal under scrutiny? Who benefits from the new law and which party is damaged by the financial consequences?
- Who has been active in (lobbying) the writing phases of the new proposal?

- Which lobbying techniques were used to mobilize and represent sectoral interests?
- How can the national positions of member states be explained by domestic politics?

Choosing the issues that one wishes to focus on carefully is important here. For example, a general interest in the 'hard' field of EU's security and defence policy (CSDP) could be translated into a research question such as how the member states cooperate in the field of military defence. As one entire policy domain may be too broad a subject of analysis (see Chapter 4 on *How We Analyze*), a further narrowing of the scope may shift the focus to the way that the EU came to decide on its battle groups for rapid response in crises situations. A simple Google search on the notion of EU battle groups may be intimidating, revealing as it does more than one million hits. But prominent in the search result are two useful links. The first leads to the pages of www.EurActiv.com, a respected EU web portal offering information on developments in EU policy sectors, the main actors and their positions. It presents policy summaries that show that the battle-group concept was not a European Commission-led initiative, but a member state project launched by the UK, France and Germany in February 2004, based upon the positive experiences with the EU-led mission Artemis in the Democratic Republic of Congo in 2004. It was tabled at the Council of EU defence ministers and then turned into a European concept, which was formally launched by the 22 November 2004 Military Capabilities Commitment Conference.

A second interesting link provided by the search engine is to the 'fact-sheets' which the Council of Ministers itself provides on its decisions (www.consilium.europa.eu). For analysts new to EU policy, it is may be initially confusing to see that the European institutions each maintain separate websites to keep track of documents and policy developments – the information on legislative procedures is effectively dispersed across several sites. There have been calls for a single EU-portal on the web, one that would include information on all legislative documents and the policies, activities, and decisions that led up to them. But until such a master source exists, it is important to know which institution is responsible for the type of policy and the stage of the cycle under examination. The researcher interested in battle groups will note that the Commission and EP sites offer far less information on the EU's security and defence policy for the simple reason that this policy domain is largely governed by the member states, united in the Council.

In terms of structuring policy-shaping research and keeping track of the different stages and events in the process under analysis, it may be helpful to sketch a detailed reconstruction of the social reality around the process. This may be a written time line, highlighting the moments

Box 6.4   Using Pre-Lex

The *Pre-Lex* database is a good source of information for retracing all EU policies since 1998. *Pre-Lex* is made up of dossiers, starting with the adoption of a Commission proposal (with the reference COM(year)number appearing) and ending when legislation is adopted. For each event in between – for example, an opinion of the Economic and Social Committee or the Committee of the Regions or the European Parliament, or the formal adoption by the Council or the withdrawal of the proposal by the Commission – *Pre-Lex* will show the date, the departments or individuals responsible, the document reference linked to the event and, where appropriate, a link to the document, a press release, or references in the *Official Journal*. *Pre-Lex* does not contain any texts, but wherever possible it gives a link to electronic texts available on other sites – for example, *EUR-Lex* (the Rapid database containing Council and Commission press releases), the Europarl site (the Bulletin of the European Union), the sites of the European Economic and Social Committee, the Committee of the Regions, and so on.). Searches can be intiated by typing, for example, the year the dossier was launched (usually when the initial proposal was sent to the Council or Parliament), or by selecting a key term from a list of options, usually the title of the initial proposal.

in a particular policy process that are relevant to the research focus, to which one can then add in the relevant actors, their positions, amendments, attempted influence, as well as the changes in the policy that occurred before it reached its final form or destination. Using subsequent draft texts of the proposal can help one retrace the input of particular member states, lobby groups, or political parties. However, policy research should never rely upon official documents as the only source. It is vital to combine paperwork with the use of authoritative media accounts, such as those of EUobserver or Euractive, policy reports of think thanks such as the Centre for European Reform or the Centre for European Policy Studies (CEPS), and interviews with insider accounts of those involved in the process as well as.

The European Commission website can be a very good source for such tracing research. The website offers organograms of DGs (useful to find relevant units and file keepers), summaries of EU legislation by policy area, with a comprehensive listing of all the relevant pieces of legislation, as well as the initiatives planned in an overall policy areas such as employment or public health. The European Parliament's legislative observatory OEIL is a database with all the decision-making procedures for new legislation. It has a 'procedure tracker', enabling one to source documents by title, reference number, topic, and so on (see Box 6.4).

EUR-Lex offers links to the budget of the European Union, the institutions' registers, as well as other documentation and information sources. For information on the development of the EU's policy in a certain field, for example, renewably energy, the 'thematic files' are useful. These are collections of legal documents on specific fields of EU activity (legislative instruments, preparatory acts, case law, parliamentary questions, and so on). Related acts and/or acts amending original acts can be consulted in the bibliographic entry for each document. Information in *EUR-Lex* is often consolidated. The Council website Consilium provides information on official documents, agendas of meetings and background notes.

It is important to keep in mind that each EU institution and each member state has its own agenda for institutional leadership and self-advancement, something that will be reflected in the particular information sources that they choose to maintain and present. Information given on websites is always 'coloured' by its provider, and as such, like any policy analysis exercise, EU policy analysis is a matter of thoroughness; one must always 'check, check and double-check' one's sources, information, and findings.

Conclusion

This chapter examined the way in which ideas and proposals for EU initiatives are developed. National and EU civil servants have a lot of impact, but there are many different (groups of) actors contributing to this phase in the policy process. This makes analysis of the shaping stages of EU policy particularly challenging. Key to EU shaping research is to structure the wealth of information available, and reconstruct the different stages highlighting important events and actors. Using a time-line, minutes of meetings, insiders' observations and document archives both at the EU institutions and within member states, questions on relative influence, success and impact, which are often central to shaping research can be tackled. Note that examination of this stage of the policy cycle includes at least a basic insight into the agendasetting and decision-making stages – how did the issue come up and what does the final deal look like?

Suggestions for further reading

Bulmer, S. and Lequesne, C. (2005) *The Member States of the European Union* (Oxford: Oxford University Press).
Greenwood, J. (2007) *Interest Representation in the European Union*, 2nd edn (Basingstoke and New York: Palgrave Macmillan).

Nugent, N. (2010) *The Government and Politics of the European Union*, 7th edn (Basingstoke and New York: Palgrave Macmillan).

Relevant websites

EU observer: day to day news on EU politics and policies (http://euobserver.com).

EURactiv: EUractiv: daily news updates across different policy domains (http://www.euractiv.com/).

EURlex: official EU law and policies, with useful search engines (http://eur-lex.europa.eu/en/index.htm).

Legislative observatory of the European Parliament's procedures (http://www.europarl.europa.eu/oeil).

Chapter 7

Decision Making

Introduction

Analyzing EU decision making is primarily about finding out how different actors have influenced new EU laws and policies and whether or not the process of agreeing on them was easy or difficult, quick or slow, fraught with conflict or relatively harmonious. In media accounts of European politics, the answer seems simple: 'Brussels has decided'. This depicts the EU as an autonomous bureaucratic monster, producing a steady stream of strictly binding rules to be passively implemented and followed to the letter by the member states. But as we have shown, the daily practices of EU policy making are a lot more pluralistic, nuanced, characterized as they are by *ad hoc* agreements, opt-outs, compromise, and bargaining, rather than straight forward 'take it or leave it' scenarios. This also holds true at the decision-making stage, where there are different procedures and where varying degrees of relative power are shared by the European Parliament and the Council of Ministers. Their (increasingly) joint agreement using majority rules produces various types of policy. The process involves permanent negotiations between many people: staff of the main EU institutions, civil servants and ministers representing different layers of government, permanent representatives of the member states, public affairs consultants and lobbyists for business and industry, social partners, citizens groups, and non-governmental and international organizations. Although top-level summits and parliamentary plenary sessions are crucial for hammering-out decisions, just as they are in national legislatures, the bulk of the work is done through informal contacts and meetings.

This chapter sheds light upon the interaction of these groups as they debate and decide upon the proposed policy options. We will show that when analyzing EU decisions one needs to look beyond the fixed occasions when political decision making occurs, the point in the process that often receives most attention in the media. We provide some academic and practical insights that might be helpful in focusing and structuring a research enquiry. The last section of the chapter offers more practical guidance: how to start (re-)searching decisions and how to attempt to reconstruct their processes that led up to them?

154

Decision making in the EU: who and what do we analyze?

This section examines the institutions and rules that govern the working of the Council, the EP, and the Commission in their capacity as decision takers. Although the Commission does not, strictly speaking, have decision-making competences, it is involved in the process through the 'various smaller' administrative decisions that follow the 'big' political decisions taken by EP and Council. Analyzing decision making will often start with the simple question: *who* decides? This is often the source of much discussion on EU decision making. In fact, the basic model of reaching agreement on new EU laws and policies is simple. In the ordinary legislative procedure (also known as 'co-decision') the Council of Ministers and European Parliament seal the laws which are drafted by the European Commission, which are then implemented and applied by the member states. In practice, however, procedures vary depending on the policy type.

Ordinarily, EU legislation and policy decisions are proposed by the Commission and co-legislated (co-decided) by the Council and European Parliament jointly. In preparatory venues such as expert committees, working groups and ambassadorial meetings (see Chapter 3), representatives of the governments of the member states are then joined by the EU institutions (the triad Commission, Council and EP), as well as by organized interests, including NGOs, lobby groups, and industry. Very often, these are the same people who featured prominently in the stages of agenda setting and policy shaping, having shaped the proposal during the formulation stages in expert committees and Council working groups.

Very often the same set of actors is involved with different responsibilities and competences. The phase of decision making is not finished in that moment that laws are published in the *Official Journal* as a huge amount of fine detail needs to be worked out regarding the practicalities of policy making. In order to identify and agree upon what are often highly technical details of policy, the Commission and member states work together in an intricate committee system known as 'comitology'.

Decisions about 'the rules of the game', such as treaty revisions and budget deals, but also the politically sensitive areas of foreign policy and criminal law, remain firmly in the hands of the member states. For these 'history making' decisions (Peterson and Bomberg, 1999), government ministers and heads of state, united in the Council of the EU and the high-level European Council, constitute the primary decision-making forum. When discussing treaty revisions, their meetings are labelled Intergovernmental Conferences (IGC). The treaty revisions signed in Amsterdam in 1997 and Nice in 2000 were the product of such IGCs. If the classical, intergovernmental and neo-realist picture of state-led diplomacy are valid anywhere, it is with regards to these political summits, where a key role is played by individual politicians, and where a lot of horse-trading goes on in order to facilitate package deals.

EU decisions can also take the form of competition rules, subsidy agreements, or research programmes. Although considerable attention is focused on the 'hard' Euro-legislation (such as directives, decisions and regulations), the annual legislative output has gone down significantly since the completion of the EU's internal market in the 1990s. There has been a shift towards new types of policy instruments, such as policy coordination and benchmarks or voluntary benchmarks and best practices – for example, in the field of employment and education policy. The adjective 'soft' refers to their non-binding character, but there can nonetheless be huge stakes involved, which can make the process of decision making for soft laws extremely political.

A key notion governing the interaction of the different players in decision making is the 'legal' or 'treaty' base, generally mentioned in the first article of the proposal, making specific reference to the relevant article in the treaty. It may be useful to identify this aspect early on in one's research, as this will automatically provide an outline of the competencies of each institution, the procedures to be followed, and, by implication the parameters of EU policy making. For example, the EU's aims in promoting cultural diversity in the member states are laid down in Title XIII, article 167 of the Treaty on the Functioning of the EU (TFEU). According to this article, the ordinary lawmaking procedure of the Council and the EP, also known as 'co-decision', described in article 294 of the TFEU, is to be used for decision making on cultural issues. This can only involve stimulating cultural exchange and diversity, however, as the same article explicitly excludes any harmonizing measure in the field of culture.

The legal base is a known source of conflict in EU policy making, with the Commission aiming for the use of qualified majority voting, and (some) member states arguing for a procedure giving them veto rights in decision making. The Council General Secretariat has a special legal team assembled on the basis of its inside knowledge of the Treaties. This legal team can play a crucial role in disputes surrounding the legal base – for expertise and information translates into power and influence. If conflict over the legal base cannot be agreed between the negotiators in the Council and the Parliament, then they are brought to Court of Justice. Although 'reactive' in the sense that it cannot decide on the cases that come before it, the Court can, as the final arbiter on EU legal matters, make a legally-binding decision on

Box 7.1   Tackling environmental crimes at the EU level

In March 2001, the Commission proposed an entirely new piece of EU law: a draft directive establishing EU-wide minimum standards for sanctions to environmental crimes, such as water pollution or the dumping of waste. The proposal suggested that member states should treat the illegal discharge of substances into the air, soil, or water as criminal offences. The Commission's proposal was considered to be bold as it touched on a particularly sensitive and topical issue. Some member states objected to any EU interference in their national criminal law, something considered to be at the core of national sovereignty. Those countries convinced the member states, united in the Environmental Council meeting of January 2003, to adopt a Framework Decision of its own accord. The focus was on the same problem – differences in national approaches to cross-border environmental pollution – but it proposed more administrative and police cooperation between the member states as the means to tackle it. The Council could take this ' intergovernmental' initiative without involving the European Commission and MEPs, since the issue fell under the competences of the intergovernmental area of Justice and Home Affairs.

The Commission saw its initiative threatened and promptly contested the legal basis on which the Council acted, launching legal action before the European Court of Justice to annul the Council Framework Decision. The Court agreed with the Commission and annulled the Council's decision in 2005, paving the way for a new proposal by the Commission. In a second ruling on the new text, issued on 23 October 2007, the Court supported the Commission's right to require criminal sanctions for 'green crimes' that caused environmental damage in the EU. However, it ruled that the Commission should leave the precise type and level of the penalties for each of the member states to decide individually. With this legal verdict, the issue was momentarily stalled at the EU level, although the discussion on how to harmonize differences in national criminal law will certainly resurface in the coming years.

the case and thereby influence the shape and direction of policy (see Box 7.1).

Here, we see what is a common phenomenon in EU policy making: draft proposals tend to bounce back and forth between the different institutional venues before the actors involved reach agreement. When opposition is particularly fierce, proposals may be shelved for a certain period, as was the case with the second proposal for a ban on tobacco advertising. The European Commission then waits for a favourable political moment (or window) to re-launch the idea. Here we witness the continual search for compromise that is a feature of all stages the

---

Box 7.2   Deciding on the Tobacco Advertising Directive

From the first proposals of the drafts which would finally become the Tobacco Advertising Directive, the European Commission's plans enjoyed the strong support of interventionist member states, such as Italy and France. In these member states, the new EU directive would lead to minimal changes in existing structures and legislation, and state intervention into the sector was supported. The proposed law to phase out tobacco advertisement was strongly opposed, however, by the more liberal member states of the north west of the EU, which have traditionally championed industry and consumer freedom. Those member states objected to the law in principle and feared high adaptation costs for their national legislation and administrative arrangements.

This configuration of forces in the Council would dominate the process of decision making on the Commission drafts for an EU-wide advertising ban on tobacco across the media, internet, radio, and sports events. Opposition by Germany, the UK, the Netherlands, Denmark, and Greece made it impossible to reach a qualified majority in the Council in favour of the proposal for many years, an example of a 'deadlock' situation. When opposing member states held the Presidency, they succeeded in momentarily stalling the discussion by simply not tabling the issue on the Presidency's Council agenda. When proponent countries took over the EU's helm, the draft texts reappeared and experts continued negotiating. In 1997, important changes in the domestic politics of the UK and the Netherlands opened a window of opportunity. General elections in the UK in 1997 resulted in a Labour

➡

---

of EU policy cycle, including that of decision making. This search for consensus is one of the norms vital for EU decision making to work. As we will show below, EU institutions and the member states normally try to reach common agreement so that the process delivers at least *some* policy output. Because they are positioned in an intricate institutional 'triangle' of interdependence, if satisfactory solutions are not found, the whole process grinds to a halt (see Box 7.2 for such a 'deadlock' situation). Without a decision, there can be no implementation or evaluation.

The Council of Ministers

In reality, there is not simply one Council of Ministers, but many, which meet roughly a hundred times a year, in nine different configurations. National transport ministers discuss decisions in the Transport Council, and economic affairs ministers in the Economic and Financial

➡

government, which expressed support for the proposal. Likewise, the new Dutch Minister of Health strongly favoured anti-smoking initiatives. The Commission did not hesitate and brought its proposal back on the table.

A tobacco advertising ban was tabled during the Health Council meeting in December 1997, and it proved to be a contentious agenda item. At one point during the meeting, the presiding Luxembourg minster deliberately chose to limit the size of national delegations. Only ministers and ambassadors were allowed to remain in the room and, together, they undertook the challenging task of trying to forge a consensus over the text. After the meeting, many participants declared that the brokering role of the Luxembourg presidency, a small but experienced member state when it comes to mediation, was vital in securing a deal. This was the basis for negotiations with the European Parliament, leading to a directive signed by both the Council and the Parliament in June 1998.

After the appeal by the German government that the directive was not based on appropriate constitutional grounds, and the subsequent ECJ annulment in 2000, the second Directive was decided upon relatively easily. By this point, the 'battles' had already been fought during the first round of negotiations – and most member states now already transposed the 1998 directive and decided to maintain the measure – meaning that the second decision-making process occurred with relative ease and the final directive could be adopted in 2003.

Source: Adamini *et al.*, 2010.

Affairs Committee (ECOFIN). Over the course of 2008, ministers convened 70 times in different 'informal' Councils – in effect, a series of working visits to the presiding member states.

The outcome of EU decision making is to a large extent determined by the constellation of actors who assert their national positions in the Council at any given moment (see also Box 7.3). Very often, the 'fit' between newly proposed legislation and existing national arrangements is crucial in determining the position of individual member states.

An institutional arrangement with an impact upon EU decision making is the rotating Presidency of the Council, held by the member states for a six-month period on a rotating basis. In an EU of 27 member states, this means that every member states is at the helm once every thirteen and a half years. The presidency's tasks involve more than merely chairing Council meetings at different levels. On the administrative side, the member state in the chair is responsible for organizing the work of the Council during its term: summoning the

Box 7.3　Regional representation in Brussels

The Council of ministers is officially composed of 'nationals representing the government of the member state'. Member states with a decentralized state structure (Belgium, Spain, and Germany) can be represented by their regional governments in the Council if decisions involve areas in which they have competences and are thus responsible. This involves, for example, environmental legislation, youth, culture, sports policy, structural funds, and territorial cohesion policies. But sub-national government representatives are actively present throughout the entire policy-making cycle, not only through their advisory role in the Committee of the Regions, but also as informal lobby groups. For example, the German *Länder*, the Spanish *Comunidades Autónomas*, and the Dutch *Provinces* all have EU representatives and offices in Brussels. They keep a close eye on the EU agenda, regularly visiting the Commission offices to discuss draft legislation. They also do a lot of networking in order to jointly represent their interests. Regional representations in Brussels can be an important access point in terms of research, as they might throw up information, contact persons in the institutions, or inside stories on a policy area or a dossier where sub-national competences are involved.

Council for meetings, directing the work of COREPER and other committees and working groups, sending out documents and timetables, and calling for a vote where deemed necessary for important political or 'process-changing' issues. The official rules of procedure, updated in 2004 to accommodate the accession of ten new member states, are the guidebook of every national presidency. Nevertheless, the Presidency can assert its prerogative, deciding, for instance, whether or not a particular working group or Council formation should be convened, or when to vote – and such issues can be critical to the outcome of negotiations. For policy analysis, it is can therefore be useful to identify which Presidency led Council negotiations for a particular issue, and to assess whether particular national concerns may have influenced how that member state dealt with the supposed 'neutrality' of the office.

The Presidency may also push preferred items onto the agenda, or leave out others which may create friction or are disputed domestically. In order to ensure coherence in the Council's agenda, a system of 'team presidencies' has been introduced. Three subsequent presidencies will now work closely together in programming the forthcoming agenda. Such a system ensures continuity, learning, and a smoother handover from one member state chair to another. It also reduces the opportunity for agenda setting by individual chairs.

Box 7.4   Protocol struggles during the EU summit

On 16 October 2008, the EU Observer reported some serious protocol issues disrupting the European Council meeting in Brussels. Polish President Lech Kaczynski had gate crashed the summit after discussions in Warsaw about whether it was the President or the Prime Minister who should lead the Polish delegation. The PM, Donald Tusk, denied the President the use of the official jet, forcing him to charter his own Boeing-737 at a cost of €40,000. The unconventional presence of President Kaczynski at the supper – where EU countries are traditionally represented by just one person – crowned a day of mini-diplomatic incidents, insults and false smiles. It began when Mr Kaczynski arrived at the summit venue one hour late, without an official badge. He eventually entered the main chamber, forcing the Polish foreign and finance ministers to leave the room in order to free up Poland's allotted chairs. The Polish President's unofficial presence at the summit also caused problems for the customary EU 'family photo'. Usually, leaders line up around the incumbent EU presidency according to strict protocol rules, with heads of state standing closer to the Chair than prime ministers. EU officials had hastily re-arranged little stickers on the floor to guide Mr Kaczynski to stand next to Mr Sarkozy, but the Polish president stood next to Mr Tusk anyway, off to the left of the group.

One way to study the influence of member states on EU decision making is by examining member states' voting behaviour in the Council of Ministers. The Council reaches decisions by different rules depending on the policy area. By default, the member states take decisions by simple majority (half plus one), although this procedure is in practice the exception to the rule. Unanimity nearly always applies for foreign policy and quite often with regards to matters of Police and Judicial Cooperation.

In most cases in fact, the Council votes on issues using qualified majority voting (QMV). Under the current Nice rules, in effect until 2014, a proposal must be backed by a majority of member states (or two-thirds in certain cases: see below) and supported by 255 votes from a total of 345 — about 73.9 per cent of the votes. Under newly applicable Lisbon rules, in force from 2014, a majority of countries (55 per cent) representing 65 per cent of the population must be in favour. To block it, at least four countries must vote against the proposal. This new system will effectively do away with the weighted vote system used at present (the Big Four have 29 votes, compared to Malta's 3 votes).

Council roll call data are made available through the Council website ('Consilium'). Together with the voting declarations that member states may attach to the Council conclusions, the data provide the policy analyst with a clear picture of what happened during Council deliberations. Only a small percentage of decisions are characterized by 'contested votes', a scenario in which Council members vote against the majority or even abstain from voting.

The voting register only gives insight into the laws on which a vote was actually taken. *Why would national ministers want to be seen to vote against a proposal on the record?* A first reason for a no-vote or an abstention (both, in practice, have the same effect) is opposition from national pressure groups or political parties, in which case government ministers need to show that they are 'toeing the party line' in Brussels and not simply deciding for themselves. Second, they may also express their opposition symbolically, knowing full well that the law (which they may even personally be in favour of, but cannot be seen to be back home) will be adopted anyway, given that they already know the position of their counterparts in the negotiation. Third, motivation for an individual no-vote can be strategic: member states may decide to please other delegations by showing support for a piece of legislation on which they don't have a particularly firm position, but about which another member state feels strongly. Of course, the assumption is that there will be some kind of 'pay-back' at a later stage, when the member state returns the favour by backing it on a political decision close to its own heart.

Despite much media attention surrounding voting procedures, only one in five pieces of legislation is formally contested in practice (Mattila and Lane, 2001). One reason for this quest for agreement is that the legislative output of the Council is binding. Regulations and directives have to be implemented and enforced by all member states. If a member state is unhappy about a decision, it may be considerably less willing to implement and enforce it, which could result in an 'implementation failure', something seen to work to the detriment of the EU as a whole (see Chapter 8). A second reason for commitment to consensus in the Council is the ongoing nature of EU negotiations. The fact that participants are government ministers from the same policy domain meeting regularly to discuss different (yet closely related) topics makes it easier to find solutions through compromise. In order to avoid the risk of its delegation getting a reputation of a 'foot dragger' in negotiations, a member states will in general 'think twice before ruthlessly seeking to maximize their individual interests' (Héritier, 1996, p.157). The voting behaviour of the Swedish delegations is a good example of this tendency. Following its EU accession in 1995, Sweden was a frequent 'foot-dragger' in the sense that it often voted against new EU legislation. However, the number of Swedish negative votes rapidly decreased in the following years, as Swedish negotiators, learning about the institutional culture of the Council – that is, norms, beliefs and practices built up gradually over time – realized this was not the way how things worked in practice.

Voting is thus a 'Damocles' sword' hanging over the negotiations – 'you are damned if you do (vote) and damned if you don't (vote)'. The prospect of a vote acts like a shadow on proceedings. The fact alone of an imminent vote influences negotiating behaviour. Experienced negotiators (civil servants in the working groups, the ambassadors and the ministers) are constantly aware of the number of votes in favour or against particular proposals. Delegations who anticipate a vote try to create coalitions and formulate compromises acceptable to all. In this way, the spread of QMV also encourages negotiators and lobbyists to inform themselves of the positions of other delegations, and to act proactively. Traditionally, domestically organized interests (often business groups) have been able to rely upon 'their' national governments to protect their position and to do all they can in an intergovernmental setting to quash (kill off) any draft legislation that will have serious repercussions (usually financial costs) for their working practices or operation. For example, national farmers' organizations can always ask their government to vote against proposed legislation in the Agricultural Council. In some cases, proceedings can turn more 'political', with member states claiming that an issue threatens national sovereignty or is too sensitive for a vote (see the French empty chair crisis, p. 75).

Despite the attention we have placed on voting systems, the Presidency, and other formal arrangements in the Council, such as the rules of procedure, one should not underestimate the relevance of informal rules in the day-to-day working of the Council (Lewis, 2003). One example is the increased prominence of important preparatory counsellor groups – for example, the Antici and Mertens groups. These two groups of national civil servants in the permanent representations, the namesakes of their initiators, play an important behind the scenes role in negotiations between ambassadors, ministers, and heads of state and government.

A second example is the creation of the Friends of the Presidency group during the *Agenda 2000* negotiations. Composed of high-level officials close to the ambassadors, the group meets on an *ad hoc* basis to discuss particular policy problems. Finally, and perhaps most crucially, there is the Council General Secretariat (not to be confused with the Secretariat-General of the Commission), an often overlooked authority in EU decision making. Its small group of A-level policy officials and lawyers, headed by the Council Secretary-General and High Representative, can have a crucial role in providing counsel (advice) to national presidencies, often producing the texts that form the basis for Council compromises.

The European Council

When the ministers in the Council cannot reach agreement, the top-level European Council may take over. The European Council originated in the 1970s as an informal political 'talking shop' for the heads of state and government of the member states to meet at 'fireplaces across Europe' (see Box 7.4). Traditionally it met once a year in the national capital of the presiding member state, but in recent years it has met twice, at the beginning and end of each presidency. With the Maastricht Treaty, it became the primary decision maker in the area of foreign and security policy. Like the Sword of Damocles scenario we mentioned above that characterizes voting in the Council, it is sometimes again as a result of the 'shadow' of European Council interference that national ministers are finally forced to reach agreement at their own level (Werts, 2008). The European Council increasingly provides an impetus for decision making if 'normal' procedures are stuck in political deadlock. Unlike the Council and Commission, which are sub-divided into policy sectors, the heads of state and government deal with all policy areas and, in so doing, can forge package deals on those issues than remain controversial in the regular meetings of the Council of Ministers. European Councils also mediate politically between Council configurations for cross-sectoral or horizontal issues. For example, in December 2008, the European Council secured agreement on an energy and climate package, covering issues that been discussed in the Environment Council in previous weeks. The summit set the famous '20–20–20' goals for greenhouse gas emissions, increasing energy efficiency and the use of renewable energy by 2020, adopted by the European Parliament just a week later.

The success of the European Council can arguably be explained by its informality, *esprit de corps* and lack of rulebook. Formal meetings of the European Council are characterized by their large numbers of participants. Heads of state are accompanied by foreign ministers, permanent representatives and large cohorts of senior officials. If negotiations become tense, the Presidency may decide to reduce numbers in the room, leaving just the heads of state and government ministers present. The standing chair of the European Council (since 1 January 2010, Herman van Rompuy, who holds the office for two and a half years) may invoke the so-called 'confessional' procedure whereby national delegations are invited to explain their positions one by one. In this case, the chair will seek to ensure that all preferences have been taken on board in any final compromise.

The European Parliament as co-legislator

Legislative work is the core business of MEPs. The European Parliament is legally obliged to give an opinion on all Commission proposals. How the Commission and the Council deal with parliamentary amendments depends on which of the legislative procedures is being used: the ordinary legislative procedure, or one of the special ones (see Chapter 2). The EP has the most impact through the ordinary legislative procedure, currently applicable in most policy areas. Although this procedure entails two 'readings' between the Council and EP, the majority of dossiers are currently decided upon on first reading. In 2008 a first reading was sufficient for 116 out of the 144 of what were referred to at the time as 'co-decision dossiers', discussed by the Council and the EP (European Commission, 2008). This procedure has led to a continuous process of informal consultation between member state representatives, MEPs and their administrative staff (some 5,000 officials), as well as Commission staff. Decision making within the EP is set in motion in the sectoral committees, in which designated MEPs take on the role of *rapporteur* and *shadow rapporteurs* (see Chapter 6). The draft report prepared on the basis of committee meetings forms the backbone of the monthly plenary meetings in the Strasbourg Louise Weiss building. At times, political battles can be very fierce and attract huge attention from the media. Lobbyists have increasingly found the EP to be an effective venue for exerting influence when it comes to draft legislation.

The EP building is often also the target of protesters, for example around the vote on the controversial directive on market access to port services (COM/2004/0654 final). There were fierce demonstrations outside the building by dock workers who had travelled to Strasbourg from a number of European countries including France, Belgium, and the Netherlands. They were demonstrating against the proposed authorization of ship crews to unload ships themselves and ship owners to run freight terminals. Trade unions claimed that such changes would lead to thousands of jobs lost, placing the economic future of European ports at risk. The Parliament resoundingly rejected the draft legislation (520 against, 120 for, 25 abstaining) on 18 January 2006, calling instead for a directive on transparency and fair conditions of competition between ports. Transport Commissioner Jacques Barrot declared: 'Today's vote is clear. It leaves no room for doubt as to Parliament's position on this proposal as submitted after the failure of the earlier proposal.' The *rapporteur,* a German Conservative, said 'an unholy alliance of rock-throwers and defenders of the status quo has won over' (adapted from Euractiv.com, 18 January 2006).

Another very political EP debate took place around the Return Directive (2008/115/EC) on EU standards for returning illegal asylum seekers. In 2007, this was the first piece of legislation on migration discussed under the co-decision procedure, and the EP wanted to make the most of its new powers. An article in the draft legislation, which held that illegal immigrants could be held in custody for up to 18

Box 7.5   Agreeing upon the EU's budget

The annual controversy surrounding the setting of the EU's budget is surprising, considering its relatively small size. The 2008 EU budget amounted to about 129 billion. The biggest share was spent on 'Sustainable Growth' (45 per cent), followed by agricultural expenditure (32 per cent). The EU has its 'own resources' to finance its expenditure. The budget also receives other revenue, such as taxes paid by EU staff on their salaries, contributions from non-EU countries to certain EU programmes, and fines on companies that breach competition rules. The annual EU budget falls within a five-year financial framework, the Financial Perspectives agreed upon jointly by the Commission, the European Parliament, and the Council of Ministers. The current agreement covers the period 2007–2013, and sets concrete ceilings for the different categories of expenditure.

In a first step, the details of the annual budget are drafted in a proposal by the European Commission. The budgetary procedure, as established in the EU treaties, runs for four months, from 1 September to 31 December, even if, in practice, it begins much earlier – preparations for the 2007 budget started before the end of 2005, for example. The Commission submits the preliminary draft budget to the Council before the budget Council meeting in July. After a conciliation meeting with the Parliament, the Council of Ministers adopts the draft budget with possible amendments. Under the Lisbon Treaty, the European Parliament has become jointly responsible for the entire EU budget, together with the national governments. Until then, Parliament did not have the final say on the categories of 'compulsory expenditure', such as the big chucks of EU spending on agriculture. At its first budget reading in October, the European Parliament may decide to amend the Council's draft. It will discuss controversial matters in 'trialogue' meetings with the Council Presidency and the Commission beforehand. Before its second reading in November, the Council has a further conciliation meeting with the Parliament and tries to reach an agreement on the whole of the budget. The Parliament may modify the Council's latest text before it votes on the final budget in December. If approved, the President of the Parliament signs the budget into law.

months, generated widespread opposition from human rights groups and the political left. In Latin America, the directive was described as the 'Directive of Shame'.

It is not only with legislation that the EP manages to show its teeth. Although it lacks the right of initiative, it may request that the Commission draft new legislative proposals. The EP also influences policy making by expressing its opinion on, and ultimately approving, the EU budget (see Box 7.5). With Lisbon, it now has greater powers over the whole budget, not just 'obligatory expenditure'. The EP can also 'sack' the Commission with a two-thirds majority, something that it threatened to do to the Santer Commission (1995–1999), who for political and strategic reasons decided to 'resign' on 15 March 2000 on their own initiative, and was then succeeded by the Commission of Romano Prodi (1999–2004). The current Commission president Jose Manuel Barroso (2004–) was given strong backing by the member states at the June 2009 summit. However, the EP, pushed by the socialists and liberals, agreed to postpone the vote until closer to the Irish referendum on 2 October 2009. A fortnight before that, on Wednesday 16 September 2009, Barroso was re-elected by the EP for a second five-year term, with 718 MEPS voting in a secret ballot, out of which 382 voted for, 219 against, and 117 abstained. Was this a political move by the EP to create positive news coverage around a more trouble-free result?

The role of the Commission in decision making: comitology

As sketched out in Chapter 6, all new policy proposals are first subject to decision making within the Commission, to be finally approved by the College of Commissioners. In the weekly meetings convened by the President, the College debates and decides upon proposals presented by the Commissioners. Consensus is the rule, but if a member requests a vote then decisions are made on the basis of a simple majority. The EP and Council approve such proposals, which by the decision-making stage have developed into fully fledged draft legislation.

There are also policy areas where the European Commission can act of its own accord. The list of these areas is small, but they are quite significant. Most crucially, in 'policing the internal market' to uphold EU competition policy, DG Competition is autonomous, issuing rules independent of national governments. The role of the European Commission in other policy areas can be described as facilitating decision making by member states and the EP, thereby closely guarding the spirit of the treaties. From the moment its policy proposals are adopted internally and sent to the member states and the EP, the Commission remains very closely involved in the decision making and implementation. To this aim, Commission representatives are always present in the council working groups and during COREPER and Council meetings. They generally sit across from the chair, held by the rotating presidency, and may explain or elaborate on policy proposals upon the request of the delegates. Outside the meetings, Commission officials are busy cultivating informal contacts and organizing meetings to defend their proposals in order to actively mediate – some might even say manipulate – the positions and amendments of other players. Throughout this time, the Commission, as former initiator of policies, retains its right to withdraw its proposal, should it come to consider that the original idea has been altered too much during the negotiations.

When the Council of Ministers and the European Parliament adopt a new law, a legal framework is created, including objectives and timeframe. But more detailed measures, for example lists of substances or products often still need to be defined. The EU policy system has developed a standing practice of further adapting the details of formally agreed legislation to fit national approaches, in an intricate committee system known as 'comitology'. According to estimates, around 80 per cent of the EU's output consists of such implementing measures. The Council and EP delegate implementing powers on the Commission, which guards this process by chairing a whole system of committees of representatives of the member states. This practice, linking decision-making activities of civil servants back to the shaping, and re-connecting it to the implementation phase, is another example of why the 'stages approach' of policy making does not resemble political reality.

Comitology is essentially a permanent discussion between the Commission and member state representatives on technical details, annexes and values of new EU policies. There are three types of committees, giving national representatives different powers to stall or overturn Commission decisions. Because the (voting) powers of Council, Commission and EP vary by procedure, many political battles are initially centred on the decision of which type of committee should become responsible for the definition of technical specifications. Consultation or advisory committees merely give opinions that the Commission must take notice of, while retaining the power of decision. So-called 'management' committees can block a proposed Commission measure by a qualified majority, while the 'regulatory' committees need a qualified majority to approve a proposed Commission measure. If a committee procedure becomes deadlocked, matters are referred to the Council and/or the Parliament. Opposition from either will block the proposed measure.

Committees often bring together exactly the same group of people who originally drafted the proposal in the Commission expert groups and the Council working groups. Committees are also frequently the place where evaluations are discussed and possible reviews prepared. This makes for a high degree of group cohesion and some continuity in the socialization among members. Certain comitology committees are very active and meet regularly, while others only meet once or twice a year. One of the oldest comitology committees is the Advisory Committee for Safety, Hygiene and Health Protection at work, composed of government, trade union, and employers' representatives. It has ten working groups on sectoral issues, which advise the Commission through intensive consultation with DG Employment. For tobacco regulation and control, DG SANCO is assisted by the Tobacco Products Regulatory Committee, which meets regularly in Brussels to review standing procedures for tobacco control.

For a long time, it was felt that the whole process of drawing up 'Commission legislation' was unduly protracted, undemocratic, and lacking transparency. As the powers of the European Parliament increased with successive treaty changes since the early 1990s, it also demanded a say in comitology. In 1999 Parliament got the right to be informed of comitology decisions and access to documents was improved, but MEPs wanted more reform. In 2006, the institutions reached agreement on introducing a new 'regulatory procedure with scrutiny'. It gave Parliament better oversight and a right of veto with the Commission implementing measures flowing from laws decided upon jointly by Parliament and Council. The agreement however implied a right only to accept or reject a proposed measure, not to amend. The Lisbon Treaty makes it possible to replace the current comitology system with a system of 'delegated acts', to be elaborated between the Commission, the EP and the Council in implementing Lisbon. The Commission has also increased transparency by providing a web-based repository which enables the user to get direct access to agendas of committee meetings, draft implementing measures, summary records of committee meetings, and voting results of opinions delivered by a committee.

National parliaments in EU decision making

Chapter 6 outlined just how much work carried out in national capitals goes into formulating negotiating instructions for national officials and ministers in the Council at the 'shaping' stage. The previous section discussed how, following decisions by the Council and EP, decisions are 'fine-tuned' for implementation on the ground through comitology, where a great deal of highly detailed and technical work is conducted by the relevant experts. However, the national parliaments of the member states play an equally important role at this particular junction between the shaping, deciding, and implementing of policy.

Parliamentarians are charged with controlling the work of their governments in Brussels. They are responsible for ratifying treaties and implementing EU decisions, as well as transposing them into national legislation. Some national parliaments are very active in EU policy making, while others are more passive when it comes to EU work. As for individual parliamentarians, a recurrent problem is that EU policy making does not attract much attention in national politics and media, at least in anything that could be considered a balanced way; it is often only sensational or ridiculous stories about the EU that seem to make the front pages of national newspapers, something that renders EU affairs less politically salient for politicians when they seek national re-election. At the same time, two developments have made national parliaments more obliged to take up EU-related work. First, problems stemming from the late and incorrect implementation of EU legislation can lead to court cases and costly legal and financial sanctions. Second, procedural changes in the treaties have come to more explicitly acknowledge the important role of national parliaments. The Lisbon Treaty grants national parliaments a right of information with regards to proposed legislation, as well as handing them competencies to rejecting proposals through a new 'yellow card' procedure. There is concern, however, that this will slow down or even stall the policy-making process. Should one third of all parliaments have concerns about proposed legislation, the Commission can be asked to submit a 'reasoned opinion' as to why it is proposing the law. Another reason for more parliamentary involvement in EU policy making is the volatile basis of public support for European integration in a number of member states. In many of those states, this has engendered special procedures for discussing the implications of new Commission documents, as well as a redoubling of the parliamentary scrutiny of national positions.

Theoretical perspectives

Understanding how the EU makes decisions means gaining sufficient insight into the forces driving the process of European integration. Why have countries chosen to cooperate at the European level and why not? This was the key question for traditional integration theorists, triggering debates between 'intergovernmentalists' and 'supranationalists' in the early fifties (see Chapter 1). Both schools of thought offered competing claims and explanations about the motives and behaviour of the member states and supra-national institutions in constructing European integration. It has been observed, for example, that the Commission, the Court of Justice, and (today even more so) the EP tend to deliberately strive for more community competences, but that it is the member states that are ultimately 'masters of the treaties', promoting interstate cooperation with a key role for national interest. It is over the question of which camp ultimately drives and controls the process that theorists differ.

In his study on EU decision making, Andrew Moravcsik's (1993) liberal intergovernmentalist perspective offered a wealth of evidence to argue that it was the member states who were dominating the process and the direction of integration through 'history-making' decisions, for example through things such as the Common Agricultural Policy (CAP), the White paper on the completion of the single market (1985), and successive negotiations on treaty change up to Maastricht. His core assumption was that the domestic and international arenas functioned separately. Domestic actors, such as interest groups, regions, and business representative, exert influence on their national governments. National governments, in turn, orchestrate careful negotiations to secure these domestic goals at the EU level. For intergovernmentalists, governments may agree to 'pool' and delegate competencies to the EU level, but only as long as it is in their own interests to do so and common goals might be achieved that would not be possible to realize on their own.

The fields of comparative politics and policy analysis, which migrated into EU studies in the 1970s, offered new lenses and tools to study decision making, including concepts from public administration such as intra-governmental bargaining and 'bureaucratic politics'. This implies taking a microscope to the internal workings of the main institutions at the various governance levels to look at power struggles and rivalries, fighting over competencies and the use of information, not just at the political level but also down the corridors of the various administrations (see Box 7.6 for a practical example of such power struggles).

Policy analysis also offers tools to open up the 'black box' of what happens within EU member states and governments. This has led to many studies on 'Europeanization', or, to put it in layman's terms, 'how member states deal with the EU' – how they influence it, adapt to it, and change their structures in accordance with it (see Chapter 4). An important theory here centres on the notion of 'goodness of fit', a reference to the congruence between existing national laws and new proposals for EU policy. The larger the 'misfit', the higher the chances that problems will occur at the implementation stages, where governments might be forced to endure adaptation costs. On the other hand, governments may also strategically use EU policy proposals as political leverage to put into effect unwanted changes to national legislation, or to achieve politically unpopular measures, measures that may not be otherwise electorally achievable. As such, EU policies can lead to domestic change, with national governments sometimes claiming 'Brussels made me do it'.

The way in which this domestic change takes place might be best described with the help of a particularly popular lens in EU decision-making studies: neo-institutionalism (see Chapter 4). Key to neo-institutional reasoning is that policy making takes place in a political context filled with 'institutions' (not to be mistaken for the supranational organizations at the EU-level) whose formal or informal rules, practices and norms constrain or enable actors, and in so doing create 'order and predictability' in policy making (March and Olsen, 2005). Depending on the lens one applies when looking at the policy process,

Box 7.6   The Services Directive

In 2006, the Council of Ministers decided upon controversial legislation on how to open up the market for services across the EU. The policy piece became also known as the Bolkestein Directive after the internal market commissioner responsible for the first drafts of the proposal. This agreement marked the end of a period of particularly heavy political struggles around a sensitive dossier. The draft directive was presented in 2004 and immediately became the subject of intense criticism by trade unions, socialist parties, and several EU member state governments, including France, Germany and Sweden, for its potential to undermine wage and safety standards. The draft was repeatedly sent back and forth between the heads of state meeting in the context of the European Council and Council meetings of the national energy and environment ministers. In the end, the vote in the European Parliament turned out to be pivotal in determining the core principle of the directive: that of the 'country of origin'. According to this principle, service providers should be allowed to operate in any member state, provided they obey the rules of their country of origin. For trade unionists in Germany, France and Belgium, the country-of-origin principle was fiercely opposed as the equivalent of social dumping. In March 2005, some 60,000 protesters rallied around the European Parliament building in Strasbourg to call for the draft law to be withdrawn. In the end, in EP introduced a new principle of freedom to provide services which became central to the final text. The deal struck in the EP over this amendment, accepted by 391 against 221 votes, was translated into a new Commission proposal. That the Austrian Presidency secured agreement in the Council during the next months was partly explained by Germany switching sides from staunch opponent to supporter of the new text. Observers did not fail to note that the leaders of both the parliamentary EPP and Socialist groups, who had drafted the compromise, were members of the domestic ruling coalition in Berlin. The Council ministers agreed to the final text, with abstentions only from the Belgium and Lithuanian delegations, resulting in Directive 2006/123/EC.

The policy process around the directive continued after it became binding EU law in 2007. Transposition of its provisions into national law caused many headaches in the member states. Among other things, the set-up of contact points for a service at the local and regional levels proved cumbersome, for example in the German *Länder*. More than half of EU governments failed to meet the December 2009 deadline for national implementation.

actor behaviour can be explained differently. Rational choice institutionalists, who take the rent-maximizing behaviour of policy making actors as their main focus, will point at the relevance of 'veto points' (rules, procedures and resources), which hamper or push individuals to act strategically. By contrast, scholars from the school of sociological institutionalism will primarily recognize the impact of common norms and political/institutional culture on realizing policy change.

Neo-institutionalism can be applied to studying EU decision making, for example, when one looks at how member states vote in the Council of Ministers. The literature offers many quantitative analyses, studies which reconstruct the exact vote distribution across member states for particular decisions. Those numbers can be explained differently, however. Rational-choice scholars will point to the relevance of strategic action by governments, which try to use a vote to demonstrate certain preferences or political courage to actors at the domestic level. Sociological institutionalism will explain the voting patterns by looking at how the consensus 'norm' influenced behaviour and outcomes.

Key issues for consideration

Examples of questions that guide research into the decision-making stage of EU policy making are:

- Which national delegations pushed for the policy in the Council, and who voted against it?
- Which lobby groups had access to MEPs, and do we see traces of this influence in parliamentary amendments on the proposal?
- Did the fact that national elections in a member state occurred at the same time that the policy was an issue of debate facilitate agreement at the Council or European Council meeting?
- How much resilience or support was there for a piece of draft legislation, and which EU institution 'won' in the end by securing what it pushed for during co-decision?

Policy analysis of EU decision making means reconstructing a political process often characterized by secrecy, strategic operations, and trade-offs between individual dossiers. It is therefore essential to open up the 'black box' to look beyond the formal highlights and get behind the scenes. This section aims to provide an idea of the different methodologies available and provide insights to help identify, use, and interpret sources of information to do with EU decision making.

There is much quantitative work available in the field of decision-making analysis. For example there are studies focusing on the amount of legislation annually adopted, how member states vote in the Council, and how political groups vote in the European Parliament. The problem with applying numbers to EU decision making is that they never tell the real story of how agreement was reached between the people involved. For example, if we wanted to see how much legislation that the EU generates annually actually has a real impact at member state level, it would not be sufficient to simply count the amount of European decisions produced each year. Total legislative output does not discriminate between entirely new legislative proposals and those which merely amend existing policies through minor technical changes to reshuffle the distribution of resources – in effect, differing little from existing laws. In addition, looking at the numbers alone would ignore the important distinctions between decisions that might have been characterized by political conflict, hard-fought battles, or intricate compromise, and those decisions that were merely written off as easy A-points in the Council. Thus, decision-making analyses differ between those based completely on qualitative research – policy reconstruction by means of documents, interviews and media accounts – and approaches that seek to combine quantitative research with qualitative methods.

Start with a time-line

As we suggested in Chapter 6, it is always helpful to start any analysis of EU policy making by drafting a time-line of events, actors and political battles. This can be done by drawing on official documents, websites, media accounts, and insiders' stories. The key message of this chapter is that EU decision making is not a clear-cut stage of inter-institutional battles in Brussels. In this sense, an effective analysis will often proceed by taking into account the events that preceded legislative negotiations – for example, what happened in the expert committees or during 'inter-service consultation', where important stakeholders from the member states and Commission discussed and perhaps discarded policy ideas – as well as the member states' various positions at the time and their particular interests that the decisions reflect. It is not rare for academic research that has been focused on EU decision making to end up in national capitals, being used for political purposes in order to explore domestic bureaucratic politics or parliamentary opposition, perhaps eventually even leading to a national delegation changing its position in the Council.

Given the huge amount of work that goes on under comitology, it is clear that decision making does not end with the publication of a new legal act in the *Official Journal*. Insight into which participants were present in the comitology committees that followed and the key battles that were fought there can be crucial in determining the factors that led to things happening as they did, and to explaining possible opposition or non-implementation. A problem the analyst faces is that the attendance lists of the committee meetings usually do not disclose the names of the participants, but only the authorities to which they belong (for example 'Slovakia, Ministry of Agriculture'). Nevertheless a good lobbyist – and policy analysts – should not find it too difficult to trace the right people within the various organizations mentioned.

Be strict when selecting

A challenge in this kind of research is to be able to narrow down the scope of the research as much as possible. One may well end up 'zooming in' more than one originally intended. A vague interest in one policy area (anti-terrorism, environment, employment policy) may evolve into more concrete questions on the 'how' and 'why' of recent policy changes (information and data distribution; chemicals policy; workers' rights) before identifying certain concrete decisions (passenger name data PNR, REACH, anti-discrimination legislation). Once the exact policy piece has been pinpointed, it will soon appear that the legal text of the actual decision is only the tip of the iceberg, and that there were a whole series of more difficult to trace sub-decisions, places where political battles occurred in the months or years preceding the decision. The challenge in every process-tracing exercise is how to identify the most relevant sources – and potentially the most revealing ones – and how to discard those that might provide less original or accurate insights. This latter category might involve those actors who were less involved in the process, those who played a passive role, or who did not gain access to the decision-making arena. Member states with no stake in a particular policy area may often turn out to be absent from Council decision making. Two helpful criteria to identify prominent issues in a certain policy decision-making process are:

- The extent to which the decision is considered radical in terms of its consequences for those involved: Does the issue require considerable financial redistribution? Does it imply organizational or policy change?
- The extent to which the policy debate was controversial: Was there much opposition against the proposal? Were fights fought out in the media?

The information surplus

There is generally no shortage of document depositories to facilitate one's quest for information. In the past, researchers had to delve deep into the archives of the institutions or the foreign ministries of the member states. In the past few years, with rapid digitalization, formal documents have become easily accessible. For decision-making queries, relevant written sources for public information on legislation are:

- Reports of legislative output such as the annual General Report by the EU institutions.
- Databases such as *Prelex, Eurlex, ScadPlus*, and so on, which give access to European Union law and institutional battles dating back to the 1950s.
- The Council of Ministers and the European Council Conclusions; for the formal accounts and voting registers.
- The *Official Journal of the European Union* (published in the early morning after every working day in two series: L (Legislation) and C (Information and Notices), for the final text of decisions.
- Annual summaries of authoritative newspapers.

Researchers often find that gaining direct access to the political affairs surrounding decision making can be quite difficult. As for the national positions of member states during negotiations, that data often proves especially elusive. Minutes of the Council of Minister sessions only cover those parts of the meeting when there are real decisions being made, or when the Council 'acts in legislative capacity'. This includes a report of statements by the Commission and/or individual or joint statements by member states. But the 'juiciest' part of the meeting is often the discussion between delegations on particular details of the subject matter, and this is not reported.

To reconstruct national preparatory decision making on instructions and mandates, access to national archives in the capitals is vital. An alternative is to request a document from the Council archives and to reconstruct national positions starting from there. The so-called 'Blue Guide' on the web is a useful tool. This is a joint effort by a group of archivists of the Foreign Affairs Ministries to pool knowledge and best practices for the conservation and consultation of documents. The guide provides a detailed summary of the location and availability of archived files and documents, and the structure of the archives of the member states and EU institutions. In addition, it can be very useful to draw on national permanent representations, as they are very much the 'eyes and ears' of the EU policy process. Many officials of the 'perm reps' take notes at the meetings they attend, be it at the working group level, or beyond. For example, the Antici Group of assistants to the Permanent Representatives take notes of the European Council discussions.

Talk with insiders

Because written sources are at best biased and at worst impossible to find, much policy analysis will rely to a large extent on people as a data source. Potential interviewees include government officials, Commission staff (including the *chef the dossier*, head of unit and members of the Cabinet), and the ambassadors of the member states and their staff (Antici, Mertens). Oral interviews can be rigidly, semi-, or loosely structured. With the permission of the interviewee, they can be recorded and then transcribed. Accounts are then often sent to respondents for their approval – and to ensure the methodological validity of the study. Always keep in mind that, as valuable as interviews are, working with people inevitably invokes the risk of irrationality, confusion, and false judgements. Conversations with people who have been directly involved will inevitably provide a personal and subjective perspective. The causes of policy failure, on the other hand, may turn out much more difficult to reconstruct than policy success. To remedy this, it is important to make use of 'triangulation', or the use of additional research methods. Peer reviews include, for example, checking the vision of civil servants in a particular Council working group, while also making use of academic experts, lobbyists, or journalists who have followed the same process or event from a certain distance.

Mind the gap between policy and practice

There are at least three serious caveats to keep in mind when analyzing EU decision making.

First, policy actors often change their preferences in the course of the process, or do not always follow their preferences as outlined elsewhere. We can illustrate this with the example of analyzing the amount of influence that the EP actually had in making new EU laws and policies. A logical research methodology is to compare the final texts of a number of EU decisions with the different drafts prepared by the Council and the EP, and then look for differences. Theoretically, there are three possibilities: (1) a final act could correspond completely to the second reading of the EP, without any amendments of the Council; (2) a final act could completely correspond to the Council's common position, without any parliamentary amendments; or (3) a final act could correspond to the compromise text reached between the Council and the EP in the conciliation committee. In our hypothetical case, the outcome of the analysis points to a small majority of Council-influenced acts that seems to suggest that the EP exerted less influence. What this analysis, using this research method, does not reveal, however, is that in the course of the shaping process, the Council could just as well have *foreseen* parliamentary concerns and purposely included them in the first reading. In other words, preferences of the actors involved in the policy process are not always the same throughout the entire process, and actors can strategically decide to deviate from their original preferences. Analyzing the policy process entirely 'on paper' will not always reveal such stories.

A second and related challenge for much EU policy research is the question of how to measure success and failure. It is very difficult to establish adequate comparative criteria to judge 'success' (see Chapter 9). Intuitively, it might seem that the degree to which an actor (government, lobby group, EU institution or interest organization) is 'successful' in Brussels corresponds to the degree to which its preferences are mirrored in the final decision. However, for daily negotiators in the EU, work is often like playing various chess games simultaneously – winning on one board comes at the expense of losing on another. Preferences and positions are often re-formulated in the course of the process, so that it is difficult or at times meaningless to assess the initial objective against the final outcome.

Finally, researchers are often confronted with what may be called 'the challenge of non-decision'. Formal records, such as the Council minutes, do not show the proposals that never made it into law. It may be just as relevant to find out why certain proposals never made it out of 'inter-service consultation' or were dismissed by the College. Which ideas were buried after intense struggles in the working group phase? Which almost-complete working group agreements were finally left by the wayside, traded off as part of a 'package deal' among national ambassadors?

These complications notwithstanding, policy research in the decision-making stage leads to the heart of the Brussels' machinery. It is often about top-level summitry, and powerful interests surrounded by intricate office politics.

Conclusion

Who won? Who lost? As with any sports game, these questions are often central to EU policy analysis. The decision-making stage often features in the political and media limelight. This is not to say that analyzing EU decision making is an easy task. The overflow of evidence and opinions available may seriously complicate research. Being strict to select is key here: validating information and assessments along the way. This chapter has offered a toolkit to be used when starting off a journey into the fascinating world of EU decision making, in which success is – as ever – in the eye of the beholder.

Suggestions for further reading

Christiansen, T. and Larsson, T. (2007) (eds) *The Role of Committees in the Policy-Process of the European Union: Legislation, Implementation and Deliberation* (Cheltenham: Edward Elgar).

Peterson, J. and Bomberg, E. (1999) *Decision-Making in the European Union* (Basingstoke and New York: Palgrave Macmillan).

Tallberg, J. (2006) *Leadership and Negotiation in the European Union* (Cambridge: Cambridge University Press).

Chapter 8

Implementation

Introduction

While the attention accorded to 'Brussels' in policy analysis has always been considerable, the last two stages of the policy 'cycle' – implementation and evaluation – have traditionally received less attention. For whatever reasons, examining how policies end up on the agenda and how they are formulated and decided upon appears to be regarded as somewhat more 'sexy' than analyzing how this policy actually fares in practice. We would argue, however, that the stage of implementation in which policy is put into effect at the 'street level', is of the utmost importance. Indeed, why bother making policy at all if it is not actually going to be put into effect in the member states? Analyzing whether policies are actually implemented is a crucial element of policy analysis as a whole, not least because, as we will outline in this chapter, the EU context embodies at least 27 separate implementation traditions.

While the existence of differing implementation traditions as such does not automatically constitute a problem, it may become problematic when some member states implement EU legislation and others do not. This disparity, referred to as the 'implementation deficit' of the EU, can be particularly acute in policy areas such as the internal market. Uneven implementation of internal market policies leads to uneven opportunities within the internal market as a whole, damaging competitiveness. There is a growing sense that implementation, when it occurs as uneven or non-existent, harms the effectiveness, not to mention the legitimacy and credibility, of the European Union, a realization that has led to more attention being paid to the implementation stage of the policy process. Over the last decade, the Commission and those who study the EU have become more and more aware of this issue. At the same time, policy analysis at the implementation stage is still in its early years, and there remains a relative dearth of information about how EU policies actually fare at the 'street level'. The lack of conclusive information about the implementation stage might be explained by the fact that doing this type of research is both difficult to undertake and very time-consuming.

180

This chapter begins by providing an overview of what implementing EU policy entails, after which we present certain state-of-the-art in implementation theories. The chapter ends by identifying the main pitfalls of doing implementation research, highlighting some key issues for consideration when analyzing the implementation stage.

Implementation in the EU: who is involved and what do we analyze?

To implement means basically 'to carry out, accomplish, fulfill, produce, complete' (Hill and Hupe, 2009, p.3). In the EU policy process, the implementation stage entails the member states putting into effect EU laws and regulations. Although relevant in all political systems, implementation is particularly important in the EU. While EU policy is decided upon in Brussels, it is carried out at the level of each member state separately, implying, in effect, 27 different 'practices'. Whenever member states fail to implement EU policy, the European Commission can intervene in order to try to ensure that they do implement it. The EU is unique amongst international organizations in having this particular recourse.

Importantly, analyzing implementation is not the same as studying effectiveness (see Chapter 9 for a more detailed account of analyzing effectiveness). Effectiveness refers to 'the efficacy of a given regulation in solving the political problem' (Neyer and Zürn, 2001, p.4). Perfect implementation can exist without it being effective, that is, without it solving the problem that the policy aims to address. There is a clear example of perfect implementation in the case of the International Montreal Protocol (on substances that deplete the ozone layer), where the protocol itself had very little substantive effect (thus low effectiveness) due to the low ambitions of the Protocol; in other words, it succeeded in what it set out to do, although in the larger sense of that purpose, it did not actually achieve very much at all (see Downs and Trento, 2004, p.20).

In the context of the European Union, different people might well refer to entirely different things when talking about 'implementation'. Talking about this topic thus requires a very clear reference to the specific actions under scrutiny, and who, in particular, is carrying them out (see Table 8.1). At the European level, the European Commission and the European Court of Justice have certain responsibilities related to implementation. At the member state level, a variety of different actors fulfill roles, including ministries, inspectorates and 'the regulated' – the latter a group that obviously differs by policy area, or even by policy instrument. This is a stage of the policy process where we see

Table 8.1   *Notions of implementation in the European context*

Member state level	European level
• Formal implementation, or 'transposition': the 'law in the books' • Practical implementation, or 'enforcement' by regulators and 'compliance' by regulated: the 'law in action'	• The Commission (in cooperation with the ECJ) as the 'guardian of the Treaties' • Direct implementation by the Commission • Comitology • European agencies

Source: based on Versluis, 2007, p.52.

relatively little involvement of lobby or interest groups (but see Box 8.1 for an example of how implementation studies can be used as a lobbying instrument).

Of all the stages of the European policy process, the implementation stage is the one where one witnesses the most direct involvement of actors at the member state level. This strong involvement of national actors stems from article 4 (TFEU), which specifies that it is the member states who are required to ensure the fulfillment of European commitments. This does not imply, however, that the member states are free to 'do as they please'. According to article 17 (TFEU), the Commission is responsible for overseeing 'the application of Union law under the control of the Court of Justice of the European Union'. In other words, there are different tasks and responsibilities related to implementation, conducted at different levels and by different actors. With respect to the notion of 'subsidiarity' within EU law, actions should normally be implemented at the lowest possible level – that is, as close to street level as possible. The following section will first describe the activities undertaken at the member state level, before then turning to the 'oversight' activities at the European level.

Implementation within the member states

The activities needed to ensure that European legislation is actually put into practice take place at the 'street level' of the member states. Which member states put EU rules into practice depends on the type of rule that is issued. Of the three binding European policy instruments, 'regulations' and 'decisions' are directly applicable, while 'directives' are only binding with regards to the results to be achieved (see Chapter 3). It should be noted that other instruments, such as opinions, communications, and non-papers have no legally binding status. With directives, in particular, confusion can arise about the meaning of the word 'imple-

Box 8.1   Implementation research as a lobbying instrument: the case of the Qualification Directive

Implementation research is certainly not conducted only by academics interested in learning more about what happens with EU policy in practice from an analytical perspective. More and more, implementation research is undertaken strategically by diverse parties for diverse ends. For example, a study of the implementation of the Qualification Directive was conducted by the United Nations High Commissioner for Refugees (UNHCR) (Brussels, November 2007). This analysis of Council Directive 2004/83/EC on minimum standards for the qualification and status of third country nationals or stateless persons as refugees, was initiated by the UNHCR in order to 'contribute constructively to discussions on the implementation of and potential amendments to the Qualification Directive' (UNHCR, 2007, p.8). The UNHCR study considered both formal and practical implementation, revealing a worrying trend. While the directive clearly led to greater conformity of legal systems throughout the EU, the persistent existence of differing chances for refugees to find protection across the various individual member states had put in place what was effectively an 'asylum lottery' (UNHCR, 2007, p.8).

For example, a situation defined as an 'internal armed conflict' is one of the circumstances that might allow people from a certain region to claim refugee status. At the time of the UNHCR's research, the situation in parts of Iraq was assessed as an internal armed conflict in France, while in Sweden it was 'merely' considered to be a 'severe conflict' – thereby precluding a claim for Swedish refugee status on that basis. At the same time, Sweden assessed the situation in Chechnya as constituting an internal armed conflict, while Slovakia, for example, did not. The report concluded with a long list of recommendations on proposed amendments to the directive (particularly to delete or amend certain articles), recommendations for the Commission (for example, to provide training and adopt guidelines), as well as for member states (for example, how to interpret certain parts of the directive). The example of the UNHCR study is telling, inasmuch as it shows how different stages of the policy process can be intertwined. This *evaluation* of the *implementation* process was conducted by the UNHCR with the aim of lobbying for change in this policy field – that is, with the aim of also influencing the *policy formulation* and *decision making* arenas of this topic.

mentation.' Often, a distinction is made between 'formal' or 'legal' implementation, on the one hand, and 'practical' or 'administrative' implementation, on the other. Formal or legal implementation implies the transposition of European directives to national legislation – basically, adapting the existing 'law on the books' to accommodate the new directive. Obviously, this understanding of implementation as transposition does not relate to regulations and decisions as they are directly applicable and simply 'absorbed' as they are within the jurisprudence (body of laws) of the member states. By contrast, practical or administrative implementation refers to the establishment of administrative agencies, the setting up of necessary tools and instruments, monitoring, and inspecting by regulators (enforcement) and the actual adherence to the law by the regulated (compliance or application). This understanding of the word implementation concerns the 'law in action'.

The actual putting into practice of EU policy thus occurs at the member state level (see Table 8.2 for a practical example). Although each member state organizes this process separately, we do see similarities. Legal implementation (the transposition of directives) is, generally speaking, arranged by the national ministry responsible for the topic at hand. For example, environmental directives are transposed by the national environmental ministries. The situation is slightly more complicated in federalized countries, where regional ministries can also be involved in the transposition process if they are responsible for the particular policy area. In Germany, for example, it is often the case that transposition responsibilities are shared between a federal ministry and the ministries of the 16 *Länder*. The involvement of national parliaments in the process depends on the type of legislation used for transposition. Member states that are more inclined to use 'primary legislation' (laws that require parliamentary approval) for transposition, such as Germany, will show more parliamentarian involvement than member states with a tradition of using 'secondary legislation' (including regulations or decrees), as is the case in the United Kingdom and Spain. Moreover, the involvement of third parties, such as regulated sectors or interest groups, varies between countries, although, generally speaking, this involvement is fairly limited as the 'room for manoeuvre' of member states in transposition is relatively low, limiting the possibilities for lobbying.

The same pattern holds for the stage of practical implementation. Member states are themselves responsible for organizing enforcement: what type of inspection bodies to appoint, whether to create specific inspection tools, and which sanctions to impose in cases of non-implementation. Federalized countries further delegate these organizational responsibilities. Enforcement in Spain, for example, is arranged by the 17 Autonomous Communities. This gives rise to a situation in which the organizational structures of inspection bodies vary both between and within member states. Some are highly centralized, using standardized operating procedures, whereas others allow more autonomy for individual inspectors; some are divided by territory (for example, labour inspectors enforce all labour policy in a fixed number of companies), others by function (labour inspectors enforce a specific part of the labour policy – for example, hazardous substances – in a wider

Table 8.2 *Implementation at the member state level – the actors involved*

Who, how or what?	*The case of Safety Data Sheets (91/155/EEC) in the Netherlands*
Aim of the directive?	To regulate a safe handling of dangerous substances (for example, sulphur or chlorine dioxide) and preparations (for example, glue or paint).
Example of a specific requirement in the directive?	Produce a 'safety data sheet' for each dangerous substance and preparations; this sheet – in 16 headings – should provide information on, for example, first aid measures and handling and storage.
Who is the transposing actor?	Dutch Ministry of Social Affairs and Employment.
How is this transposed?	Safety Data Sheets Decree of 29 April 1993 (transposition delay of 23 months, as the required deadline was 30 May 1991).
Who are the 'regulated'?	Manufacturers, importers, and distributors of dangerous chemical substances and preparations.
What do the regulated mainly have to do?	Make and regularly update safety data sheets for all their dangerous substances and preparations.
Who deals with the enforcement?	The Dutch Inspectorate of Housing, Spatial Planning and the Environment.
What do the enforcers mainly have to do?	Inspectors have to check whether companies have safety data sheets for all their dangerous substances and preparations, whether these sheets have the correct format and content and whether they regularly update this information.
What are the main 'implementation difficulties' in this case?	The smaller and medium-sized companies that need to comply with this directive often lack the expertise to make and update good safety data sheets, thus resulting in sheets of bad quality. Inspectorates in various member states do not find this directive the most important topic to check, and thus enforcement only takes place occasionally.

Source: based on Versluis, 2007.

region); some work with detailed inspection tools such as computerized checklists, others do not. In sum, the organizational structure of enforcement is a purely domestic, sometimes even regional, responsibility, and varies widely across the EU.

Implementation at the European level

While the member states are busy implementing (or not) they are being 'watched'. Certain activities at the European level are concerned with 'oversight', ensuring that the member states are doing their job as they should. First of all, the Commission is the 'guardian of the Treaties'. As guardian, the Commission is, together with the European Court of Justice, and through the infringement procedure (articles 258 and 260, TFEU), responsible for ensuring the proper application of EU legislation in all member states. When confronted with non-implementation – for example, the incorrect transposition, or the absence of application – the Commission can first issue a 'letter of formal notice', then a 'reasoned opinion', followed by a referral to the European Court of Justice. In the final instance, financial sanctions can be imposed. Over the years, a growing number of infringement proceedings have been initiated: in recent years an average of about 1,700 letters of formal notice have been issued, leading to an average of 550 reasoned opinions and 200 referrals to the Court of Justice per year (European Commission, 2008b). Given that around 70 per cent of the complaints regarding non-implementation that reach the Commission are actually solved before a letter of formal notice is sent, we might conclude that the Commission is relatively successful as guardian or 'watchdog' of the Treaties. The Commission does not have officials working in the member states whose sole aim is to locate infringements. Rather, it depends on third parties to notify it about shortcomings. In the environmental sector, NGOs are especially active in informing the Commission of cases of non-implementation.

Next to this concrete function of the Commission as the guardian of the Treaties, there are three other activities at the European level in which references to implementation can be made. A first activity concerns the Commission's tasks in directly overseeing the application of European legislation in specific policy fields – for example, the administration of the EU's humanitarian aid programme, or the common fisheries policy. Most important is the field of competition, in which the Commission can, for example, directly prevent mergers from taking place. These exceptions were put in place in fields where differing interests between member states were likely to arise, and where we arguably need the Commission as an 'objective' partner.

Secondly, 'comitology' (see Chapter 7 for a more detailed description) is also sometimes described as part of implementation. The existence of comitology in the EU highlights the difficulties of using a 'policy process' approach that distinguishes between different stages as an analytical tool. As comitology committees actually take decisions, it is debatable – and will doubtless vary by case – whether this particular activity can be considered as a final part of the decision-making stage, or the first part of the implementation stage.

There is one 'implementation-related activity' at the European level that is fairly new. Since the 1990s, we have observed an increasing trend for specific tasks to be delegated to independent agencies within the European Union. By agencies, we mean a 'variety of organizations – commissions, boards, authorities, services, offices, inspectorates – that perform functions of a governmental nature, and which often exist outside the normal departmental framework of government' (Majone, 2000, p.290). Currently, there are about 30 in total, but their numbers are rapidly increasing. Most agencies can be labelled as 'regulatory' agencies, and some within that category have tasks that relate specifically to implementation, agencies in the area of transport being a salient example. For example, the European Maritime Safety Agency (Lisbon) and the European Aviation Safety Agency (Cologne) – both of which exist in order to ensure safety in their respective fields – can conduct inspections in the member states. Currently, the number of agencies with such far-reaching tasks is limited, their tasks still restricted to inspecting the inspectors – that is, inspecting the work of the national inspectorates but not directly inspecting the actors actually being regulated. Only the future will tell whether this becomes a new trend in the EU, and whether or not we will continue to depart from the principle whereby, according to article 4, member states are responsible for implementation.

Theoretical perspectives

The above description of implementation in the European policy process shows 'oversight' activities by the European Commission, the European Court of Justice, and European agencies, as well as the more concrete act of putting policies into practice at the member state level. Implementation research tends to concentrate on this last element. Importantly, there is no such thing as one specific theoretical approach when studying implementation in the EU context. Theorizing about this topic has its origins in the context of nation-states. Implementation research developed out of the notion that there was a gap between decisions and the reality of policy, that policy did not necessarily lead to the expected outcomes. In light of this, the first implementation studies tended to be somewhat pessimistic in nature, appearing as they did out of a frustration over failed policy. The 'founding fathers' of implementation research are the US scholars Pressman and Wildavsky whose book, *Implementation: How Great*

Expectations in Washington are Dashed in Oakland, is seen as a departure point in implementation studies, tackling the question of why policy aimed at reducing poverty had failed. Since its publication in 1973, the area of implementation studies has been rapidly growing in the United States, although in the European Union context, implementation studies are also beginning to take off (for an overview see Mastenbroek, 2005; Sverdrup, 2005; Treib, 2006). In particular, the Europeanization research agenda (see, for example Cowles *et al.*, 2001; or Héritier *et al.*, 2001) with its shift in focus to the member state level, has generated an increased amount of academic interest in the field, just as questions about the impact of the EU on its member states has focused attention on EU policy implementation in places such as Berlin, Athens, and Warsaw.

Because policy implementation takes place in different types of political systems, theorizing about implementation has also developed with different contexts in mind. Although traditionally, implementation research originated in the nation-state context, with more and more international cooperation taking place, theorizing about implementation has also evolved beyond state boundaries. The following section will move from a national, to a European, and then to a more international perspective on implementation research (see Box 8.2 on pp. 190–1 for an example of implementation research).

Implementation research in the nation-state context

Traditional implementation research began with the debate between the 'top-down' and the 'bottom-up' approaches. Top-down scholars (for example, Meter and Horn, 1975; Mazmanian and Sabatier, 1981) start from the perspective of the policy maker, analyzing how a decision moves from the 'top', where it is made, to the 'bottom', where it is executed. Implementation failure is largely analyzed in terms of a lack of clarity in policy objectives and (lack of) available resources. This approach departs from the perception that it is the policy type and content that shapes implementation, and these scholars believe in the possibility of a clear-cut differentiation between policy formulation and policy implementation. They hold that those stages can be neatly separated and that after a decision has been made, implementation starts as its own distinct stage, which can be guided from above.

Bottom-up scholars (for example, Lipsky, 1980; Hjern 1982), on the other hand, start from the perspective of the street-level bureaucrat and claim that variation in implementation can largely be explained by examining the amount of discretion that local level implementers enjoy. According to the bottom-up perspective, it is the implementation itself that shapes the nature of policy. Here, instead of asking whether and how a particular policy is implemented from the top, analysis should start with what is actually happening at the level of the target population.

As one can imagine, the two approaches identify different reasons for implementation failure. While 'top-downers' analyze how and why failure exists because policy is not carried out properly (for example, due to lacking financial resources, lack of trained staff, inadequate infrastructure, or fraud), and seek solutions for better steering from above, the 'bottom-uppers' identify unsuccessful policy (for example, due to poor legislation, overly idealistic policy, or policy that requires too much adaptation) as the 'bad apple', arguing for a better drafting of legislation to take into account more realistically the situation at it exists at street-level.

In an attempt to move away from the top-down versus bottom-up debate, more legal-sociologically oriented scholars have started to explore 'regulatory' or 'implementation styles'. Coming to prominence in the 1980s, this 'school' drew on case studies to describe and explain variation in implementation styles between inspectors, agencies, countries, or policy areas (see, for example, Braithwaite, 1985; Vogel, 1986; Hutter, 1989; Kagan, 1989). In this tradition, implementation styles are generally classified in terms of extremes: an implementation style can, on the one hand, be characterized as *legalistic* – also known as a 'compulsory', 'sanctioning', 'coercive', or 'penal' style – or, on the other hand, it can be characterized as *conciliatory* – a 'compromising', 'cooperative', or 'advisory' style. The legalistic style is typified by a tendency to resort to formal legal methods, with tracking down cases of infringement and sanctioning those responsible being seen as the most important aspect of the regulator's job. The conciliatory approach places the emphasis on negotiation, consultation, and persuasion, with sanctions seen as the last resort when all else fails. Vogel (1986), for example, compares the regulatory styles of the United Kingdom and the United States in the field of environmental policy. He concludes that the British style resembles the conciliatory version, while the American style is more legalistic. Variations in implementation styles are explained by the following categories of independent variables: *legal design* factors (for example, the complexity and visibility of the regulatory problem at stake, legal powers, the specificity of the rule), *organizational* factors (for example, the resources available to enforcement agencies), *political* factors (for example, the role of interest groups and the preferences of political authorities, which in turn are induced by factors such as catastrophes, economic circumstances, or electoral shifts), and *social* (or task environment) factors – for example, the relationship between the regulator and the regulated, the degree of willingness of the latter to comply, and the visibility of violations (see

Box 8.2   Implementation of the Seveso II Directive

The explosion of a chemical plant in Flixborough (United Kingdom) in 1974 led to 28 fatalities. The next year, a naphtha cracker exploded in Beek (The Netherlands), killing 14 employees. A year later, two accidents occurred in Italy: one in Manfredonia, and one in Seveso, where a vapour cloud containing lethal dioxins escaped from a chemical plant and resulted in 2,000 people having to be treated for dioxin poisoning. These accidents – demonstrating the agenda-setting role that crises can play, as we saw in Chapter 5 – led to a call by the European Parliament to introduce European legislation to regulate the safe handling of dangerous substances. After three years of negotiations, the Seveso Directive was adopted in 1982. Further explosions and new insights provided by research led to an amendment in 1996: the Seveso II Directive (96/82/EC). Under this directive, chemical companies that house a quantity of dangerous chemicals beyond a certain threshold need to write a 'safety report', in which they demonstrate how they will contain the potential hazards presented by these chemicals (that is, which safety measures they have in place), and how they respond (what their emergency plans are) in case something does happen.

Research into the implementation of this directive (Versluis, 2003), provides a clear example of how uniform European rules do not necessarily lead to uniform practices. Using a qualitative approach – interviewing and sending questionnaires to both the inspectors charged with enforcing this directive, and the chemical companies required to comply with it – we managed to obtain a picture of what actually happens with this specific directive at the 'street level'. What emerges are the huge differences between member states. While in the Netherlands, inspectors on average spend 20–40 days assessing the safety report of a chemical company, Spanish inspectors only spend 5–20 days carrying out these checks. In a similar vein, Dutch chemical companies spent on average 11 months and involved 4 to 5 people to draft a safety report, while their Spanish colleagues managed to write the report in 3 months with 2 to 3

→

especially Kagan, 1989, for a clear overview of independent variables used in this tradition).

This particular school did not attempt to analyze *implementation failure* as such (as top-down and bottom-up scholars did), but strove to *analyze how implementation works* by describing styles and analyzing which factors called into being that particular style of implementation.

→

people. How can we explain these differing results? Why do Dutch inspectors and companies spend more time on the implementation of this directive compared to their Spanish colleagues?

This research – conducted for a PhD dissertation – demonstrated that a combination of factors were at play here. Firstly, legal design factors – in other words, the wording used in legislation – influence the implementation style of different countries. Annex II of the directive outlines what needs to be included in a safety report – nothing if not a remarkable example of vague wording. According to this Annex, safety reports should include a 'detailed description of the possible major-accident scenarios and their probability or the conditions under which they occur including a summary of the events which may play a role in triggering each of these scenarios'. It is not specified, however, what a scenario is, or what is expected by a detailed description of such a scenario. Such a scenario is thus open to interpretation, and, indeed, analysis into the interpretation of the directive in different member states shows that this ambiguity leads to major differences in practice. Spain, for example, literally translated the vague wording into Spanish legislation, effectively providing both inspectors and chemical companies with little explanation of what precisely what would be expected from them – paving the way, in turn, for difficulties in implementation. The Netherlands, on the other hand, provided a long document in which it clearly explained what all companies needed to do to comply with this policy. Clearly, imprecise wording of EU legislation can lead to significant variations in implementation styles of across different countries.

The differences between the Dutch and Spanish reactions to this directive were exacerbated by already existing differences in experience with the topic of the directive. While the Netherlands already had a history of experience in regulating this field, the topic was a relatively new one for Spain. In other words, a lack of experience and expertise clearly influenced the less 'insistent' approach of the Spanish inspectors.

Implementation studies in the EU: the influence of Europeanization

Following this nation-state tradition in implementation literature, the first real empirical study of the European situation, by Siedentopf and Ziller (1988), set the scene for a wide range of EU implementation research. While those authors demonstrated that after the stage of transposition, directives are treated exactly the same as national legislation, others have argued that implementation is relatively easier in more linear administrative systems, such as centrally organized governments (Peters, 2000). Harding and Swart explicitly state that there is 'a basic difference between enforcing Community law and enforcing national law. To achieve a satisfactory level of enforcement is considerably more difficult for the Community than it is for a State effectively to enforce its laws' (Harding and Swart, 1996, p.1). The EU comprises a wide variety of actors involved in the policy implementation process. Both top-down and bottom-up scholars have argued that an increase in the number of actors involved will most likely result in an increase in the amount of potential implementation difficulties. Taking this into consideration, scholars in the European context have deviated from the more nation-state dominated traditions, developing their own approaches – even if many of the explanatory variables initiated by this top-down and bottom-up debate are also relevant at the European level.

There have been no attempts to develop a specific theory that explains implementation at the European level. Although many would have difficulties labelling it a 'theory' – and criticism of its explanatory power has grown over years – the 'Europeanization' school comes closest to what we can label a specifically 'European' approach to studying implementation. Europeanization can most generally be defined as studying the impact of European integration at the national level. While the wider research agenda aims at understanding how and to what extent EU activities influence domestic polities, politics and policies, a large portion of this agenda has ended up focusing on specific cases of implementation of EU legislation at the member state level. The main issue addressed in these studies has been how to explain variations in the implementation of EU legislation between member states.

The first studies began with the assumption that domestic adjustment – that is, the implementation of EU legislation – is only to be expected in cases where a 'misfit' exists between the European rule and the domestic situation. If such a misfit occurs, the second step is to identify the mediating or facilitating factors that eventually make change possible. Implementing EU policy at the member state level has generally been assumed to be a question of the 'goodness of fit' between the specific EU law and the domestic situation, and by the availability of mediating factors to stimulate implementation. According to Börzel and Risse (2003), the mediating factors all fall into the framework of new institutionalism, and can be grouped under either rational choice institutionalism or sociological institutionalism. According to the rationalist perspective, the two mediating factors are 'multiple veto points' and 'facilitating formal institutions'. The absence of both will stimulate (or strengthen the chances in favour of) implementation. According to sociological institutionalism, both the presence of 'persuasive change agents' and a consensus-oriented or cooperative decision-making culture, encourage socialization. Socializing or bringing together the relevant actors on a cooperative basis is fundamental for effective policy implementation.

The more Europeanization studies that appeared, the stronger criticism of the 'goodness of fit' hypothesis became. Mastenbroek and Kaeding (2006), for example, argue that hypothesis has not been borne out in any significant sense by the empirical evidence, and that there is little link between goodness of fit and ease of implementation. They conclude that goodness of fit is not even a necessary condition for domestic change, and that it would be theoretically more sound to concentrate on domestic preferences and beliefs in trying to understand why implementation proceeds as it does. In sum, 'Europeanization' has not been able to provide a common framework for understanding implementation either.

The wider international scene: the role of IR theories

The Europeanization framework is especially concentrated on the implementation of EU policy at the member state level, and in particular aims at explaining differences in implementation between member states. There is, however, a third possible framework that can be used to analyze the implementation stage of the EU policy process. The International Relations (IR) traditions provide insight into our understanding of why nations comply, or do not, with international rules. While IR theories are generally used to understand how international regimes work in general – one can think of studies of the WTO, IMF, OECD, climate change regimes, and so on (for example, Luck and Doyle, 2004) – their insights are just as applicable to studies of the implementation of EU legislation. Three dominant traditions in IR compliance theory – rationalism, management, and constructivism – each provide a different explanation as to why compliance problems occur, identifying distinct independent variables to explain non-compliance.

First, rationalism sees compliance as an intentional mechanism: actors (member states) make a rational choice whether or not to comply (whether or not to implement EU policy) based on cost/benefit calculations. Whenever non-compliance occurs, this is seen as a preference because the costs of compliance are considered to be too high. Non-compliance can also occur out of opposition, or, indeed, in protest at having been outvoted during negotiations in the Council (Moravcsik, 1993). It is suspected that countries that are unable to 'upload' their preferences during the decision-making process are more like to not implement the policy in the spirit of opposition (Falkner *et al.*, 2004). Here, implementation becomes an opportunity to assert oneself by taking a deliberately stubborn stance and resisting the process. The explanatory variables that explain non-compliance lie in the monitoring and sanctioning capacities of the regulator(s). Countries will only comply with international rules when there is an effective system to detect and respond to violations and infringements. Explaining implementation processes in the EU according to such a rationalist perspective would thus entail research into the functioning of the Commission as the guardian of the treaties, and an investigation of behaviour of member states as rational actors in this process.

The management approach – induced by Chayes and Chayes (1993) – begins from the opposite assumption – that is, that countries are generally willing to comply with international rules – and goes on to stress the unintentional mechanisms behind compliance. Whenever non-compliance occurs, it can generally be explained as a result of incapacity or rule ambiguity. Explanatory variables can be located in the financial, technological, scientific, administrative, or other capacities of the regulated, as well as in poorly drafted legislation (see also in the 'bottom-up school'). The new member states of Central and Eastern Europe are thought to be vulnerable to these sorts of incapacities. Explaining EU implementation from this perspective requires an analysis of member state capacities, as well as of the way policy is formulated.

A third perspective, that of constructivism, is grounded in a vision of a more normative mechanism, viewing non-compliance through the lens of a lack of internalization of the norms of appropriate behaviour. According to this line of reasoning, the longer a state is exposed to a certain set of international laws, the more likely it will be that this state 'internalizes' those rules as the 'right thing to do', and thus the more likely it is that compliance will take place. Whether or not the regulated actors comply with the regulations depends to a large extent on how such a process of social learning takes place. There are circumstances that can stimulate this internalization or socialization: for example non-state actors such as NGOs, research centres or the media can act as a catalyst in persuading the right actors that implementation should take place. The analysis of EU implementation processes from a constructivist approach requires research into the ability of member states to undergo such socialization processes.

As non-compliance can rarely ever be attributed to a single factor, or explained from a single perspective, scholars from the different 'schools' acknowledge that the different IR compliance perspectives are not always in opposition. The question is not which model is 'true', but how much of the variance in compliance can be explained by each model (Underdal, 1998).

In summary, there are different traditions in the study of implementation, with variations in scope, from the domestic, to the European, to the international level (see Table 8.3).

Key issues for consideration

With the various theoretical perspectives used to analyze the implementation processes, this section will explore the 'dos and 'don'ts' of implementation research. What are the main pitfalls, and more importantly, what are the key issues for consideration?

Problems and pitfalls

When doing implementation research, one should be aware of three potential traps: implementation as a research object is a 'slippery concept' (Hill, 1997), there is a danger of having an overload of potential explanatory variables, and there are risks in not taking into consideration certain serious methodological constraints.

Implementation as a slippery concept

The first thing every scholar who analyzes implementation processes should be very clear about is what he or she actually means by the concept of 'implementation'. As the section on theories suggested, we can in actual fact be referring to very different things when we talk about the implementation of EU policy. Does one analyze transposition results, or does one concentrate on the role of the Commission as the guardian of the Treaties? Sinclair (2001) points out how various implementation studies fail to discuss their theoretical assumptions and/or conceptual boundaries explicitly and thus do not specify what is understood by 'implementation' in their particular cases. In the EU context, Treib (2006, p.10) shows that many authors do not systematically distinguish between the stages of transposition and enforcement and application, thereby postulating the entire implementation process as following a single theoretical logic. Moreover, many implementation studies fail to specify clearly what is actually meant by successful implementation (Lester and Goggin, 1998).

All this suggests a larger quandary: how to measure implementation? While traditionally the top-down school has concentrated on measuring implementation as *goal-achievement* (that is, to what extent the goals in a certain policy are attained in practice), in recent years, some scholars have called for a redefinition of implementation as *output* (measuring the performance of the implementers in implementing the

Table 8.3   *Comparative overview of different theoretical approaches*

School	Main question	Main independent variables
Nation-state context		
Top-down versus bottom-up	How do we explain implementation failure?	Organizational factors (top-down) versus policy factors (bottom-up)
Regulatory style	How do we explain variation in implementation styles?	Legal design, organizational, political, and social factors
EU context		
Europeanization	How do we explain differences in implementation of EU policy between member states?	Goodness of fit, mediating factors (such as veto players, change agents, or facilitating formal institutions)
Wider international context		
IR compliance theories	How do we explain why nations comply with international policy?	Strength of the enforcement system, capacity and rule ambiguity, strength of non-state actors

policy) or *outcome* (measuring the effects of policy on the target population) (for example, Winter, 1999; Sinclair, 2001). Winter (1999) claims that goal-achievement is not an effective standard for measurement because goals always have certain values (it might be far from straightforward for everybody to agree on what the actual goals of a given policy are) and it may not always be the real intention that ostensible goals be fully achieved. Measuring implementation via outcome is no less susceptible to problems than measurement via goal achievement. Who or what decides what constitutes a successful outcome? Regulators may well have a different opinion as compared to those being regulated. Implementation studies may often misrepresent the full picture when they use such situated concepts as 'good' or 'poor' to describe implementation results, even if such typologies might help policy makers grasp the degree of implementation success or failure. What are the standards used to evaluate the results? The first pitfall of an implementation researcher is failing to clearly define what is meant by 'implementation' – yet at the same time, again, there is not necessarily any agreement at the outset of the process that might ensure a common understanding by all actors of how implementation will eventually be measured.

Difficulties related to the many potential explanatory variables

The title of Goggin's 1986 article suggests an inherent major trap within the implementation research field: 'The "too few cases/too many variables" problem in implementation research'. In addition, O'Toole (2004) lists the use of more than 300 variables to explain implementation, arguing that the number of variables offered by scholars as plausible explanations for implementation results continues to grow. Meier once ironically labelled implementation theory as the theory of 'forty-seven variables that completely explain five case studies', suggesting that 'any policy implementation scholar who adds a new variable or a new interaction should be required to eliminate two existing variables' (Meier, 1999, p.5). How useful, then, are all the theoretical approaches and their explanatory variables, if each new case study on implementation might alternatively be explained by new variables?

The examples given in the theoretical section above reflect this problem. In order to explain the process of implementing European legislation, researchers can call upon different traditions, ranging from nation-state oriented, to Europeanization or even IR theories. While there is some overlap in the types of explanatory variables used, all approaches contain their own focus. Yet at the same time, all of these perspectives resort to factors relating to legal design – for example, all claim that implementation can be explained by looking at the wording and structure of the policy at hand. It is often the case that the type of research question one aims to answer already helps one to identify the most useful theoretical perspective. As Table 8.3 shows, a research question concentrated on understanding why nations comply with international rules is better answered by IR theories than by the top-down or bottom-up approach. In other cases, however, it might not be as obvious which theoretical approach is the most suitable. In such a situation, the researcher must make his or her own selection.

It has been argued that the overload in explanatory variables is caused by the complexity of the topic. Pressman and Wildavsky (1973) have noted that implementation is even extremely complex under 'normal' circumstances where there is no conflict between ends and means. In this sense, a second pitfall in implementation research is the potential overload of explanatory variables that one might use to explain the case at hand – where and how to start to make a selection?

Methodological constraints

While the problem of too much analytical choice is essentially theoretical in nature, anyone embarking upon implementation research should also take the following methodological constraints into consideration. First of all, implementation research shows an incredible reliance on single case studies (Sinclair, 2001). In the European context, qualitative case studies prevail, often with a focus on environmental and social directives. Such *small-n* research creates problems of 'generalizability' – the degree to which one can make a larger generalization based on what may be limited evidence and patterns observed in other cases. How do we know that the variables that seem to explain case A will also be applicable to case B? How can we test the generalizability of implementation research findings given the heavy reliance on single case studies? What does research on the water directive in Germany tell us about the implementation of directives in the financial sector in Poland, or about implementation of EU policy in general? Furthermore, it has been suggested that the first generation of implementation studies suffered from a biased case selection and may have been too focused on policy failures. Some have argued that implementation studies have overlooked the fact that 'everyday and on every level of government, new programs are introduced that, to some degree or another, work' (DeLeon, 1999, p.321). This attention on exceptional failure – leading to the nickname 'misery research' (Rothstein, 1988, quoted in Saetren, 2005, p.572) – led to bias in the implementation research product, as case studies that show up glaring evidence of implementation failure are perhaps more 'newsworthy' to the academic and politician than a totally unexpected success story, let alone a run-of-the-mill performance or a reasonable outcome. We are more likely to ask ourselves 'what went wrong?' than 'what went right?'

When examining EU implementation studies, we witness another bias, leading to a second methodological constraint. A large portion of EU implementation studies is concentrated on the transposition stage of the first pillar only. Of the 39 studies on implementation in the EU in the period 1986–2005, analyzed by Mastenbroek (2005, pp.1105–7), 69 per cent focus (mainly) on transposition. Despite some exceptions (for example, Demmke, 2001; Falkner *et al.*, 2005; Versluis, 2007), questions of practical implementation are still largely ignored. This can be explained to a large degree by the availability of data. 'Transposition scholars' access databases containing national transposition measures or infringement data provided by the European Commission, thereby allowing them to proceed with a more quantitative approach. By contrast, information on practical implementation is difficult to obtain because opportunities for detection are scarce; 'data on these dimensions are tremendously hard to gather, which is why they have received only scant attention so far' (Mastenbroek, 2005, p.1114). What is needed is to gather empirical data at the street-level – for example, by conducting interviews and/or setting out surveys in the member states to reveal levels and practices of compliance and enforcement, as well as investigating the motives or motivation of actors.

Practical insights

Keeping in mind the potential traps to be avoided, the next, and arguably more interesting, question with regards to implementation research is: how to go about it then? Where to start and what to do when analyzing the implementation stage of the EU policy process?

General guidelines

As suggested in our description of potential pitfalls, the first lesson that should be retained from the above is that any researcher analyzing implementation should first of all clearly identify what is meant by implementation. As we have seen in this Chapter, the EU implementation stage consists of many different elements that can all be analyzed, and it is advisable that the researcher clearly indicates what he or she seeks to concentrate on specifically. In order to achieve some sort of generalizability, implementation research should include a clear theoretical perspective, explicitly operationalize the explanatory variables, and show variation in the object of analysis. Regarding case selection – and also to enable the generalization of results – EU implementation research can draw on empirical insights from a wider range of policy sectors. There is a pressing need for more data on the implementation of regulations, decisions, recommendations, and OMC instruments across a many different policy domains beyond the current focus on directives in the environmental and social domains. Furthermore, it is not only instances of policy failure that should be selected if we are to gain a balanced understanding of the variables influencing implementation success or failure.

As we have seen, the most common element studied in the EU context is the transposition process, but research into the practical implementation stage, the role of the Commission as the guardian of the Treaties, or the functioning of agencies at the implementation stage can be of equal interest. Any study should first make clear which specific element of implementation it intends to concentrate on. The next steps are to identify which theoretical perspective appears most suitable, to explain how implementation is to be measured, and to identify an appropriate methodological approach. The remainder of this section will specify in more detail how to go about this process when undertaking the two of the most common types of EU implementation studies: transposition and practical implementation.

Researching transposition

As we have suggested, the most common object of study in EU implementation research is the transposition stage, as this is the stage where the largest quantity of data is available. Transposition research is generally comparative in nature, either comparing different member states' transposition results, or different policy sectors in a single member state. Research often focuses on the timeliness, the completeness, or the correctness of transposition of EU directives into member state legislation. The main theoretical perspective here is grounded in the Europeanization tradition. The nation-state and IR perspectives on implementation are less suitable for this type of research, as transposition is a very specific EU activity that is not applicable to the implementation of domestic or other international legislation. Transposition scholars analyze the extent to which transposition deadlines and requirements are met at the member state level, and provide explanations for their outcomes – for example, how do we explain the fact that country A transposes on time and country B does not, or why country C transposes correctly in the field of X but not in the field of Y?

These sorts of exercises can be approached by consulting the information that the Commission provides on its website 'Application of Community Law', including timetables for implementation measures and the notifications by member states of their national transposition measures. Although this website provides the general statistics, if one wants to undertake research into single cases, one can also make use of the EUR-LEX site. For example, if one is researching the implementation of the Tobacco Advertising Directive, looking up this directive via its number (year 2003, number 33), and clicking on the 'biographical notice' will provide a list of all notified national transposition measures ('display of national execution measures'), organized by the member states and their dates – a convenient and instantaneous overview of the timeliness of transposition activity. However, one should never rely on this information alone, for these lists will not specify whether transposition is in fact complete. They list only those measures communicated by the member states, making no reference to instances where a country has only transposed a part of a directive, and where more transposition measures are pending. Indeed, evidence has been found of member states notifying draft laws that were not in actual fact adopted (Falkner *et al.*, 2005). In this sense, it is vital to double-check this information with statistics from member states' national websites, for example.

This initial method only provides information on timeliness. In order to analyze the completeness and/or correctness of transposition, one needs to delve into the texts of the legislation in question.

This implies reading and analyzing both the EU directive and the national transposition measures to assess whether all the elements of the directive have indeed been transposed (completeness) and whether or not they have been transposed properly (correctness). Such an exercise requires the linguistic expertise to be able to judge whether or not the content of the directive has been adhered to, because the documents will be written in the language of each member state. Once the researcher is able to assess the timeliness, completeness, and correctness of transposition, it is then possible to analyze the results. How to explain the variation in outcomes between member states or between policy sectors? Here, the variety of variables used in Europeanization research discussed above comes into play.

Researching practical implementation

Research into the practical implementation stage – the enforcement by inspectors and the compliance with or application of the rules by the regulated – is relatively rare (while there are numerous examples of problems in this stage; see Box 8.3). It is not so much that this type of research is highly complicated. Rather, the problem lies more in the time-consuming nature of researching practical implementation. As the Commission only keeps track of transposition measures of which member states provide notification, there are no statistics available on the Commission's website that can be used to provide an insight into practical implementation, nor is there an easily accessible database with information about how inspectors enforce EU legislation, or how the regulated comply with it. In order to obtain that sort of information, one needs to 'descend' to the street level of the member state to gather the information oneself. One method is through interviews or questionnaires. Just as with transposition research, research into practical implementation is largely comparative in nature. The researcher is interested in providing insight into variation in results –why does member state A enforce a certain piece of legislation differently from member state B – and in providing explanations for that variation. As practical implementation is an activity that is not strictly limited to EU legislation – national and other international legislation is also put into practice at the street level – the researcher can draw upon the wide variety of approaches introduced in the theoretical section above, selecting one that is appropriate to the type of policy area in question.

How does one undertake this type of implementation research? The first task, before being able to conduct an analysis, is to gather empirical information on enforcement and compliance practices. This can only be done by researching specific practices in the member states.

> ## Box 8.3   Implementing the Tobacco Advertising Directive
>
> As outlined in the previous chapters, the Tobacco Advertising Directive saw a long and turbulent history before it was finally adopted in 2003. The transposition deadline was set for 31 July 2005. Germany – already successful in achieving annulment of the first attempt to this Directive – decided to 'try again' and asked the ECJ to review the validity of the directive. Germany argued, in particular, that tobacco advertising in local newspapers should not be subject to EU law as it did not affect trade between EU member states. In December 2006, the ECJ dismissed Germany's challenge, and this ruling led to the Commission becoming active as the guardian of the Treaties, as Germany up until that point had not yet transposed the directive. The infringement procedure went as far as a referral to the ECJ before Germany finally managed to transpose the directive. In the end, with a delay of about two years, all member states managed to transpose the directive. Reporting on the implementation of the Tobacco Advertising Directive in 2008 (European Commission, 2008c, p.4), the Commission even states that 'the tobacco advertising and sponsorship bans in Member States are wider than and/or go beyond the bans laid down in the Directive and apply also to activities at local level, such as advertising in cinemas'.
>
> While reporting positively on transposition, the Commission – in this same report – is more sceptical about the status of enforcement in the member states, arguing that there is a need to streamline monitoring and provide guidance to member states, as well as to develop mechanisms for cross-border enforcement. The main reason for this being that controlling advertising is difficult because wrongdoers can easily relocate themselves.

One should first find out which actors are actually responsible for enforcing the legislation (the regulators) and which actors are required to comply with it (the regulated). Generally speaking, the legislation itself will clearly identify whom it targets, thus providing insight into the nature of the regulated. Although the regulators in a given situation are not always clearly defined, the researcher should try and identify which actors are in general responsible for enforcing the specific policy field in question. When identifying how EU legislation is enforced, the best approach is to actually ask the regulators – through oral interviews or questionnaires, for example – how inspections are arranged, a type of information that is generally not provided on inspectorates' websites. Questions might concentrate on the number of inspectors that enforce a piece of legislation, the amount of time they spend doing so, the style or working method used in the inspections, or the use of sanctions. The same sort of techniques are required to understand how the regulated comply with the EU requirements. Companies will not provide such information on their websites; one needs to ask for it explicitly. Typical questions might centre on who is responsible for compliance, how this is arranged, or how much time is spent on that activity.

Research into practical implementation, by nature, is explorative and qualitative. This does not imply that *small-n* research is the only way to understand practical implementation. Treib (2006) suggested that we need to make more use of *medium-n* comparative qualitative case studies. In order to move towards the generalizability of data, international teams of (PhD) students could be set up to study the enforcement of, and compliance with, diverse EU policy instruments (not only directives), in a wide variety of member states (with a special focus on the new members), and in various policy sectors (not only the environmental and social domain).

Conclusion

Doing implementation research requires different strategies and tactics in different stages. Analyzing transposition requires a different approach compared to analyzing practical implementation. While transposition studies are numerous, the practical implementation to a large extent remains a black box. Currently, EU scholars do not have a complete picture of the working and functioning of the EU policy process at the implementation stage. In order to be able to contribute to the ongoing debate about whether or not the EU suffers from an implementation deficit, with all its consequences for the EU as a legitimate and credible political system, we need further research into the practical implementation of EU policy.

Suggestions for further reading

Hartlapp, M. and Falkner, G. (2009) 'Problems of operationalization and data in EU compliance research', *European Union Politics*, 10(2): 281–304.
Hill, M. and Hupe, P. (2009) *Implementing Public Policy* (Los Angeles: Sage).
Zürn, M. and Joerges, C. (2005) (eds) *Law and Governance in Postnational Europe* (Cambridge: Cambridge University Press).

Relevant websites

EU homepage on the application of Community law, with links to the annual reports by the Commission, the quarterly tables with transposition scores per member state and per sector, and infringement cases: http://ec.europa.eu/community_law/index_en.htm.

For researching single cases on transposition, EUR-LEX: http://eur-lex.europa.eu/en/index.htm.

Chapter 9

Evaluation

Introduction

Looking back over half a century, one might evaluate the 'success' of the EU itself as an integration project by recognizing the emergence of supranational institutions with expanding competences, the pooling of sovereignty by the member states, or the legal or regulatory output of the Commission and the European Court of Justice. Look at the outcomes, in terms of what has actually spilled down to shape the day-to-day of the citizens, such as free movement (the Schengen area), student mobility (the Erasmus programme), free-trade (the internal market), high-speed rail (TGV, Eurostar) that has 'shrunk' space; a single currency (the euro) and its potential psychological impacts on identity; a constitution of sorts (the Lisbon Treaty); and the promotion of things such as citizenship and multilingualism.

It would be particularly difficult to evaluate the EU at large because no targets were set at the beginning – it was a political venture into the unknown. In this sense, it is difficult to judge the European project as a success or failure because integration has occurred organically and extended into areas that few foresaw at the outset. Who could have imagined that pooling coal and steel would have led to all this? In short, without baseline indicators that measure the status quo at the outset, and without targets to work towards being explicitly laid down, it is difficult to assess the degree to which any intervention has contributed to the achievement of any clearly defined goals. Of course from a political perspective one could – and we see that politicians regularly do – make grand claims and sweeping gestures about the success of integration, for example with the 2008 celebrations marking 50 years since the Treaties of Rome, looking back at all that has been achieved.

Terms like 'success' and 'failure' are subjective and value-driven. Even when targets are set down, measurement is often fraught with difficulty, not least given the constraints with which the evaluator is faced: limited financial (and hence, intellectual) resources, problems of access to stakeholders, poor reporting by those implementing, and time pressure. In most cases, there is no black and white, but merely *degrees* or *shades* of success or failure. Actors will undertake their own evaluations and use them to claim success, but often these claims are competing and contradictory. Certain stakeholders may claim policy success or failure by

Table 9.1   *Questions posed* before, during, *and* after *policy evaluation*

Questions for the future ('ex ante')	Questions for the present ('mid-term')	Questions for the past ('ex post')
Will policy be achievable given the constraints of resources, time, and support?	Is policy on course to be carried out as planned?	Was policy carried out on time and within budget?
	Are the limited resources being used effectively?	In which areas were benefits most or least felt?
Will the benefits exceed the costs?	Are the benefits being felt and if so, by whom	Were the goals achieved?
Are the outputs foreseen really worth it?	mostly?	Did policy work and what did it produce? How can it be improved in the future?
	Have the goals been understood by all?	
Are the goals clear?		Should policy continue?
Which is the best alternative in terms of value for money?	What problems can we recognize and why?	

brandishing the results of their latest, highly technical quantitative evaluations, to try to offer conclusive proof of policy success or failure based on complex data modeling. Others may simply base their evaluations on interviews and discussions in order to present a more human account of what happened when 'doing policy'. In reality, most evaluations will mix methods, combining quantitative and qualitative analysis.

In public policy, evaluation is about assessing the processes and consequences of innovations in policy or organizations (Payne and Payne, 2004, p.80). Research is undertaken to assess the *potential worth* (looking forward to future policy) or the *relative success* (looking backwards to implemented policy). Here, evaluation is about how policy 'fared in action'. It assesses the 'effectiveness of public policy in terms of its perceived intentions and results' (Gerston, 1997, p.120). Evaluation has two keys aims: *accountability* and *learning*. In other words, the idea is to justify the validity and worth of the actions taken, and to learn from what went well and what didn't, with a view to improving procedures. Hogwood and Gunn (1984, p.219) justify the need for evaluation: 'If we lived in a world of complete certainty and perfect administration there would be no need for evaluation: having selected the best option and put it into operation we would know in advance what its effects would be. However, we rarely have such certainty. Our understanding of many issues, especially social [and political] problems, is imperfect or even contested. Our understanding of how government intervention will work and what its effect will be is therefore also limited.'

Evaluation usually focuses on a single piece of legislation, operational programme, or individual project, given that these are the bite-sized initiatives through which policy budgets are normally channelled, with the explicit aim of achieving certain policy goals. That is, policies are translated into workable 'courses of action', generally for a fixed duration, and with a projected cost. However, evaluators are interested not only in the policy outputs and impacts, but in taking the policy-making process as an equally valid object of study. While this chapter will not disregard research into political feasibility and 'forward-looking' evaluation (sometimes referred to as 'appraisal'), in line with most academic research, it will concentrate largely on the process of delving into the recent past to examine how policy was experienced, to try to determine relative success or failure (see Table 9.1).

Evaluation in the EU: who is involved and what do we analyze?

Most EU policy will be subject to evaluation, some areas more so than others. Certainly, some policy areas that are characterized by more visible achievements will be easier to evaluate than those in more politically sensitive areas, or where policy does not build or construct anything and it is harder to identify tangible outputs. It may be fairly straightforward to assess the impact of a quota within the EU's fishery policy or the results of an environmental programme by DG Environment to clean up rivers. By contrast, it may be less simple to evaluate a foreign policy mission as part of the CSDP.

Evaluation is fundamental to the EU, given the need for accountability (what is it doing exactly with taxpayer's money?) and measurement of performance (how effective are EU policies really and what is ultimately the value-added?). It is important for institutions in charge of managing and steering policy on a day-to-day basis to be able to justify their performance and their very *raison d'être*. After all, if their policy is not working, why not do away with the institutions, or find other actors who can perform better – such as the member states? It should be borne in mind that many key policy actors, particularly those inside the European Commission, are non-elected, and in this sense there may be great importance placed on justifying the worth of their activities. Programme administrators may be obliged to set loose targets, even though doing so creates risk. If policy performs badly, institutions will have 'shot themselves in the foot', so to speak, by making it easier for evaluators to find fault when targets have not been reached. In such a case, there may be some contention as to whether the measurement techniques were accurate, or if suitably representative data was collected or a wide enough cross-section of stakeholders sampled – a reasonable question to ask, given that where evaluation is voluntary, it is often those with extreme views who most willingly volunteer their opinions, something which may in turn serve to cloud the 'reality' for the majority in the centre of the spectrum.

Evaluation actors

Nearly all policy stakeholders – that is, those with vested interests in policy outcomes – will engage in some form of evaluation, not just before and after, but while policy is being put into effect. This means politicians, bureaucrats, non-governmental actors such as lobbyists and business interests, as well as the public, are all involved in overseeing policy in practice. Each actor engaging in evaluation will have his/her own agenda, so it is worth considering, especially when coming across an evaluation report, the position that a particular institution may have started from when it engaged in an evaluation (what were its motives? is it objective?), the purpose of the evaluation (what were they intending to use it for?), and how comprehensive it was (what were its resources? how, when and by whom was it conducted?)

EU evaluation occurs in many venues, and in both a formal and an informal sense (see Box 9.1). Even public protests outside the Berlaymont and voting (or, indeed, not voting) at EP elections might be considered forms of political evaluation. Opinions are vocalized or registered based on approval or rejection, disengagement or disenchantment (sometimes disgust) of political performance, which is, after all, merely the overall performance of all the government's policies during a certain term in office. Political groupings within the European Parliament and parties at member state level will also keep a close eye on EU institutions, particularly the Commission. Likewise, the Commission will be eager to secure external evaluation to place alongside those evaluations produced by member states. Government and civil society groups may also communicate through focus groups, tasks forces, and consultation exercises.

The Committee of the Regions (CoR) and the European Economic and Social Committee (EESC), as representatives of the regions and key stakeholder groups such as trade unions and business, seek to evaluate and monitor not only policy content, but also the policy-making process – particularly as they have no decision-making powers). For example, in its 80th plenary session on 17–18 June 2009, the CoR published its 'own-initiative opinion' in a White Paper on multilevel governance, with which it launched a general consultation to canvas the views of local and regional authorities, associations, and other stakeholders, calling on them to submit their

Box 9.1 Evaluating EU institutions

Some of the new EU agencies are not permanent bodies, but rather set up with a temporary remit to undertake specific tasks, often to do with implementation. The work of the agency must then be evaluated by the Commission at a mid-point to determine the degree to which the agency is achieving its goals. Unsurprisingly, it is not infrequent for evaluation to recommend an extension of these activities, or even an expansion of resources and tasks. It might be argued that this is an incidence of cultivated spillover, as, here, the Commission's own evaluation recommends strengthening the EU's institutional architecture.

A case in point might be the European Network and Information Security Agency (ENISA), established in order to 'enhance the capability of the Community, the member states and consequently the business community to prevent, address and respond to major network and information security risks'. Created on 14 March 2004, it was initially meant to operate for five years. In Article 25 the ENISA Regulation (460/2004) of the European Parliament and of the Council of 10 March 2004 establishing the European Network and Information Security Agency) the Commission was mandated to evaluate the ongoing work of the agency before March 2007 – in particular, to determine whether its duration should be extended, assess its impact on achieving its objectives and tasks and its working practices, and make any appropriate proposals.

In agreement with the ENISA Management Board, the Commission launched an independent evaluation with an external panel of experts to provide a formative assessment of the Agency's working practices, organization, and remit, as well as making recommendations for improvements, if appropriate. As specified in the terms of reference, the external evaluation took account of the views of all relevant stakeholders. According to a Commission press release of 13 June 2007, the evaluation produced many valuable findings that were critical of both the good functioning of ENISA and its impact on network and information security, in particular regarding the internal market dimension. The Commission largely agreed with the evaluation findings, which were positive in terms of how the Agency was seen to have reflected the original policy goals, even if the evaluation also noted that the Agency's size and the organization of its work at that point was unlikely to be adequate for meeting its future challenges – in effect, both of these findings provided an opportunity to argue in favor of prolonging the life of the agency. Accordingly, Regulation 1007/2008 extended its remit until 13 March 2012.

Source: http://ec.europa.eu/information_society/newsroom/cf/itemdetail.cfm?item_id=3462 – date accessed 10 August 2009.

comments – based on experience – on the best way of implementing multilevel governance in Europe, with the aim presenting a more inclusive vision of the 'Community method' of policy making to the EU institutions.

One should not forget the role of the courts in all of this. The Court of Justice reviews legislative actions to determine whether they respect constitutional principles. In the context of the EU, this means whether they respect the Treaties. Likewise, when money is spent on programme implementation, the European Court of Auditors is very active evaluating procedures and conduct as concerns the spending of the EU budget. It conducts spot-checks on all EU institutions to investigate the eligibility of expenditure and the processes used to account for funds.

Given that the evaluation units in most DGs contain a handful of desk officers, with few real evaluation experts in-house, much Commission evaluation activity is outsourced. It regularly advertises public tenders on its website. Bids are submitted by mixed consortia of academics and experts with specializations either in the policy area, or in conducting evaluation. These groups, competing for the job, put together research proposals outlining the methodology and the approach to use, and, of course, indicating their price. An example is the European Policies Research Centre at Strathclyde University, which houses experts in both cohesion policy and the evaluation of Structural Funds. One of their evaluation projects from 2008–9, in which academics and private consultants collaborated, sought to assess the coherence and added value of EU Cohesion Policy and EU Common Agricultural Policy in terms of sustainable rural and regional development. It drew lessons from experiences on the ground in five countries and identified needs for future policy. Another 2007–8 project evaluated the contribution of regional policy instruments in 2007–2013 to the Lisbon and Gothenburg objectives for growth, jobs, and sustainable development. Some evaluation tenders might even be aimed specifically at developing indicators for use in future policy making, in order to develop the tools to monitor and evaluate programmes and projects more effectively. As the types of actors involved in evaluating EU policy differ so widely across types of evaluations carried out, we have saved much of the description of who is involved in EU evaluation for the next section.

Theoretical perspectives

We can distinguish between three essential categories when discussing theoretical approaches to evaluation and the related academic literature. The types of actors most likely to be involved in these different categories are mentioned in Table 9.2.

Table 9.2   *Types of evaluation*

Evaluation Type	Aim / Focus	Undertaken by
Administrative	Examines efficient delivery, determines value for money (use of budget), the achievement of priorities and goals, managerial performance, respect of democratic procedure	Government (Commission) or by specialized executive agencies, private consultants, think-tanks, banks
Political	Attempts to label a policy as a success or a failure based on preferences and ideology often with calls for termination or change; neither systematic or technically sophisticated, can be biased, impartial	All actors with interests in political life (political lobbies, NGOs, EP groupings, business interests, EESC, CoR)
Judicial	Examines issues related to how programmes are implemented, assesses legality of government action and codes of administrative conduct	Judicial courts (ECJ, ECA)

Source: draws in part on discussion in Howlett and Ramesh, 2003, pp.210–16.

Administrative evaluation

Much of the literature that has been written on the subject has taken policy evaluation as neutral, technical, objective, systematic, and empirical: were targets reached? Were goals achieved? This of course presupposes that such things as targets or goals were explicitly and clearly stated, and remained static throughout the process – largely unrealistic assumptions. The majority of public policy literature and the conceptual frameworks for engaging in policy analysis that have been provided are aimed at practitioners, planners, decision makers, or civil servants – that is, people who either have to appraise the political feasibility of policy alternatives and/or, once decisions have been made and policy implemented, assess how well the programmes have fared in action.

Importantly, such an approach assumes that considerations of *how to evaluate* are made at the outset, and that vague objectives can be seamlessly translated into specific operational goals, which can then be themselves made to correspond to measurable targets. The difficulty is having sufficient baseline data to actually work with and make projections to then be able to evaluate relative 'success', before one even begins to determine how success will actually be judged. In many senses, the degree to which once can *expect* effective evaluation – that is, one that follows a clear, well-designed methodology, establishing early on what will be measured – will largely depend on the design stage. This means evaluation being given due consideration at the policy formulation stage (see Chapter 6).

Monitoring and indicators

Two fundamental ingredients of any effective administrative evaluation are monitoring and indicators. Strict and consistent monitoring is a vital precondition for evaluation at all stages of the policy process, but particularly during implementation. As mentioned earlier, many policies are implemented through programmes and projects. Using qualitative means such as written reports, communications materials, and surveys, it is possible to gauge how policy is experienced by those 'doing policy' on the ground (street-level implementation). Practically, this means tracking whether pre-defined 'actions' have been completed as planned. Using a limited set of quantitative indicators, it is possible to follow and aggregate the delivery of outputs and cumulative total of results over the project lifetime. However, impacts may only be registered in the final stages of project reporting once vital infrastructure is in place or new services are up and running. Monitoring should allow the evaluator to detect general trends and changes in the dynamism or in the trends, patterns, and phenomena that signal the scale and scope of integration.

Reporting during the implementation stage may reveal poorly conceived or limited institutional structures, management weakness, ineffective distribution of internal resources, inappropriate governance systems and reporting methods, blocked communication channels, and a lack of common norms and values. Evaluation may in this way be a useful practice for determining the potential for future learning. By using a system of continuous monitoring, implementation stakeholders such as project managers can provide insights into how the project is being 'felt' on the ground. In short, monitoring is useful for evaluating not merely *after* implementation is complete but *during* the process. At the end of a project, desk officers may reappraise a whole series of implementation reports in order to identify the general strengths and weaknesses of partnership dynamics over time – which obstacles arose and what types of solutions were found (or not) to overcome them?

Comparative and voluntary monitoring

A significant amount of academic research over the course of the last five years has focused on evaluation and monitoring through peer review and the joint surveillance of national policies as one of several activities that takes place within the Open Method of Coordination (OMC), a new pattern of governance based on voluntary policy coordination, rather than that obliged by legislation. Targets and deadlines are signed up to informally. The term emerged in the conclusions of the Lisbon Summit in March 2000, in an attempt to reconcile the legitimacy of the EU's policy-making system with its effectiveness (Radaelli, 2003; Borrás and Jacobsson, 2004; Casey and Gold, 2005; De la Rosa, 2005; Schäfer, 2006). In this sense, a vital part of pursuing the convergence of national policies in EU governance is about effective monitoring. Member states may prefer this to new legislation. An important aspect of this new mode of governance is its capacity to foster learning. As Borrás and Jacobsson (2004, p.195) assert, 'the political expectation of a "mutual learning process" relies on the assumption that coordination will be achieved through changes in national policies conveyed by the explicit political commitment to common goals'. The process should thus trigger a *diffusion of knowledge and experiences*, lead to *persuasion* through peer review and dialogue, encourage the development of common discourse and indicators (knowledge work), and foster repetition and mimicking of best practice. However, the authors wonder if the process isn't more like a beauty contest, whereby member states show off their best policies, rather than showing themselves to be versatile, malleable and willing to absorb new ideas and ways of doing.

Political evaluation and learning

Whereas much of the early literature attempted to develop qualitative systems for policy evaluation, later scholars began to view evaluation as political (Anderson, 1979; Kerr, 1976; Manzer, 1984). Fundamentally, as Howlett and Ramesh (2003, p.218) have pointed out, this means that political conditions can be interpreted quite differently by different political analysts (as we suggested in Chapter 4) and, as such, 'there is no definitive way of determining who is right'. It is much about providing convincing arguments based on suitable data and/or reasoning. Can we really expect then any purely rationalist methodologies in terms of political evaluation? It would seem not. But what we can do is examine the politics of evaluation, that is to say, the focus of our attention may not be the *effectiveness* or *efficiency* of policy (as administrative evaluation might investigate), but rather the evaluation of *conduct* and *culture*, to understand why results did or did not influence successive policy and what the impacts have been on institutions – in terms of learning, structural change, political strategy, and behaviour.

- What has ultimately led to shifts in political power and knowledge?
- How have actors used the information and expertise involved in, and emerging from, the evaluation process to further their own agenda?
- How were results received by the myriad of multi-level stakeholders?
- How can we explain objection and why were recommendations glossed over or ignored?
- Which policy effects were disguised or concealed?
- Was evaluation seen as a threat?

In short, evaluation must be recognized as a political (that is, irrational, biased, partial, unsystematic) exercise. Political scientists should also approach the topic fully aware that while even the task of administrative evaluation may appear to be about refining and improving tools and methods 'for the greater good of policy', in fact, much like what occurs at the agenda-setting stage, it is a 'continuation of the struggle over scarce resources or ideologies'. Policies may well change as a function of the politically driven process of assessing past performance – even if this is not always the case. It may be a case of reading for the politics between or behind the lines (Sanderson, 2002; Howlett and Ramesh, 2003). As far as analyzing evaluation goes, for the researcher, it may be largely a question of *asking questions about the questions evaluators asked*. Which issues were probed? What aspects of policy were enquired about? How were the questions phrased and why? Who were the questions aimed at and why? What were the possible political motivations at play? Which institutions had the most to gain or lose, depending on the outcomes?

Evaluation as learning

As we explained in the introduction to this chapter, it is useful to think of evaluation as being about accountability and learning. As Pressman and Wildavsky (1973) acknowledge, evaluation may produce the most benefits in terms of the education process. Different types of learning can occur – for example about the performance of policy instruments, the extent of public support, the obstacles during implementation, or the articulation of goals. The assumption is that actors actively engaged in policy making will actively learn and their lessons will result in improved policy or processes. Learning also refers to both the intended and unintended consequences of pursuing policy choices (Howlett and Ramesh, 2003). Indeed, one reason why institutions may engage in evaluation is to learn how to do things better. An area of particular interest to political scientists is *learning* (Heclo, 1974; Hall, 1993) and *lesson-drawing* from other policy areas that leads to an inward process of 'policy transfer' (Rose, 1991). Learning has been

Table 9.3   *Types of learning*

Type of learning	Description
Political learning	When policy-makers react to changes around them and what they do to make sure their policies keep up with the new policy environment
Policy-oriented learning	When deep or long-lasting changes in the approach to making policy occur, because of experience built up or altered thinking or beliefs
Lesson-drawing	When policy makers learn from the good and bad experience of others to see what worked and what didn't and adapt their policy accordingly
Social learning	When policy is adjusted based on insight into how previous policy fared and making the most of new information and techniques
Government learning	When governments become generally wiser and better at governing, which improves the effectiveness of the policies they are carrying out

Source: own descriptions drawing on discussions in Bennett and Howlett's classic journal article (1992).

defined as 'a deliberate attempt to adjust the goals or techniques of policy and new information so as to better attain the ultimate objects of governance' (Hall, 1993, p.278) and as a 'a relatively enduring alteration in behavior that results from experience; usually this alteration is conceptualized as a change in response made in reaction to some perceived stimulus' (Heclo, 1974, p.306) (see Table 9.3).

Any analysis of learning should also consider who learns and whether they merely identify mistakes *or* actually learn lessons. Bennett and Howlett (1992, pp.275–94; Howlett and Ramesh, 2003, pp.221–2) distinguish between, on the one hand, 'endogenous' learning, where actors within the policy subsystem, such as those within the institutional apparatus of the EU, learn about policy instruments and adjustments, and, on the other, 'exogenous learning,' where a multitude of actors in the wider 'policy universe' undergo a much more fundamental experience whereby they actually adopt a new perception of the problem or what the goals should be. In some senses, this may imply a complete paradigm shift in terms of approaching the problem, or, indeed, thinking about the result, if external events influence the image or framing of the existing problem that policy is currently trying to tackle. Here, it is useful to think back to Chapter 5 on agenda setting. Hall refers to this more universal and all-encompassing process as 'social learning', for it may actually stem from outside the policy subsystem/process, and derive from major shifts or a sea-change (broad transformations) in socio-political beliefs, such as about the role of the state, public/private ownership, the fairness of redistribution policies, or fashions in global economic policy.

Epistemic communities and expertise

Institutions rely heavily on the policy knowledge and expertise of academic scholars and the research community. The Commission, in particular, by financing research through grants and tenders, such as the 7th Framework Programme, Marie Curie, and the Community Research and Development Information Service, has cultivated an epistemic community (Haas, 1992) – that is, a community of analysts organized within mixed consortia that now account for a large proportion of officially commissioned programme evaluations. These 'communities' (or issue networks) possess policy-relevant knowledge. They usually share a set of causal beliefs and ideas and, as a group, favour certain policy scenarios over others. As we suggested in the case of tobacco legislation, the Commission has encouraged the emergence of interest groups and lobbies, such that in many policy areas it effectively promotes research networks whose evaluation findings may support its policy-making activity.

How to evaluate areas of 'high politics' – always political?

Much of what we have discussed so far in this chapter concerns the political and administrative evaluation of policies that aim at redistribution and regulation. But what about policies in the fields of justice and home affairs (JHA) and common foreign and security policy (CFSP)? How can one pursue evaluation activities in such high-politics areas where there may not even be consensus or support for concerted action? Examples of such areas might be military action in Afghanistan, crisis intervention in Kosovo, or the guarding of the EU's external border in southern Spain.

As Peen Rodt (2008) asserts, essential to any debate of whether the EU is successful in foreign policy is the question of what constitutes success in this new sphere – and the existing literature has yet to agree on anything approaching a shared notion. A theoretical framework in which to evaluate the success rate of CSDP military conflict management missions has yet to be developed. Working towards the development of any analytical framework depends first on agreeing on definitions of 'conflict,' and then distinguishing between conflict 'management', 'prevention,' and 'resolution'. She maintains (ibid., p.4),

Box 9.2 EU foreign policy and crisis management – always an official success?

In term of real-life cases, Emerson and Gross (2007) investigate intervention in the Balkans. Juncos (2007) looks at the EU's first ever 'police mission' back in 2003 in Bosnia and Herzegovina, addressing 'effectiveness' and 'learning by doing'. Ioannides (2007) examines 'effective multilaterlism' and perceptions of success and their link to transparency and information sharing. The authors show that with the rapid growth of CSDP, EU officials have been aware of a continued and important learning process – whereas military operations have benefited from better and more established structures and processes than the civilian crisis-management missions, the latter have shown up the importance of developing capacity and improving human resources through trained personnel, having better procurement procedures. The authors show that certain 'growing pains' exist in doing policy and question whether lessons are always learned and applied. Nonetheless, evaluation shows the practical challenges of coordinating crisis management when attempting to stabilize a region.

Failure? In practice, some argue that the objectives of EU missions may often be formulated so narrowly that it is very hard in fact to fail. The obvious thing that the EU does is 'to contribute to' the stability of a country through its interventions, not necessarily provide stability itself. In the case of Aceh (Indonesian region hit by the tsunami in 2004) the EU was keen simply to 'monitor the security situation on the ground' in the most narrow sense. Human rights were beyond this particular remit. After little over year in the jungle, the Head of Mission (Feith, 2007) claimed it was 'nothing less than a success', yet Schulze (2007), discussing lesson-learning shows that the mission was 'not so impossible' anyway. It may be that the EU is to some extent risk-averse in its choice of missions. Lesson learned, as in many policy areas may largely focus on 'improved coordination'.

But how to measure the success of negotiation, mediation and diplomacy that actually avoids missions and the deployment of troops, and which maintains the peace? The diplomatic aspect of policy is an equally important part that is regularly overlooked. Can we ever adopt a purely technical, administrative evaluation approach when assessing something as politically contentious as EU military intervention? Or will evaluation inherently be a mix of biased political evaluation (ideologically based opinion), coupled with a host of targets and operational objectives on paper, which just give the impression of a systematic means for evaluating success?

'conflicts do not necessarily develop in a linear and logical fashion but indeed often move back and forth between different stages of violence and non-violence'. And what is success exactly? In its most general form, success means 'to reach a favorable or desired outcome' (ibid., p.7) – but according to whom, and to what? (See Box 9.2.)

Success is at the very heart of foreign policy analysis, yet it remains a disputed concept among scholars. Does one evaluate success from the perspective of the policy actor, the target, or according to theoretically defined standards (for example human and minority rights) or principles (for example Just War Theory) (Baldwin, 2000; Pushkina, 2006). In practice, a narrow understanding of success reflecting the interests and intentions of the policy actor alone is often applied. The success criteria are here referred to as internal, because they are articulated by the policy actor itself in its stated policy objectives and implementation plan (Peen Rodt, 2008, p.7).

Thus, whether a policy has been successful might be assessed in terms of whether it has reached its stated objective; in other words, the EU should be judged on its own merits alone. As such, whether an CSDP military conflict management mission is successful depends solely on whether it fulfills its 'mission mandate' as planned. Peen Rodt (2008, pp.7–8) claims that such a definition is problematic: first, it does not allow one to evaluate whether the chosen option was the most 'appropriate' policy option; second, evaluating the EU against the objectives it has set itself means it could be evaluated as being highly successful at attempting to do very little – regardless of the chaos and disarray a mission may leave behind (the absence of failure does not equal success); and third, it does not allow for evaluation of the means by which the policy actor sought to reach its goal. Like Ross and Rothman (1999), Baldwin (2000) and Pushkina (2006), she thus rejects such a narrow internal definition of success.

The alternative is to use external criteria to judge success according to the interests of the target – often associated with so-called 'higher values of peace and justice' – or according to a set of theoretical standards or principles. In fact, many CFSP scholars argue in favour of a combination of the two. Scholars have sought to evaluate different concepts: Ginsberg (2001) has put forward 'impact'; Hill (1993, 1998) has examined a 'capability–expectation-gap'; Allen and Smith (1990) analyze 'presence'; and Bretherton and Vogler (2006) conceive of 'actorness'.

Judicial evaluation

The European Court of Justice (and Court of First Instance, which deals with the majority of cases) will make decisions based on a legal evaluation of the cases brought before them, analyzing the circumstances and deciding whether or not existing legislation (regulations, directives) are in indeed in respect of the Treaty, as well as the consequences for the members states. Any third party – civilian, business concern, or member state – may bring a case to the court, based on a belief that it is prejudicial to its activities or freedoms. Conversely, a third party may be brought to the court by the EU institutions for failure to transpose legislation correctly, usually by a specific deadline. In some cases, the EU institutions have even taken each other to court, an example being the case of EU transport policy. In the 1980s, the European Parliament took the Council of Ministers to the ECJ, accusing it of failure to develop a proper EC transport policy. In 1985, the ECJ indeed found the Council guilty, that is, in breach of its Treaty obligations, ordering that stated commitment and responsibility for such policy be elaborated.

Thus, an area of particular interest for EU political analysis is the degree to which the decisions of EU institutions can actually account for common policy progress (as opposed, for example, to a more intergovernmentalist belief in member state gate-keeping), and to what extent they provide other institutions with room for manoeuvre in promoting change. In the case of transport policy just mentioned, the legal decision by the ECJ created a political space conducive for rapid policy development (see also the example in Box 9.3). This, combined with effective leadership and an entrepreneurial Commission, as well as the wider political consensus supporting the Single Market programme, can together account for policy developments in recent years.

In short, anyone interested in judicial evaluation, rather than developing conceptual frameworks, may be interested in how the EU institutions choose a legal basis on which to ground their new legislation – in other words, how the issue is framed (with the chapter on agenda setting in mind) and the way in which legislation is itself a potential policy instrument for securing political change among a range of alternatives. Which type of legislation should be favoured? Moreover, of further interest, as some scholars claim, is the notion that the jurisprudence of the EU has developed a judicial consensus largely in support of integration *per se*. This means explicitly recognizing that EU law is not only applied but is also largely *interpreted*.

Key issues for consideration

Evaluation design

Even twenty-five years, ago Hogwood and Gunn (1984, p.228) recognized that evaluation literature had become too caught up in how to improve methodologies, to the detriment of reconsidering the pur-

Box 9.3   The Tobacco Advertising Directive: an example of judicial evaluation

In July 1998, the Community enacted Directive 98/43, banning all direct and indirect advertising of tobacco products and sponsorship of events. Member states had until 30 July 2001 to implement it. Germany, the UK, and the Netherlands were – and remain – the EU's principal cigarette manufacturers. Perhaps unsurprisingly, Germany challenged the legality of the Directive, bringing an action before the ECJ to annul it. Were the articles that were used at the time, 100a, 57(2), and 66 of the EC Treaty, proper legal bases for the Directive prohibiting tobacco advertising and sponsorship in the EU? Germany felt that banning tobacco advertising was not an internal market measure, but one designed to protect public health. It also claimed that provisions in the Directive did not contribute to facilitating free movement of goods and services, but actually hindered them.

The ECJ had to engage in *judicial evaluation* of the legality of the legislation in accordance with the Treaty. It questioned whether the Directive aimed to prevent the emergence of future trade obstacles resulting from multifarious development of national laws. The Directive's preamble defined the 'obstacles' as barriers to: (1) the movement of products serving as the media for tobacco advertising and sponsorship; (2) the freedom to provide services in that area; and (3) the removal of distortions of competition. Thus, the Directive would have been properly adopted in light of Articles 100a, 57(2), and 66, if it helped prevent obstacles to the free movement of goods, provision of services, and removal of distortions of competition.

The ECJ overruled the Directive, but indicated the potential validity of legislation with a more limited scope, confined to areas with more obvious trade obstacles. The Court specifically cited banning tobacco advertising in printed products and of the tobacco sponsorship of cross-border events as types of advertising permitted under the EC Treaty. It was not possible to annul the Directive partially, so it was annulled wholly in October 2003. By indicating what *would* be a legally acceptable policy, the ECJ clearly stepped into the seat of policy shaper, or even decision maker, demonstrating again how judicial evaluation can loop back into the 'earlier' stages of the policy process.

Source: Adamini *et al.*, 2010.

poses, practical limitations, and political contexts of evaluation. More recently, Hansen (2005, p.449) asked how evaluation sponsors and evaluators decide how to design evaluations with so many models to choose from, asserting that design should be determined by the purpose of the evaluation, the object of evaluation, and with a specific consideration of the agency or programme in question. Various models focus on different aspects – results (goal-attainment, effects), process, system, economics (cost-efficiency, cost-effectiveness, cost-benefit), and actors (client-oriented, stakeholder, peer review). Methodologies are important, and each one certainly has its own technical pluses and minuses. However, in the final instance, the 'appropriateness' or 'best-fit' should be determined by the fundamental purpose of the exercise: should evaluation imply a quick assessment of short-term impacts in the early stages of policy in order to consider future funding or identify problem areas, or should it require a longitudinal qualitative study *ex post* into impacts on institutional change?

Any research methodology for evaluation must be *valid* – that is, it must be sufficiently consistent to allow for conclusions to be logically drawn, conclusions that can demonstrate a clear link to the original project goals. It must enable one to systematically judge the empirical reality of the impacts of what was implemented (Nagel, 1990, p.430). A second criterion is that it is *important* – research design should allow for an appropriate focus on those issues/impacts, making a substantial contribution to regional integration. Third, research should be *useful* to those requesting the evaluation – it should, as far as possible, be able to speak to their needs. Fourth, research must be *original*, contributing unique insights and identifying hitherto undetected – or at least unmeasured – phenomena. Fifth, evaluation should provide added-value or be *additional* to the wider evaluation activities being carried out across the project, not merely replicate research already being conducted at lower levels. Finally, research should be *feasible* – that is, practical, realistic, and able to deliver given the resources available and the recognized constraints.

The use of indicators opens up a potential minefield, and often even those dealing with them on a regular basis fail to properly distinguish between an output, a result, and an impact. But as mentioned earlier, in many policy areas, such as fisheries, environment, transport, education, and social policy, indicators will be established to structure the evaluation of a policy programme. The policy programme budget will be the main *input*, allowing for the hiring of staff and financing implementation activity. In the first instance, *outputs* may be seminars, meetings, or reports. A logical link should be established between outputs, results, and impacts. Tight definitions are essential to make clear what is being measured and what is not. In general, indicators are useful for gathering quantitative data for aggregation. They might measure increases in length, size or volume, but not necessarily quality, intensity, or strength. As a rule, outputs, results, and impacts sit in a pyramid formation, with many clearly identifiable (project) outputs at the bottom, all of which contribute to fewer (programme) results and with a small number of measurable (policy) impacts at the top.

Table 9.4   *Policy evaluation indicators*

Indicators	In real terms...	Effectiveness	Efficiency
Output	What is built, produced or organized; often what one buys with the money; what is visible or tangible	Actual v. planned output	Output v. cost
Result	How this leads to changes in behaviour, activity, organization, beliefs	Actual v. planned result	Result v. cost
Impact	The overall effect (reduction, increase, improvement) on policy targets/ objectives	Actual v. planned impact	Impact v. cost

Source: inspired by and draws on Ekins and Medhurst's scheme for evaluating Structural Funds (2006, p.487).

Indicators should be SMART (specific, measurable, applicable, relevant, and time-constrained) or TURC (technically sound, understandable, relevant, and cost-effective) (Crawford *et al.*, 2004). A comparison between the actual and planned outputs, results, and impacts, indicates the *effectiveness* of the programme. A comparison between outputs, results and impacts, and the costs (financial inputs) indicates the *efficiency* of the policy program (Ekins and Medhurst (2006, p.486) (see Table 9.4).

Those engaged in administrative evaluation will be interested in *delivery* (cost-effectiveness, timeliness, budget, implementation) and seek to assess the *results* and *impact* of policy programmes using a variety of methods, as described in detail by Hogwood and Gunn (1984, pp.228–34). First, mathematical *modelling* to analyze project outputs is useful from the outset of a project in order to forecast outcomes based on presumed causal relationships. Such models are intricately developed before project implementation, and rest on fixed assumptions calculated by project promoters who must engage in extensive data collection beforehand. These models often fail to assume changes in the external environment. Second, *retrospective cost–benefit analysis* often presumes that all can be counted, but fails to measure intangible, non-quantifiable impacts. It relies on detailed data collection but may only gauge short-term benefits – and, of course, many benefits are derived only after a project ends, just as impacts are felt in the long-term after evaluation activities have ended. Also, aggregated data may not be useful for measuring redistributive projects where geographical impacts are uneven. Third, *mitigation* analyses the set objectives of stakeholders against the positive and negative impacts felt throughout the project cycle, using pre-established monitoring tools. A popular, traditional project evaluation approach is simply a loose, common sense *before-and-after-study*, examining project results after project completion to see how the situation has changed, either since the implementation of the project, or, in the case of several projects having been implemented, since a specific start date. Evaluation often uncovers what would have happened in the project's absence, as opposed to what did happen. In fact, the most commonly adopted approach may be *experimental methods*, relying on surveys, questionnaires, and statistical analysis, to isolate very specific effects of projects. Such evaluation can be time- and cost-intensive, relying on identifying control groups and target samples, but this is precisely what the Commission often pays for when it tenders out evaluation activity as it seeks to find out 'what has gone on out there'.

Evaluators usually produce highly technical reports, accompanied by an executive summary. Research findings are often presented in complex language, which may make it difficult for decision makers to understand the approach, method, or findings. As Hogwood and Gunn (1984, p.238) assert, if findings are to be utilized properly, they need to be communicated in a comprehensible language: 'Such communication must include an indication of the limitations of the findings, whether resulting from conceptual focus, measurement problems, quality of data collected, or method of analysis. Not surprisingly, some evaluators have found it difficult to avoid defending their findings, regardless of the limitations of their research'. In short, though the limitations of the research may give political actors ammunition to place doubt on or even dismiss the findings as inconclusive, it is better to flag them up openly. After all, evaluation as an exercise will never escape politics.

Drawing conclusions

Given that evaluation will never escape politics, we must realize that this particular exercise can be highly contentious. While it is supposedly a technical, objective affair, in fact, as much recent academic research has shown, it is by no means free of politics, and as such, political interference and manipulation – particularly in the EU policy system, where a plethora of actors and institutions are fighting to champion their own agenda and their preferred course of action to remedy problems, as we discussed in Chapter 5 on agenda setting. How those who have requested (and/or importantly, paid for!) evaluation research actually use the results is also highly political. As the British prime minister, Benjamin Disraeli, is famously reported to have once said, 'There are lies, damn lies – and statistics'. Data, measurements, percentages, and figures can all be used in evaluation selectively to highlight or conceal strengths and weaknesses or success or failure, with the aim of convincing key stakeholders and securing preferences for a future course of action (policy re-formulation), perhaps to argue that policy was not sufficiently resourced, or to claim that there were winners but also losers, that latter of whom are now due compensation.

Not everybody will necessarily agree with the findings of official EU reports, especially those conducted on behalf of the Commission. For example, in the field of public services, known in EU jargon as 'services of general economic interest', the Public Services International Research Unit, part of Greenwich University (UK), conducted an evaluation of the European Commission's own 2004 analysis (EC SEC(2004) 866) of public service industries. Their report spoke of 'a devastating critique of EU evaluation', asserting that the Commission 'manipulates results' of research it conducts. It claimed, '[t]he [Commission] report is biased and disregards evidence in its own research that is critical of liberalized public services. The Commission spin doctors the results. Research for the Commission that argues that liberalization of services of general economic interest does not contribute to long-term dynamic efficiency and does not contribute to long-term labor productivity is simply ignored. Findings that clearly link liberalization with a loss of employment are twisted and do not show up. The Commission continues to contravene demands of the European Parliament which has argued for open and transparent debate and independent analysis. The Commission is not capable of considering its own work critically' (Hall, 2005).

From all this, one might conclude that academic analysis of political evaluations can expose bias and uncover the truth. Reading the small print, however, reveals that this 'academic evaluation' of the Commission's evaluation was actually requested by the *European Federation of Public Service Unions*, which represents *more than 200 unions* and 8 million public service workers. Not only might such a large federation be well-financed, but it might also have a political agenda. In short, not only is EU evaluation inherently political, but evaluations themselves are regularly scrutinized and criticized by other vested interests – EU evaluation culture is political and pluralistic, characterized by a variety of organizations willing to pay significant sums of money to finance research that may produce data in support of their political views.

Bearing this in mind, a number of key issues should be considered when seeking to measure impact or cooperation. Evaluation techniques for impact assessment should acknowledge that the long-term and indirect impacts from projects may not be measurable immediately upon project closure. Evaluators in public organizations seeking to assess *effectiveness* may be concerned with environmental impacts, natural

---

Box 9.4 How would one evaluate the success of ERASMUS?

By counting:
the number of students who have taken part
the number of friends and contacts made abroad
the number of mixed nationality marriages that resulted

By recording:
percentage attendance rates of university classes abroad
average exam scores for university exams taken abroad
number of 'contact' or class hours given in foreign language environment

By assessing:
the quality and duration of the friendships made
how each individual's language skills improved
improved understanding of key EU history and jargon
new insights into European culture and traditions
how pro-European each participant became in their political views

By investigating:
how many participants end up working for EU institutions
the total cost of funding all participants with a calculation of the extra EU-GNP generated by their future employment
the financial amount channelled to each EU region and the multiplier effect this student expenditure will have had on the regional economy

---

resource management, biodiversity, literacy, energy efficiency, or human/social capital. Large EU projects, through their life cycle, have many impacts beyond those which can be easily observed or quantified in the short-tem, hence the need to identify tools for measuring and analyzing the broader process across a wider conceptual territory. Longer-term impacts may only be felt after evaluation activities have ceased being financed by private actors. NGOs, public agencies, and universities many be more interested in *longitudinal surveys* and/or *qualitative research* that looks to non-tangible benefits or outcomes that impact upon society, community, and the environment – that is, research that looks not just at the frequency or propensity to use the project outputs, but the changes in attitude, values, and behaviour around the project as a whole. Rather than seeking out macro-economic data to assess financial, technological, and physical change, it may be more realistic to look for indicators of change in firms and institutions, as well as in communities and society, in order to get a *feel* for general change across stakeholder groups or transformation in the regions.

There are surely alternative ways of evaluating the impact of EU policies beyond focusing on the visible, tangible impacts, or engaging in quantitative research (see Box 9.4). What about looking at the changes in attitude or behaviour? Aside from project outputs, it may be useful to examine the partnership itself and the *process* of doing policy. Examining the *human experience* of carrying out EU policy programmes on human and social capital generation and development can be particularly insightful since EU projects often involve an array of actors from different countries, regions, institutions, industrial sectors, and language groups, all with a vested interest in working for successful implementation. There will have been many, often overlooked, impacts upon individuals themselves within the various teams, groups, partnerships and committees. Cooperation might be assessed in terms of its *quality*, *intensity*, *frequency* and *density* of human interaction. The impacts on the group may include increased learning, socialization, awareness, new ways of doing, knowledge transfer, development of trust, empathy and confidence, and incentives for future cooperation. On generating social capital Bourdieu (1986) or Hooghe and Stolle (2003) are useful further reading. Human and social benefits may be evaluated by questionnaire, survey, or interview.

Policy failure?

If a policy is evaluated as being successful, it may continue largely in its existing form. Yet the very culture of evaluation (and the resources involved) means there are expectations that the exercise will flag up 'room for improvement'. Thus, in most cases, recommendations are made for policy to be refined or redirected. According to the textbooks, this process of feedback suggests a loop back to the policy formulation stage. But in some rare cases, policy is deemed to have failed entirely, in which case it is terminated, bringing policy making back as far as the agenda-setting stage (Pierson, 1993; Howlett and Ramesh, 2003). In many ways, any policy feedback will result in incremental adjustment and fine-tuning or 'tweaking', rather than altering the larger structure or organization of the policy area. There is an element of 'path dependency' at play, whereby the way that policy started out largely dictates how it continues; in other words, it is set on a trajectory and becomes 'locked in' (Arthur, 1989). Hence, there is great scope for academic analysis of how we can explain the shape, content, and direction of policy today, in light of successive rounds of policy making.

Conclusion

This fifth policy stage of evaluation brings together consultants, experts, analysts and academics. Sets of actors conduct evaluations on behalf of a variety of multilevel institutions, who compete for their own findings and conclusions to be recognized as authoritative, comprehensive, impartial and reflecting what actually occurred. The goal may be to defend recent performance (or criticize it) and to influence the shape of future policy. Ideally, evaluation should provide feedback and learning, and 'loop back' to the earlier stages of the policy cycle. In short, considerable evaluation may be about learning, be it by policy elites, institutions or the wider policy community. EU scholars and political scientists should be conscious of the politics, financing and culture of evaluation in Brussels. There is great scope to investigate whether national and supranational institutions draw lessons and translate them into better policy, by examining how they collect and interpret data and then use their findings to advance their own interests at the agendasetting and policy-shaping stages.

Suggestions for further reading

Carter, N., Klein, R. and Day, P. (1995) *How organisations measure success – The use of performance indicators in government* (London: Routledge).
Fitzpatrick, J., Christie, C. and Mark, M.M. (2009) *Evaluation in Action. Interviews with expert evaluators* (London: Sage).
Rossi, P.H., Lipsey, M.W. and Freeman, H.E. (2004) *Evaluation. A systematic approach*, 7th edn (London: Sage).

Journal

Evaluation: The International Journal of Theory, Research and Practice was launched in July 1995 and is published by Sage.

Relevant websites

The *European Evaluation Society's* goal is to promote the theory, practice, and utilization of high-quality evaluation, especially, but not exclusively, within the European countries. This goal is obtained by bringing together academics and practitioners from all over Europe and from any professional sector. The society was founded in the Hague in 1994. The first official board was elected in autumn 1995 and started its work in January 1996. http://www.europeanevaluation.org/.

The *University of Strathclyde's European Policies Research Centre (EPRC)* has extensive competence and experience in comparative research on regional problems and policies in Europe and on the evaluation of Structural Funds programmes and projects, as well as a wide range of other regional policy and planning studies. Many evaluation reports can be freely downloaded. http://www.eprc.strath.ac.uk/eprc/publications.cfm.

Think Tank Directory Europe provides a list of organizations monitoring and evaluating EU activity. It is useful to contrast think-tank evaluations with those conducted by universities, member states, EU institutions, and European business federations, not only in terms of their style and methodology, but also in what they ultimately find, conclude, or even recommend. http://www.eu.thinktankdirectory.org/.

Conclusions

Analyzing policy making in the European Union means to examine, scrutinize, assess, and question the very core of what is done in the name of the EU member states. Policy is made not only by political actors at various levels of governance, but also by a pluralistic community of stakeholders, including administrators, bureaucrats, businesses, lobbyists, academics, NGOs, and civil society. The EU makes policy not for policy's sake, but rather as a means to address problems that many of those groups of actors argue require a solution. Thus, Brussels policy making is a creative process, and one that involves options, choices, scenarios, variables, and what-ifs. To choose means to opt for an alternative with implications for the wealth, security, and health of EU citizens. In turn, choices also affect the power, prestige, and influence of those promoting their own policy solutions.

Policy analysis in the EU is essentially about trying to work out how, why, and by whom those alternatives emerged and were then framed, articulated, fleshed out, approved (or rejected), put into action, and fell on the ground. Thereafter, it is about measuring what the chosen alternative achieved, and perhaps, assessing if the evidence suggests it was the right one after all. The other essential ingredient is time. Analysis is needed to reconstruct why policy developments occurred at a particular moment or in a certain sequence relative to developments in other policy domains, and whether they could be considered to have happened slowly or fast.

Analyzing this entire process is an ambitious, even, one might well conclude, foolhardy, task, given the almost endlessly complex web of human interactions and the wealth of communication that will have taken place to influence the shape of policy outcomes. Even a network of flies on the wall of every EU meeting room would not be able to completely reconstruct reality to explain the provenance, evolution, and emergence of policy. Not least because EU policy making is about more than just committees, working groups and summits, or draft proposals and binding legislation. It is about all the interactions that go on in the policy-making environment, including media reporting, mass protests, the signing of petitions, book launches, cocktail parties, and chats down the corridors. It's about formal procedures and debates, which can be traced in minutes, records and agendas. It also concerns that which defies precise recording – that which occurs informally, or behind closed doors: conversations over dinner, opinions expressed in the lift. It's about officially invited audiences, but also about gate-crashing and one-upmanship at high-profile events. It's about flashy PR and glossy public affairs campaigns, but also about the intelligent use of information and expertise to put forward data as fact or incon-venient reality, often subtly, out of the spotlight, from the side-lines.

These features of the contemporary policy-making environment are similar to those taking place in any government centre, be it the national capitals of the member states or the United States. There, as well as in the EU setting, the system continues to face pressure to be more transparent, more accountable, or more legitimate. Political actors are publicly forced to demonstrate and justify their activities. Paradoxically, the relative openness that begins to result as political actors make more and more concessions to transparency on one level, may lead them find new ways to secure access and influence at other levels less susceptible to scrutiny – bringing new sorts of secrecy and opaqueness to the process, and further complicating the task of the policy analyst. Although the EU institutions are making efforts to try to address this problem, it is a contentious characteristic of any policy-making process, and one that reinforces to the idea cultivated by out-siders that the EU is a mysterious, distant, bloated and wasteful, out-of-touch beast.

The distinctiveness of the EU policy process

The EU, like post-war Europe in general, continues to evolve as a polity – its existing institutions in flux, its policies spawning new ones. It might be described as a Byzantine system, involving policy processes that warrant a thousand adjectives: fuzzy, blurry, vague, complex, multi-faceted, opt-outs, comprise. Its outputs are similarly diverse, involving bargaining, negotiation, compromise, consensus, and package deals. EU practices are often referred to as the politics of the lowest common denominator, although with the complex characteris-tics of the EU system in mind, this does not seem entirely justified. The value of the EU, regardless of policy outputs, must be as an entity, the essence of which is the maintenance – and therein the acceptance – of such a process of mutual accommodation and understanding. The implication of all the political soul-searching and cooperation from among 27 member states and all the policy communities that have grown up in Brussels is that things are, so to say, a bit complicated.

A key feature of the EU policy process is its ability to evolve by incremental, step-by-step, gradual shifts through the often highly tech-nical nature of regulatory policy making. It can be complex, often unpredictable, often highly emotional, but rarely is there sudden rupture. Policy making is largely about maintaining an acceptable and workable status quo. In most policy areas, the process is all about fine-tuning or 'tweaking' what has already been in place for several years. However, on some occasions there is a need for a rapid response, and what then emerges may not only be unpredictable in terms of objectives or common position, but in actual results.

The architecture of the *sui generis* (one-of-a-kind and in the making) EU is certainly distinctive. The policy-making environment is a hybrid, something holistic, not just the sum of all the different bit-parts of national political systems. Some may argue that it is a French style bureaucracy with a Germanic corporatist element. At the same time, its architecture has been 'Swedified' through the recent proliferation of agencies. Others may see it as giant rhetorical mouthpiece, analyzing discourse, speeches, policy statements, language, and metaphor, loaded with conditionality, norms, values, and promises.

There is no centre of ultimate power or authority in the EU. The power and effectiveness of all participating actors is bound up with others. There is an element of mutual dependence through the process of *engrenage* or being tied inextricably to each other. And at the same time this linking of national political systems through policy making at the supranational level creates all sorts of possibilities for political actors to use and abuse the two-level game (Putnam, 1988) to justify their actions home or away.

But whatever characterization one deploys, it is clear that the EU policy process involves policy entrepreneurs at many levels and from different walks of life. Commission desk officers, business and industry representatives, parliamentarians, campaigners, civil society and national civil servants are all seeking to advance their ideas. In so doing, they are advancing an agenda: pursuing a strategy that advocates a certain course of action (policy) that will ultimately serve their own interests to increase their power, in terms of money, influence, or knowledge. Most actors in the policy-making environment, not just those in communications and PR, will articulate, frame, and promote their ideas, finding ways to make their solutions palatable or desirable – be it on the grounds of supposed urgency (stressing the imperative for immediate coordinated action), efficiency (low cost), effectiveness (results), or legitimacy (acceptability).

To talk of the EU policy process is in some senses misleading, for one should really talk in the plural – of processes, conscious of the many policy processes going on at any point in time, across the EU institutions. Many are underway, not only pursued by institutional actors across policy domains, but also within a single domain or institution (Young, 2010, p.47). Even inside a Commission Directorate-General, different units of 12–15 policy makers may be formulating different policies and programmes, which should be complimentary. To take the example of transport policy, in DG TREN, clean urban transport is a policy in itself, pursued by its own unit. This part of the organization must work in harmony with, and not contradict, the work of policies (units) on maritime transport, trans-European networks, traffic management, and satellite. As such, there are many policy cycles actually going on within any institution. Each unit with a Commission DG may find its generalist administrators and technical experts to be engaged in discussion, consultation, negotiations, bargaining with representatives from other DGs or EU institutions. They also are in regular contact with lobbyists, who can provide valuable expertise and information on the topic at hand.

EU and member state institutions are not unitary actors. There are numerous 'black boxes' inside the 'black box' of the policy process. Analysis should pay attention to the dynamics not only between but also inside institutions, where power is fragmented and compartmentalized. There may be sets of norms/values/cultures juxtaposed or competing within institutional parts, moulding the way in which policy emerges. Most EU institutions boast marked, often rigid, hierarchies, and display strong path dependency (historical institutionalism). Good analysis is conscious of these intra-institutional power games and rivalries, while recognizing the importance of linkages between institutions through committees, high-level groups, and working groups. This includes not only their (semi-)permanent role in COREPER and during comitology, but temporary, *ad hoc* and extraordinary groups. In short, there is great differentiation in the EU policy process: in the object of study (Single Market, macro-economic, functional, sectoral, external and budgetary policies are all colourful and varied); in the instruments available (regulations and directives, Open Method of Coordination, enhanced cooperation, flexibility); and in the way power is exerted: the use of authority (legal power), treasure (money), nodality (information), and organization (formal institutions).

The constantly changing policy making environment

EU policy is not only shaped by those gathered in Brussels or in national capitals. Increasingly, EU policy is influenced by other polities, international organizations, and regional blocs. Mutual dependencies inherent in global politics and economics have intensified the trans-nationalism and interdependence of policy making worldwide. Moreover, the EU has found that it must tackle global problems such as climate change, drug trafficking, pollution, terrorism, security, and finance, as part of an international community. The financial crisis of 2008–2009 shows how interlinked the EU policy cycle is with the US and the Far East. It also exposes the tensions between EU regulatory activity and national *laissez-faire* attitudes towards the market which have been 'innocent until proven guilty'. The paradox is that this has only strengthened arguments in favour of state control and monitoring of the markets, opening up new areas into which the EU might extend its policy reach.

While the EU has become more complex in the last 60 years since the early days of European integration, policy makers must rethink problems and alternative solutions as part of a much wider policy community. This can make the internal squabbles between supranational actors and member states over the distribution of powers and competences pale into insignificance. In this sense, analyzing EU policy will likely become a more ambitious task in the years to come. The EU policy process is not comparable to the process at member state level, where it is principally 'member governments' who engage in policy making, as Wallace *et al.* (2010) assert. The Lisbon Treaty – which entered into force in December 2009 after more than five years of political headaches and uncertainty – brings new opportunities for both civil society and national parliaments to engage further in this process at the agenda setting and policy formulation stage. It has at least four practical implications for the role of EU institutions in the EU policy process, worth briefly mentioning here.

First, the policy process is likely to become more *efficient*, with the extension of QMV to new policy areas supposedly making decision making faster. Second, the process should be more *stable* given the election of a President of the European Council for two and a half years. Troikas of member states will work together for eighteen-month periods to ensure effective handover. Certain issues may remain on the agenda longer, instead of simply being dropped when one country's presidency ends. The policy cycle should thus become smoother, less jerky and myopic. Third, the policy process should become more *democratic*, with national parliaments more greatly involved in scrutinizing new proposals and the European Parliament strengthened by making co-decision the 'ordinary legislative procedure'. Fourth, existing initiatives such as the voluntary register for lobbies (and think-tanks), but also the introduction of the 'one million signatures' idea to enable citizens to call on the Commission to launch proposals, should make the process more *transparent*.

What are the practical implications of these four optimistic adjectives? First, the extension of QMV might lead to more 'behind-the-scenes' negotiations to secure member state votes from those member states fervently for or against a given proposal. Consider the case of the Tobacco Advertising Directive, with Germany lobbying Spain instead of member states lobbying institutions or lobbyists. Such a scenario would make consensus essential, but might lead to a lower common-denominator politics. Moreover, it may make the policy process less insightful for individual analysts. Second, the new presidential role could lead to greater inter-institutional tensions between the Council and Commission. Already it seems there is ambiguity over responsibilities and tensions between the Council Secretariat and DG RELEX, and between the new post-Lisbon function of Commission President Barroso, High Representative Baroness Ashton, and European Council President Van Rompuy. This observation would imply that political leadership will be vital. If the European Council is to become ever more powerful as an agenda setter, will policy analysts be able to trace when issues emerge? The Treaty may signal a more intergovernmentalist turn and a period of relative emasculation for the Commission. It seems doubtful that the EU is even capable of acting collectively in foreign policy on the world stage – it is telling that six of its twenty-seven member states still refuse to recognize the existence of Kosovo in its own backyard. Perhaps it is this peculiar kind of disparity, even absurdity, that so fascinates certain policy analysts. Third, national parliaments are already overloaded with national legislative processes. The new tasks they have been given with successive Treaty changes may cause them to buckle, actually slowing down the policy process if they are unable to react to subsidiarity requests within deadlines. Fourth, there is the prospect of the Citizens' Initiative becoming practice. One million signatures are actually not that many, and the notion of collecting them may be open to abuse by organized interests. Will all proposals demanded be followed through, or is there a need to police this process? Already it seems that the Committee of the Regions and the European and Economic Committee may be involved in monitoring and filtering activity in this regard. In short, in the wake of the Lisbon Treaty we can expect to see more analysis of the role of national parliaments, the Council and EP, and political leadership mixed with (shaped by) national political cultures.

The Lisbon Treaty is supposedly about reinforcing the EU's norms – reiterating the values of freedom, solidarity, and security, as evidenced, for example, with the introduction of the Charter of Fundamental Rights. These norms will be promoted on the world stage as the EU takes on a single legal personality, develops its new European External Action Service, works to protect energy supplies, and engages with third countries and international organizations (WTO, UN, World Bank, IMF) and regional bodies (Mercosur, Asean, Saarc) to both tackle larger world issues (terrorism, poverty, pollution, drugs, climate change) and to negotiate on trade and financial issues. Global governance is about the EU *vis-à-vis* the rest of the world. Multi-level governance debates must increasingly acknowledge this fourth level above the regional, the national and the supranational level of governance. There might thus be greater potential for analysis of discourse and rhetoric, through speeches and policy documents, and more constructivist explanations of policy integration, but also attention to IR perspectives.

The media is an increasingly relevant actor in shaping public discourse, until now predominantly at the national level. Media will continue to play a hugely significant role in reporting the EU, and in turn, framing issues through text and image story telling. It can potentially play a massive role in furthering transparency and securing greater citizen inclusion, particularly through interactive websites. At the same time, readerships are becoming more fragmented and varied, as citizens use multiple sources to compare and contrast, but still rely heavily on television. It is important to remember that issues ultimately reach the attention of decision makers on the basis of a social construction of reality, whereby it is ultimately the perception that counts. The media is key in this construction, influencing citizens and policy makers, many of whom might find it difficult to fully grasp the technical nature of what is presented – indeed (see Chapter 5), the supposed technical nature of an issue may be used as a smokescreen.

Long-term questions about the EU policy-making process concern enlargement (if and when?) and deeper integration (multi-speed or 'enhanced cooperation'). These developments have obvious implications for the policy process. For example, how to regulate society in an EU of thirty plus members? Also, about instruments: whether or not this is essentially now just about 'fine-tuning' in most internal market areas, or whether there are still areas with a huge scope for common policy making to regulate, harmonize, and establish more uniformity. As for executive activities, one question is whether or not the Commission will be allowed to expand, or if its implementation activity will be increasingly conducted by EU agencies. In the light of their specialist rather than generalist nature, these agencies' contribution to policy shaping and decision making may be set to grow. The advantage of this for member states is the ease by which they can control agency activity through management board supervision. Implied in the way that these configurations develop, in turn, are larger questions of the transparency and visibility of the EU policy process as a whole, as well as the level of insight that will be available to individual analysts.

The usefulness of the policy cycle and its stages

It has been shown in the previous chapters how the policy cycle offers a guiding approach to analyzing the policy process. It provides a model with discrete stages in which different institutions and interests are involved. At each stage, policy analysis essentially means problem solving (Howard, 2005). However, one should not be fooled into thinking that policy making itself can actually be encapsulated in such a systematic and linear fashion. If only it did, analysis would be much simpler! But the European policy process is by no means a straightforward, linear process. While all policy processes demonstrate examples of non-linearity, linkages, overlap, or irrationality, the EU is a very specific case. First, a series of authoritative, highly political choices are made for policy during the decision stage (which itself influences shape and content) where the Parliament and Council seek to exert influence. Then, we witness a great deal of more technical and often incremental but highly complex activity, as the Commission takes charge of further policy formulation activities at the implementation stage, where a whole array of more minor decisions are necessary. There is thus a constant interplay between the stages of formulation, decision making, and implementation at the EU level. As we suggested in Chapter 5, on agenda setting, often solutions exist first and policy makers may end up searching for a problem – that is, policies go looking for an issue. And what to think of comitology? How should this particular EU activity be framed within a policy cycle? When analyzing the activities undertaken by these committees, we could argue for categorizing them as policy shaping, decision making or even implementation. In other words, the order of the stages may actually be reversed, skipped, or show evidence of stalling, braking, and standstill, due to resistance or disagreement.

Using a policy cycle approach suggests a 'process-oriented', often rational or logical model, for something that can be highly irrational, illogical, and value-driven, precisely because it involves politics. The stages within the cycle might be best perceived as 'activity episodes' or 'time-action capsules' (Hogwood and Gunn, 1984), inasmuch as each activity, from agenda setting to evaluating, occurs across a specific period of policy-making time. Certain activities may be drawn out, taking longer than others, while others may be compressed or hurried through. For example, while it might take decades for an issue to make it onto the political agenda, the decision-making process might take just six months. Implementation and evaluation activities will often have their time periods prescribed in the legislation or contractual documents. These activities may well overlap – evaluation of policy in practice (programmes and projects) will occur as policy objectives and priorities are being reformulated (renegotiated) for the future. Likewise, the 'ping-pong' of opinions back and forth between EP and Council will largely shape the ceilings, quotas, and targets that are central to securing a policy's main aims. Interests are at play at every stage, hence the proliferation of lobbies, representations, federations, and watchdogs, all with their ear to the ground, as it were, maintaining firm positions on where they stand on proposed legislation in order to protect and advance their members' financial and political interests. In fact, 'interests' is a rather convenient euphemism for many things dear to the heart of EU businesses – costs/profit, market share, political control, and influence – but also areas that are important for EU citizens – fairness, safety, longevity, justice, quality of life, welfare, opportunity.

It should thus be acknowledged that the stages of the policy process do not in themselves say anything about the dynamics of the policy-making process. If anything, they merely indicate activities and general direction. It is the task of policy analysis to detect those dynamics, based on the frequency and density of policy-making activities, and the expression of preferences by what is normally a highly pluralistic policy community. The history of policy making in particular domains will already give clues about policy-making dynamics, as will its general high/low politics character, the legal base, voting procedures and, of course, the amounts of money (subsidy) that are involved.

Concentrating on a single stage of the policy cycle allows one to zoom in on a particular episode in policy-making time. This can help provide suitable focus and narrow down the scope of a research project. However, no single-stage analysis should ignore the other stages completely – what came before and what happened next are important considerations. It is vital to stand back from the legislation or recent policy development, in order to contextualize policy analysis. Specific developments must be understood in relation to the history of policy integration in the whole domain. EU policy is not encompassed in a single document, but equates to the whole history of decisions and non-decisions that have been taken at the Community level with regard to potential action in a specific policy domain. EU policy analysis must take on board the evolution of the policy field, and contextualize new legislation or developments against a backdrop of other developments, not only in that field, but in other policy areas, in order to understand why policy has come about in the first place.

There is clear path-dependency in policy development. For example, agriculture dominated the agenda for decades after the Treaty of Rome, to the detriment of transport policy, which only got underway after that neglect was recognized by the ECJ. Likewise, recent initiatives to regulate alcohol consumption can only be understood as a corollary to attempts to ban tobacco advertising – a process where the Commission actively stimulated a health lobby in Brussels – but also progress in public health legislation overall. As we have seen in the EU tobacco case described throughout this book, each policy cycle of a legislative proposal will be unique, each with its own twists and turns, some veritable rollercoaster rides for all stakeholders involved (see Table C.1). Policy analysis usually means glancing back in retrospect, and often with some regret. In the tobacco case, the original choice of legal base (internal market) was probably a mistake. This initially affected outcomes but, through a subsequent legal case, ultimately led

Table C.1   *The policy cycle stages and the case of EU tobacco regulation*

Stage of the policy cycle	Key activities associated with stage	What happened in the EU tobacco case?
Agenda setting	Bringing issues, ideas,problems to the attention of policy makers	• was on and off the EU agenda for many years • rose up due to key political personalities (for example, Mitterrand) and the actions of the Commission and the WHO • was framed as causing cancer
Policy shaping	Agreeing on objectives, solutions, identifying alternatives, demands	• Commission promoted a health lobby • resistance from large tobacco companies and certain member states • strategic role played by the EP, accepting the fragile Council compromise; see link decision-making phase
Policy decision	Taking decisions or not, choosing legal or tax-based, voluntary or binding instruments	• strong power play between member states in the Council; deadlock for many years • strategic use by Presidencies (withdrawing the item from the agenda; see link agenda-setting phase) • example of strong brokering / mediation by the Luxembourg Presidency
Implementation	Setting targets, taking agreed action, working to deadlines, imposing sanctions and fines	• a textbook example of transposition being late (more than two years delay), but after the action by the Commission and ECJ, completed • more questions about the status of enforcement and practical implementation
Evaluation	Measurement of inputs, outputs / results / impacts, success / failure, efficiency / effectiveness, learning	• useful example of how judicial evaluation by the ECJ refers the policy cycle back to the policy-shaping and decision-making phases

to a result, where once one might not previously have been possible. In this way, the policy process itself can build momentum for change, strengthen the policy community, and be important for disseminating key messages about the direct links between cause and effect – in this case, smoking and cancer.

In light of what has been said about the dynamics of the policy cycle in the EU, how might we visualize the EU policy making process? Here are six attempts to provide a schematic representation (see Figure C.1). Is it:

1. An arrow going round in a clockwise circle, in five broken lines?
2. Five arrows all proceeding horizontally, from left to right, at different speeds?
3. An arrow coiling and recoiling like telephone wire, in a general forwards direction?
4. An arrow zigzagging down, wide at the top and narrower at the bottom?
5. Many arrows being pinballed around in all directions in a chaotic and random manner?
6. A graph with arrow rising to its apex half-way along the x-axis and then descending?

Doing EU policy analysis: key issues for consideration

This book has introduced a kaleidoscope of theories and research methods that can be embraced in tandems or trios for comparative policy analysis. These might be plucked individually to describe the whole cycle, or the applicability of several compared and contrasted at individual stages. Theories have been drawn from public policy, political science, and International Relations. Most contemporary academic policy analysis examines the lifecycle of new or recent EU legislation. It may be an attempt to retrace interactions between the EU institutions and member states. It can focus on the technocratic nature of multi-level administrative governance and the influence of policy networks and epistemic communities. Theory can provide lenses in research, allowing the analyst to focus on particular actors, features, and phenomena. Theories may also offer valuable building blocks (conceptual frameworks, toolkits) for categorizing and sorting data, interpreting it, and then constructing a convincing, evidence-based case. This can drive home one small point that is valuable in its originality, shed new light on the dynamics of the policy process in that domain, and thus contribute to understanding.

Doing policy analysis means making choices from the outset. It urges the researcher to reconsider options: analysis for/of policy, formal/

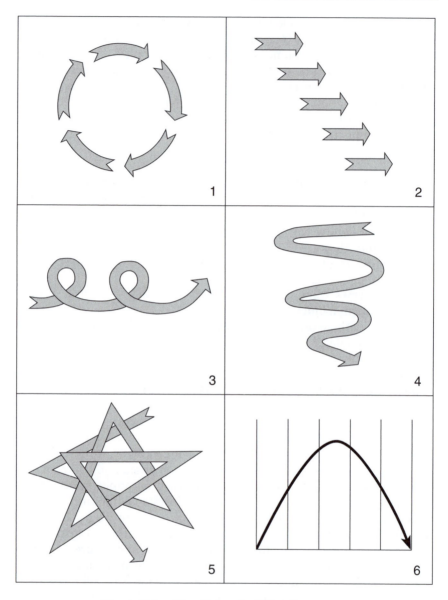

Figure C.1   *Visualizing the EU policy process*

informal, longitudinal/snapshot, rational/constructivist, qualitative/
quantitative, actors/institutions, politics/administration, numbers/
words. These choices determine the analytical approach. For many
analysts, students or professionals, what determines choices is the
limited data initially available (which already tells a 'story so far').
Added to this are individual hunches, gut-feelings, assumptions, and

suspicions, these based on what one has learnt in the past about EU policy making in a particular field or the predictable behaviour of a certain institution. No researcher is a clean slate, but at the same time, few are mediums, able to channel a crystal-clear image of the policy past. Even in the most meticulous, exhaustive research, there will remain grey areas, where there is no black-or-white, clear-cut evidence to prove causality. One must construct an argument using the available, sensible, relevant evidence, just as evaluators of EU policy 'extrapolate' results, 'guesstimating', and projecting results and impacts.

Policy is a big, impressive-sounding, even intimidating word. EU policy is indeed big and impressive, and might well seem intimidating as a result of its technicality and objectives, aimed at fulfilling the lofty ambitions of political actors. However, when it comes down to the actual doing, analysis often focuses on small, incremental developments, changes in long-standing, slowly emerging, integrated policy, particularly in 'low politics', or what were previously first pillar policies. Early on in the process, one will find oneself addressing how issues are articulated, and then how power is exerted. However, much of the time – particularly during implementation and evaluations – policy is effectively operational programmes and projects – the small manageable bite-sized chunks of policy action on the ground, in line with key policy goals.

Drowning in documents, feeling overwhelmed by data, unable to see the wood for the trees: these are experiences that most students or scholars of the EU will have felt at one time or another. Doing EU policy analysis is in itself very much a learning experience. Even the most elaborate research design will have its weaknesses, and gaining original insight into policy developments may mean deviating from plans. Once an interview that one is conducting has begun, it might quickly become clear that the most effective way to proceed is to ignore one's own tightly constructed questionnaire. It is important not to be too rigid or stubborn – going off on tangents and down unexplored avenues can at times be very helpful.

Finally, policy analysis in the EU can have many objectives: to lead to a better understanding of tensions in the EU policy area, the dynamics at play in the EU policy process, or the (in)applicability of the policy cycle and/or its stages. Through the application of theory to an empirical case, it can seek to test that theory with a view to refining it, or even to expose its limitations. It can contribute to the existing literature in a specific field of public policy or European Studies politics by concentrating on the internal dynamics of the policy process, such as the role of committees, or by provoking debate around bigger questions with a political theory dimension, such as the implications of a policy with regards to the supposed democratic deficit of the EU. And although it can concentrate on the thematic content of policy as an output, it is more likely to concern itself with policy making as a process and all the struggles within it.

As Howlett and Ramesh (2003, p.248) assert, 'social [and by extension, political] phenomena are shaped by highly contingent and complex processes, which require an appropriate research methodology to accommodate the uncertainty', thus in some senses 'the mode of analysis [the policy process as a cycle of stages], itself becomes just as a much a subject of analysis and reflection as the object of analysis [here the EU]'. The aim of this book has been to show that analyzing *how the EU policy process is analyzed* can be as vital and potentially rewarding line of enquiry as analyzing the EU policy process itself.

Bibliography

Adamini, S., Versluis, E. and Maarse, H. (2010) 'European policymaking on the tobacco advertising ban: the importance of escape routes', *Health Economics, Policy and Law*, forthcoming.

Alegre, S. and Leaf, M. (2004) 'Mutual Recognition in European Judicial Cooperation: A Step Too Far Too Soon? Case Study – The European Arrest Warrant', *European Law Journal*, 10(2): 200–17.

Allen, D. and Smith, M. (1990) 'Western Europe's presence in the contemporary international arena', *Review of International Studies*, 16(1): 19–37.

Anderson, C.W. (1979) 'The Place of Principles in Policy Analysis', *American Political Science Review*, 73(3): 711–23.

Andersson, J.J. (2006) *Armed and Ready? The EU Battlegroup Concept and the Nordic Battlegroup* (Stockholm: Swedish Institute for European Policy Studies).

Arnull, A. and Wincott, D. (2002) (eds) *Accountability and Legitimacy in the European Union* (Oxford: Oxford University Press).

Arthur, W.B. (1989) 'Competing technologies, Increasing Returns, and Lock-In by Historical Events', *Economic Journal*, 99: 116–31.

Aspinwall, M. and Schneider, G. (2001) *The Rules of Integration – Institutionalist Approaches to the Study of Europe* (Manchester: Manchester University Press).

Baldwin, D. (2000) 'Success and failure in foreign policy', *Annual Review of Political Science,* 3: 167–82.

Bardach, E. (2005) *A Practical Guide for Policy Analysis: The Eightfold Path to More Effective Problem Solving* (Washington, DC: CQ Press).

Baumgartner, F.R. and Jones, B.D. (1993) *Agendas and Instability in American Politics* (Chicago and London: University of Chicago Press).

Beach, D. (2004) 'The unseen hand in treaty reform negotiations: the role and influence of the Council Secretariat', *Journal of European Public Policy*, 11(3): 408–39.

Bechhofer, F. and Paterson, L. (2000) *Principles of Research Design in the Social Sciences* (London: Routledge).

Benford, R.D. and Snow, D.A. (2000) 'Framing Processes and Social Movements: An Overview and Assessment', *Annual Review of Sociology*, 26: 611–39.

Bennett, C.J. and Howlett, M. (1992) 'The lessons of learning: reconciling theories of policy learning and policy change', *Policy Sciences*, 25: 275–94.

Bijsmans, P. and Altides, C. (2007) 'Bridging the gap between EU politics and citizens? The European Commission, national media and EU affairs in the public sphere', *Journal of European Integration*, 29(3): 323–40.

Birkland, T. (2005) *An Introduction to the Policy Process. Theories, Concept, and Models of Public Policy Making* (Armonk, NY: M.E. Sharpe).

Boessen, S. (2008) *The Politics of European Union Health Policy-Making. An Actor-Centred Institutionalist Analysis* (PhD Thesis, Maastricht University).

Borrás, S. and Jacobsson, K. (2004) 'The open method of co-ordination and new governance patterns in the EU', *Journal of European Public Policy*, 11(2): 185–208.

Borrás, S., Koutalakis, C. and Wendler, F. (2007) 'European Agencies and Input Legitimacy: EFSA, EMeA and EPO in the Post-Delegation Phase', *Journal of European Integration*, 29(5): 583–600.

Börzel, T.A. (2002) 'Pace-setting, Foot-dragging and Fence-sitting. Member state responses to Europeanisation', *Journal of Common Market studies*, 40(2): 193–214.

Börzel, T.A. and Risse, T. (2003) 'Conceptualizing the Domestic Impact of Europe', in K. Featherstone and C. Radaelli (eds), *The Politics of Europeanisation* (Oxford: Oxford University Press): 57–82.

Bourdieu, P. (1986) 'The forms of capital', in J. Richardson (ed.), *Handbook of Theory and Research for the Sociology of Education* (New York: Greenwood Press): 241–58.

Bovens, M. (2007) 'New Forms of Accountability and EU Governance', *Comparative European Politics*, 5(1): 104–20.

Braithwaite, J. (1985) *To Punish or Persuade. Enforcement of Coal Mine Safety* (Albany: State University of New York Press).

Bretherton, C. and Vogler, J. (2006) *The European Union as a Global Actor* (London: Routledge).

Bulmer, S. (1983) 'Domestic Politics and European Community Policy-Making', *Journal of Common Market Studies*, 21(4): 349–63.

Burgess, W., Cappier, B., Gore-Both, P. and Zolotas, X. (1960) *A Remodelled Economic Organisation* (Paris: Organisation for European Economic Cooperation).

Burnham, P., Gilland Lutz, K., Grant, W. and Layton-Henry, Z. (2008) *Research Methods in Politics*, 2nd edn (Basingstoke and New York: Palgrave Macmillan).

Casey, B., and Gold, M. (2005) 'Peer Review of Labour Market Programmes in the European Union: What Can Countries Really Learn from One Another?', *Journal of European Public Policy*, 12(1): 23–42.

Chayes, A. and Chayes, A.H. (1993) 'On Compliance', *International Organization*, 47(2): 175–205.

Checkel, J.T. (1998) 'The Constructivist Turn in International Relations Theory', *World Politics*, 50: 324–48.

Checkel, J.T. (2001) 'Why Comply? Social Learning and European Identity Change', *International Organization*, 55(3): 553–88.

Checkel, J.T. and Moravcsik, A. (2001) 'A constructivist research programme in EU studies?', *European Union Politics*, 2(2): 219–49.

Christiansen, T. (2002) 'The role of supranational actors in EU Treaty Reform', *Journal of European Public Policy*, 9(1): 33–53.

Christiansen, T. and Kirchner, E. (2010) (eds) *Committee Governance in the European Union* (Manchester: Manchester University Press).

Cini, M. (1996) *The European Commission. Leadership, organization and culture in the EU administration* (New York: Manchester University Press).

Cobb, R.W. and Elder, C.D. (1972) *Participation in American Politics: The*

Dynamics of Agenda-Building (Baltimore and London: The Johns Hopkins University Press).

Cohen, M.D., March, J.G. and Olsen, J.P. (1972) 'A Garbage Can Model of Organizational Choice', *Administrative Science Quarterly*, 17(1): 1-25.

Compston, H. (2009) *Policy Networks and Policy Change: Putting Policy Network Theory to the Test* (Basingstoke and New York: Palgrave Macmillan).

COPA/COGECA (2000) *Position of COPA and COGECA on the Use of Gene Technology in Agriculture*, Pr(00)06F1/P(00)06F1, Brussels, 21 January.

Corbett, R., Jacobs, F. and Shackleton, M. (2007) *The European Parliament*, 7th edn (London: John Harper).

Cowles, M., Caporaso, J. and Risse, T. (2001) (eds) *Transforming Europe* (Ithaca: Cornell University Press).

Crawford, P., Perryman, J. and Petocz, P. (2004) 'Synthetic Indices: A Method for Evaluating Aid Project Effectiveness', *Evaluation 2004*, 10: 175–92.

Crum, B. (2006) 'Parliamentarization of the CFSP through informal institution-making? The fifth European Parliament and the EU High Representative', *Journal of European Public Policy*, 13(3): 383–401.

Dahl, R. (1961) *Who Governs?* (New Haven, CT: Yale University Press).

De la Rosa, S. (2005) 'The Open Method of Coordination in the New Member States-the Perspectives for its Use as a Tool of Soft Law', *European Law Journal*, 11(5): 618–40.

DeLeon, P. (1999) 'The Missing Link Revisited: Contemporary Implementation Research', *Policy Studies Review*, 16(3/4): 311–38.

Demmke, C. (2001) 'Towards Effective Environmental Regulation: Innovative Approaches in Implementing and Enforcing European Environmental Law and Policy', Jean Monnet Working Paper 5/01, Cambridge: Harvard Law School.

Den Boer, M. and Monar, J. (2002) '11 September and the Challenge of Global Terrorism to the EU as a Security Actor', *Journal of Common Market Studies*, 40(s1): 11–28.

Dinan, D. (2005) *Ever Closer Union? An Introduction to the European Community*, 3rd edn (Basingstoke and New York: Palgrave Macmillan).

Dostal, J.M. (2004) 'Campaigning on Expertise: How the OECD Framed EU Welfare and Labour Market Policies – And Why Success Could Trigger Failure', *Journal of European Public Policy,* 11(3): 440–60.

Downs, G.W. and Trento, A.W. (2004) 'Conceptual Issues Surrounding the Compliance Gap', in E.C. Luck and M.W. Doyle (eds), *International Law and Organization* (New York: Rowman and Littlefield): 19–40.

Duina, F. and Oliver, M.J. (2005) 'National Parliaments in the European Union: Are There Any Benefits to Integration?', *European Law Journal*, 11(2): 172–95.

Duke, S. and Ojanen, H. (2006) 'Bridging internal and external security: Lessons from the European Security and Defence Policy', *Journal of European Integration*, 28(5): 477–94.

Dunn, W.N. (2004) *Public Policy Analysis. An Introduction* (Upper Saddle River, NJ: Pearson).

Dye, T. (1972) *Understanding Public Policy* (Englewood Cliffs, NJ: Prentice-Hall).

Egeberg, M. (2006) (ed.) *Multilevel Union Administration* (Basingstoke and New York: Palgrave Macmillan).

Ekins, P. and Medhurst, J. (2006) 'The European Structural Funds and Sustainable Development: A Methodology and Indicator Framework for Evaluation', *Evaluation*, 12: 474–95.

Emerson, M. and Gross, E. (2007) (eds) *Evaluating the EU's Crisis Missions in the Balkans* (Brussels: Centre for European Policy Studies).

Eulau, H. (1963) *The Behavioral Persuasion in Politics* (New York: Random House).

European Commission (1989) *Proposal for a Council Directive on the Advertising of Tobacco Products in the Press and by Means of Bills and Posters*, COM (89) 163, 18 April 1989.

European Commission (2002) *Life Sciences and Biotechnology – A Strategy for Europe*, COM (2002) 27, 2 March 2002.

European Commission (2004) *A New Partnership for Cohesion: Convergence, Competitiveness, Cohesion*, Third Report on Economic and Social Cohesion, 18 February.

European Commission (2008) *General Report on the EU's Activities* (Brussels: European Commission).

European Commission (2008a) *Eurobarometer 70: Public Opinion in the European Union*. First Results, December 2008.

European Commission (2008b) *25th Annual Report from the Commission on Monitoring the Application of Community Law*, COM (2008) 777 final, 18 November.

European Commission (2008c) *Report on the Implementation of the EU Tobacco Advertising Directive*, COM (2008) 330 final, 28 May.

European Council (1999) *Presidency Conclusions, Tampere, 15 and 16 October*, Europa website.

European Council (2001) Conclusions and Plan of Action of the Extraordinary European Council Meeting on 21 September.

European Parliament (1988) *Official Journal of the European Union*. Annex. Debates of the European Parliament, 1988–9, no. 2–367.

Falkner, G., Hartlapp, M., Leiber, S. and Treib, O. (2004) 'Non-Compliance with EU Directives in the Member States: Opposition through the Backdoor?', *West European Politics*, 27(3): 452–73.

Falkner, G., Hartlapp, M., Leiber, S. and Treib, O. (2005) *Complying with Europe. EU Harmonisation and Soft Law in the Member States* (Cambridge: Cambridge University Press).

Farmer, D.J. (1995) *The Language of Public Administration: Bureaucracy, Modernity and Post-modernity* (Tuscaloosa: University of Alabama Press).

Farrell, H. and Héritier, A. (2005) 'A rationalist/institutionalist explanation of endogenous regional integration', *Journal of European Public Policy*, 12(2): 273–90.

Featherstone, K. and Radaelli, C. (2003) (eds) *The Politics of Europeanisation* (Oxford: Oxford University Press).

Feith, P. (2007) *The Aceh Peace Process: Nothing Less than Success* (Washington, DC: The United States Institute of Peace).

Fischer, E. (2004) 'The European Union in the Age of Accountability', *Oxford Journal of Legal Studies*, 24(3): 495–515.

Follesdal, A. and Hix, S. (2006) 'Why there is a democratic deficit in the EU: a response to Majone and Moravcsik', *Journal of Common Market Studies*, 44(3): 533–62.

Fossum, J.E. and Schlesinger, P. (2007) (eds) *The European Union and the Public Sphere. A Communicative Space in the Making?* (New York: Routledge).

Franklin, M. (2001) 'How Structural Factors Cause Turnout Variations at European Parliament Elections', *European Union Politics*, 2(3): 309–28.

Geradin, D., Muñoz, R. and Petit, N. (2005) (eds) *Regulation through Agencies in the EU: A New Paradigm of European Governance* (Cheltenham: Edward Elgar).

Gersick, C. (1991) 'Revolutionary Change Theories: A Multilevel Exploration of the Punctuated Equilibrium Paradigm', *Academy of Management Review*, 16(1): 10–36.

Gerston, L.N. (1997) *Public Policy Making: Process and Principles* (New York: M E Sharpe).

Ginsberg, R.H. (2001) *The European Union in International Politics: Baptism by Fire* (Lanham, MD: Rowman & Littlefield).

Goggin, M.L. (1986) 'The "too few cases/too many variables" problem in implementation research', *Western Political Quarterly*, 38: 328–47.

Gornitzka, A. and Sverdrup, U. (2008) 'Who Consults? The Configuration of Expert Groups in the European Union', *West European Politics*, 31(4): 725–50.

Graziano, P. and Vink, M.P. (2008) (eds) *Europeanization: New Research Agendas* (Basingstoke and New York: Palgrave Macmillan).

Greenwood, J. (2007) *Interest Representation in the European Union*, 2nd edn (Basingstoke and New York: Palgrave Macmillan).

Greer, S.L. (2008) 'Choosing Paths in European Union Health Services Policy: A Political Analysis of a Critical Juncture', *Journal of European Social Policy*, 18(3): 219–31.

Groenleer, M., Kaeding, M. and Versluis, E. (2010) 'Regulatory Governance through EU Agencies? The Role of the European Agencies for Maritime and Aviation Safety in the Implementation of European Transport Legislation', *Journal of European Public Policy*, 17(8), forthcoming.

Haas, E.B. (1958) *The Uniting of Europe. Political, Social and Economic Forces, 1950–1957* (Stanford: Stanford University Press).

Haas, P. (1992) 'Introduction: Epistemic Communities and International Policy Coordination', *International Organization*, 46(1): 1–35.

Hakim, C. (2000) *Research Design: Successful Designs for Social and Economic Research* (London: Routledge).

Hall, D. (2005) 'Evaluating the impact of liberalisation on public services, a critique of the European Commission 2004 report "Horizontal Evaluation of The Performance of Network Industries Providing Services of General Economic Interest" EC SEC(2004) 866, by David Hall, Director, PSIRU. A report commissioned by EPSU. Paper freely accessible at website of European Federation of Public Services Union (EPSU) at http://www.epsu.org/a/1049; accessed 9 May 2010.

Hall, P.A. (1993) 'Policy Paradigms, Social Learning, and the State: The Case of Economic Policymaking in Britain', *Comparative Politics*, 25(3): 275–96.

Hansen, H.F. (2005) 'Choosing Evaluation Models: A Discussion on Evaluation Design', *Evaluation*, 11: 447–62.

Harding, C. and Swart, B. (1996) (eds) *Enforcing European Community rules: Criminal proceedings, administrative procedures and harmonization* (Aldershot: Dartmouth).

Hawkins, J., Blaine, D., Nielson, D. and Tiernan, T. (2006) *Delegation and Agency in International Organizations* (Cambridge: Cambridge University Press).

Hay, C. (2002) *Political Analysis – A Critical Introduction* (Basingstoke and New York: Palgrave Macmillan).

Hayes-Renshaw, F. and Wallace, H. (2006) *The Council of Ministers* (Basingstoke and New York: Palgrave Macmillan).

Heclo, H. (1972) 'Review article: policy analysis', *British Journal of Political Science*, 2: 83–108.

Heclo, H. (1974) *Modern Social Politics in Britain and Sweden: From Relief to Income Maintenance* (New Haven: Yale University Press).

Heclo, H. (1978) 'Issue networks and the executive establishment', in A. King (ed.), *The New American Political System* (Washington: AEI Press): 87–124.

Héritier, A. (1996) 'The accommodation of diversity in European policy-making and its outcomes: regulatory policy as a patchwork', *Journal of European Public Policy*, 3(2): 149–67.

Héritier, A., Kerwer, D., Knill, C., Lehmkuhl, D., Teutsch, M. and Douillet, A. (2001) *Differential Europe. The European Union Impact on National Policymaking* (Lanham, MD: Rowan & Littlefield).

Hill, C. (1993) 'The Capability-Expectations Gap, or Conceptualizing Europe's Foreign Policy', *Journal of Common Market Studies*, 31(3): 305–28.

Hill, C. (1998) 'Closing the Capability-Expectations Gap', in J. Peterson and H. Sjursen (eds), *A Common Foreign Policy for Europe: Competing Visions of the CFSP* (London, Routledge): 91–107.

Hill, M. (1997) 'Implementation Theory: Yesterday's Issue?', *Policy and Politics*, 25(4): 375–85.

Hill, M. (2009) *The Public Policy Process* (Harlow: Pearson/Longman).

Hill, M. and Hupe, P. (2009) *Implementing Public Policy* (Los Angeles: Sage).

Hindmoor, A. (2006) *Rational Choice* (Basingstoke and New York: Palgrave Macmillan).

Hix, S. (2005) *The Political System of the European Union*, 2nd edn (Basingstoke and New York: Palgrave Macmillan).

Hix, S. (2007) *Democratic Politics in the European Parliament* (Cambridge: Cambridge University Press).

Hix, S., Noury, A. and Roland, R. (2005) 'Power to the Parties: Cohesion and Competition in the European Parliament, 1979–2001', *British Journal of Political Science*, 35(2): 209–34.

Hjern, B. (1982) 'Implementation Research – The Link Gone Missing', *Journal of Public Policy*, 2: 301–8.

Hoffmann, S. (1966) 'Obstinate or Obsolete? The Fate of the Nation State and the Case of Western Europe', *Daedalus*, 95(3): 862–915.

Hogwood, B.W. and Gunn, L.A (1984) *Policy Analysis for the Real World* (Oxford: Oxford University Press).

Hood, C. (1986) *The Tools of Government* (Chatham: Chatham House).

Hood, C. and Margetts, H. (2007) *The Tools of Government in a Digital Age* (Basingstoke and New York: Palgrave Macmillan).

Hooghe, L. and Nugent, N. (2006) 'The Commission's Services', in J. Peterson and M. Shackleton (eds), *The Institutions of the European Union* (Oxford: Oxford University Press): 147–68.

Hooghe, M. and Stolle, D. (2003) (eds) *Generating Social Capital – Civil Society and Institutions in Comparative Perspective* (Basingstoke and New York: Palgrave Macmillan).

Howard, C. (2005) 'The policy cycle: a model of post-Machiavellian decision-making?', *Australian Journal of Public Administration*, 64(3): 3–13.

Howlett, M. and Ramesh, M. (2003) *Studying Public Policy – Policy Cycles and Policy Subsystems* (Oxford: Oxford University Press).

Hutter, B.M. (1989) 'Variations in Regulatory Enforcement Styles', *Law & Policy*, 11: 153–74.

Ioannides, I. (2007) 'Police mission in Macedonia', in M. Emerson and E. Gross (eds), *Evaluating the EU's Crisis Missions in the Balkans* (Brussels: Centre for European Policy Studies): 81–125.

Jeffery, C. (2006) 'Social and Regional Interests', in J. Peterson and M. Shackleton (eds), *The Institutions of the European Union* (Oxford: Oxford University Press): 312–30.

Jenson, J. (2007) 'The European Union's Citizenship Regime. Creating Norms and Building Practices', *Comparative European Politics*, 5: 53–69.

Juncos, A. (2007) 'Police mission in Bosnia and Herzegovina', in M. Emerson, and E. Gross (eds), *Evaluating the EU's Crisis Missions in the Balkans* (Brussels: Centre for European Policy Studies): 46–79.

Kagan, R.A. (1989) 'Editor's Introduction: Understanding Regulatory Enforcement', *Law & Policy*, 11: 89–119.

Kassim, H., Peters, G. and Wright, V. (2000) (eds) *The National Co-ordination of EU Policy: The Domestic Level* (Oxford: Oxford University Press).

Kerber, W., and Eckardt, M. (2007) 'Policy Learning in Europe: The Open Method of Coordination and Laboratory Federalism', *Journal of European Public Policy*, 14(2): 227–47.

Kerr, D.H. (1976) 'The Logic of "Policy" and Successful Policies', *Policy Sciences*, 7(3): 351–63.

Keulen, M. van (2006) *Going Europe or Going Dutch? How the Dutch Government Shapes European Union Policy* (Amsterdam: Amsterdam University Press).

Kiiver, P. (2006) *The National Parliaments in the European Union: A Critical View on EU Constitution-Building* (The Hague: Kluwer Law International).

King, G., Keohane, R.O. and Verba, S. (1994) *Designing Social Enquiry: Scientific Influence in Qualitative Research* (Princeton, NJ: Princeton University Press).

Kingdon, J.W. (2003) *Agendas, Alternatives, and Public Policies*, 2nd edn (New York: HarperCollins College Publishers).

Koremenos, B., Lipson, C. and Snidal, D. (2003) (eds) *The Rational Design of International Institutions* (New York: Cambridge University Press).

Kousser, T. (2004) 'Retrospective voting and strategic behaviour in European Parliament elections', *Electoral Studies*, 23(1): 1–21.

Krotz, U. (2009) 'Momentum and Impediments: Why Europe Won't Emerge as a Full Political Actor on the World Stage Soon', *Journal of Common Market Studies*, 47(3): 555–78.

Kurpas, S., Groen, C. and Kaczynski, P. (2008) *The European Commission after Enlargement: Does Mmore Add Up to Less?* (Brussels: Centre for European Policy Analysis).

Laffan, B. (2006) 'Financial Control. The Court of Auditors and OLAF', in J. Peterson and M. Shackleton (eds), *The Institutions of the European Union* (Oxford: Oxford University Press): 210–28.

Lasswell, H. (1935) *Who Gets What, When and How* (New York: Whittlesey House).

Lavenex, S. (2004) 'EU external governance in "wider Europe"', *Journal of European Public Policy*, 11(4): 680–700.

Leonard, M. (2005) *Why Europe Will Run the 21st Century* (London: Fourth Estate).

Lester, J.P. and Goggin, M.L. (1998) 'Back to the Future: The Rediscovery of Implementation Studies', *Policy Currents*, 8(3): 1–9.

Lewis, J. (2003) 'Integration and construction of the Council', *Journal of European Public Policy*, 10(6): 996–1019.

Lijphart, A. (1971) 'Comparative Politics and the Comparative Method', *American Political Science Review*, 65(3): 682–93.

Lindberg, L.N. (1963) *The Political Dynamics of European Economic Integration* (Stanford: Stanford University Press).

Lindstrom, G. (2007) *Enter the EU Battlegroups*, Chaillot Paper No. 97 (Paris: Institute for Security Studies).

Lipset, S.M. (1960) *Political Man* (New York: Doubleday).

Lipsky, M. (1980) *Street-Level Bureaucracy* (New York: Russell Sage Foundation).

Luck, E.C. and Doyle, M.W. (2004) (eds) *International Law and Organization* (New York: Rowman & Littlefield).

Luo, C.-M, (2008) 'Interpreting the Blair Government's Policy-making on European Monetary Union: An Examination of Public Policy Theories', *Journal of Contemporary European Studies*, 16(3): 443–8.

Majone, G. (1994) 'The rise of the regulatory state in Europe', *West European Politics* 14(3): 77–101.

Majone, G. (1996) *Regulating Europe* (London: Routledge).

Majone, G. (2000) 'The Credibility Crisis of Community Regulation', *Journal of Common Market Studies*, 38(2): 273–302.

Manzer, R. (1984) 'Policy Rationality and Policy Analysis: The Problem of the Choice of Criteria for Decision-Making', in O.P. Dwivedi (ed.), *Public Policy and Administrative Studies* (Guelph: University of Guelph).

March, J. and Olsen, E. (2005) 'Elaborating the 'new institutionalism'', *Arena Working Papers*, no. 5 (Oslo: Arena).

Marks, G., Hooghe, L. and Blank, K. (1996) 'State-centric versus Multi-level Governance', *Journal of Common Market Studies*, 34(3): 343–78.

Mastenbroek, E. (2005) 'EU Compliance: Still a 'Black Hole'?', *Journal of European Public Policy*, 12(6): 1103–20.

Mastenbroek, E. and Kaeding, M. (2006) 'Europeanization Beyond the Goodness of Fit: Domestic Politics in the Forefront', *Comparative European Politics*, 4(4): 331–54.

Mattila, M. and Lane, J-E. (2001) 'Why unanimity in the Council? A roll call analysis of Council voting', *European Union Politics*, 2(1): 31–52.

Mazmanian, D. and Sabatier, P.A. (1981) (eds) *Effective Policy Implementation* (Lexington, Mass.: Lexington Books).

McNamara, K. (2006) 'Managing the Euro', in J. Peterson and M. Shackleton (eds), *The Institutions of the European Union* (Oxford: Oxford University Press): 169–89.

Meier, K.J. (1999) 'Are We Sure Lasswell Did It This Way? Lester Goggin and Implementation Research', *Policy Currents*, 9(1): 5–8.

Meter, D.S. van and Horn, C.E. van (1975) 'The Policy Implementation Process: A Conceptual Framework', *Administration and Society*, 6(4): 445–88.

Moran, M. (2002) 'Review article: understanding the regulatory state', *British Journal of Political Science*, 32: 391–413.

Moravcsik, A. (1993) 'Preferences and Power in the European Community: a Liberal Intergovernmentalist Approach', *Journal of Common Market Studies*, 31(4): 473–523.

Moravcsik, A. (1999) *The Choice for Europe: Social Purpose and State Power from Rome to Maastricht* (London: UCL Press).

Nagel, S.S. (1990) 'Conflicting Evaluations of Policy Studies', in N.B. Lynn and A. Wildavsky (eds), *Public Administration: The State of the Discipline* (Chatham, NJ: Chatham House).

Neyer, J. and Zürn, M. (2001) 'Compliance in comparative perspective. The EU and other international institutions', *IIS-Arbeitspapier*, no. 23/01, Universität Bremen.

Nugent, N. (2010) *The Government and Politics of the European Union*, 7th edn (Basingstoke and New York: Palgrave Macmillan).

O'Toole, L.J. (2004) 'The theory–practice issue in policy implementation research', *Public Administration*, 82(2): 309–29.

Parsons, W. (1995) *Public Policy: An Introduction to the Theory and Practice of Policy Analysis* (Cheltenham: Edward Elgar).

Payne, G and Payne, J. (2004) *Key Concepts in Social Research* (London: Sage).

Peen Rodt, A. (2008) 'Defining and evaluating success in European Union military conflict management', conference paper presented at ISA 2008.

Peters, B. G. (2000) 'The Commission and Implementation in the European Union: Is There an Implementation Deficit and Why?', in N. Nugent (ed.), *At the Heart of the Union: Studies of the European Commission* (Basingstoke and New York: Palgrave Macmillan): 190–205.

Peters, B.G. (2010) *Comparative Politics: Theory and Methods*, 2nd edn (Basingstoke and New York: Palgrave Macmillan).

Peterson, J. (2005) 'Policy networks and European Union policy making: a reply to Kassim', *West European Politics*, 18(2): 389–407.

Peterson, J. (2006) 'The College of Commissioners', in J. Peterson and M. Shackleton (eds), *The Institutions of the European Union* (Oxford: Oxford University Press): 81–103.

Peterson, J. and Bomberg, E. (1999) *Decision-Making in the European Union* (Basingstoke and New York: Palgrave Macmillan).

Pierson, P. (1993) 'When Effect Becomes Cause: Policy Feedback and Political Change', *World Politics*, 45: 594–628.

Pierson, P. (1996) 'The path to integration: a historical institutionalist analysis', *Comparative Political Studies*, 29(2): 123–63.

Plachta, M. (2003) 'European Arrest Warrant: Revolution in Extradition?', *European Journal of Crime, Criminal Law and Criminal Justice*, 11(2): 178–94.

Pollitt, C. and Bouckaert, G. (2000) *Public Management Reform: A Comparative Analysis* (Oxford: Oxford University Press).

Pressman, J. L. and Wildavsky, A.B. (1973) *Implementation: How Great Expectations in Washington are Dashed in Oakland* (Berkeley, CA: University of California Press).

Princen, S. (2002) *EU Regulation and Transatlantic Trade* (The Hague: Kluwer Law International).

Princen, S. (2009) *Agenda-Setting in the European Union* (Basingstoke and New York: Palgrave Macmillan).

Princen, S. and Rhinard, M. (2006) 'Crashing and Creeping: Agenda-Setting Dynamics in the European Union', *Journal of European Public Policy*, 13(7): 1119–32.

Pushkina, D. (2006) 'A recipe for success? Ingredients of a successful peace-keeping mission', *International Peacekeeping*, 13(2): 133–49.

Putnam, R.D. (1988) 'Diplomacy and Domestic Politics: The Logic of Two-Level Games', *International Organization*, 42(3): 427–60.

Radaelli, C. (2003) 'The Open Method of Coordination: A New Governance Architecture for the European Union?', SIEPS Reports, No. 1.

Rochefort, D.A. and Cobb, R.W. (1994) (eds) *The Politics of Problem Definition. Shaping the Policy Agenda* (Lawrence, KS: University Press of Kansas).

Roemer, R., Taylor, A. and Lariviere, J. (2005) 'Origins of the WHO Framework Convention on Tobacco Control', *American Journal of Public Health*, 95(6): 936–8.

Rosamond, B. (2000) *Theories of European Integration* (Basingstoke and New York: Palgrave Macmillan).

Rose, R. (1991) 'What is Lesson-Drawing?', *Journal of Public Policy*, 11(1): 3–33.

Ross, G. (1995) *Jacques Delors and European Integration* (New York: Polity Press).

Ross, M. H. and Rothman, J. (1999) *Theory and Practice in Ethnic Conflict Management: Theorizing Success and Failure* (Basingstoke and New York: Palgrave Macmillan).

Saetren, H. (2005) 'Facts and Myths about Research on Public Policy Implementation: Out-of-Fashion, Allegedly Dead, But Still Very Much Alive and Relevant', *Policy Studies Journal*, 33(4): 559–82.

Salmon, T. (2005) 'The European Security and Defence Policy: Built on Rocks or Sand?', *European Foreign Affairs Review*, 10(3): 359–79.

Sanderson, I. (2002) 'Evaluation, Policy Learning and Evidence-Based Policy-Making', *Public Administration*, 80(1): 1–22

Sandholz, W. and Stone Sweet, A. (1998) *European Integration and Supranational Governance* (Oxford: Oxford University Press).

Sandholtz, W. and Zysman, J. (1998) '1992: Recasting the European Bargain', *World Politics*, 42(1): 95–128.

Schäfer, A. (2006) 'Resolving Deadlock: Why International Organisations Introduce Soft Law', *European Law Journal*, 12(2): 194–208.

Scharpf, F.W. (1996) 'Negative and Positive Integration in the Political Economy of European Welfare States', in. G. Marks, F.W. Scharpf, P. Schmitter and W. Streeck (eds), *Governance in the European Union*, (London: Sage): 15–39.

Scharpf, F.W. (1997a) *Games Real Actors Play: Actor-Centered Institutionalism in Policy Research* (Oxford: Westview Press).

Scharpf, F.W. (1997b) 'Introduction: The Problem-Solving Capacity of Multi-Level Governance', *Journal of European Public Policy*, 4(4): 520–38.

Scharpf, F.W. (1999) *Governing in Europe: Effective and Democratic?* (Oxford: Oxford University Press).

Schattschneider, E.E. (1960) *The Semi-Sovereign People. A Realist's View of Democracy in America* (New York: Holt, Rinehart & Winston).

Schendelen, M.C.P.M. van (2006) *Machiavelli in Brussels: The Art of Lobbying the EU* (Amsterdam: Amsterdam University Press).

Schneider, G. (1991) *Time, Planning and Policy-Making: An Evaluation of a Complex Relationship* (New York: Peter Lang Publishers).

Schön, D.A. and Rein, M. (1994) *Frame Reflection: Toward the Resolution of Intractable Policy Controversies* (New York: Basic Books).

Schulze, K. (2007) *Mission Not so Impossible: The Aceh Monitoring Mission and Lessons Learned for the EU* (Berlin: Friedrich Ebert Stiftung).

Scully, R.M. (2005) 'Rational institutionalism and liberal intergovernmentalism', in M. Cini and A.K. Bourne (eds), *Palgrave Advances in European Union Studies* (New York: Routledge): 19–34.

Shackleton, M. (2006) 'The European Parliament', in J. Peterson and M. Shackleton (eds), *The Institutions of the European Union* (Oxford: Oxford University Press): 104–24.

Siedentopf, H. and Ziller, J. (1988) (eds) *Making European Policies Work. The Implementation of Community Legislation in the Member States. Volume I, Comparative Syntheses* (London: Sage).

Sinclair, T.A.P. (2001) 'Implementation theory and practice: uncovering policy and administration linkages in the 1990s', *International Journal of Public Administration*, 24(1): 77–94.

Smith, M. (2004) 'Between two worlds? The European Union, the United States and world order', *International Politics*, 41(1): 95–117.

Snidal, D. (2002) 'Rational choice and international relations', in W. Carlnaes, B. Simmons and T. Risse (eds), *Handbook of International Relations* (New York: Sage): 73–94.

Sverdup, U. (2005) 'Implementation and European Integration: a review essay', ARENA working paper no. 25 (Oslo: Arena Centre for European Studies).

Sverdrup, U. (2006) 'Administering Information: Eurostat and Statistical Information', in M. Egeberg (ed.), *Multilevel Union Administration* (Basingstoke and New York: Palgrave Macmillan).

Tallberg, J. (2003) 'The agenda-shaping powers of the EU Council Presidency', *Journal of European Public Policy*, 10(1): 1–19.

Thygesen, N. (2008) 'Comparative Aspects of Peer Reviews: OECD, IMF and European Union', in K. Tanaka (ed.), *Shaping Policy Reform and Peer*

Review in Southeast Asia. Integrating Economies amid Diversity (Paris: OECD Publishing).

Treib, O. (2006) 'Implementing and complying with EU governance outputs', *Living Review European Governance*, No. 1.

Trondal, J. and Veggeland, F. (2003) 'Access, voice and loyalty, the representation of domestic civil servants in EU committees', *Journal of European Public Policy*, 10(1): 59–77.

Underdal, A. (1998) 'Explaining Compliance and Defection: Three Models', *European Journal of International Relations*, 4(1): 5–30.

UNHCR (2007) *Asylum in the European Union: A Study of the Implementation of the Qualification Directive* (Brussels: UNHCR).

Versluis, E. (2003) *Enforcement Matters: Enforcement and Compliance of European Directives in Four Member States* (Delft: Eburon).

Versluis, E. (2007) 'Even Rules, Uneven Practices: Opening the "Black Box" of EU Law in Action', *West European Politics*, 30(1): 50–67.

Vink, M.P. and De Groot, G.R. (2010) 'Citizenship attribution across Europe: International framework and domestic trends', *Journal of Ethnic and Migration Studies*, 36(5).

Vogel, D. (1986) *National Styles of Regulation: Environmental Policy in Great Britain and the United States* (Ithaca: Cornell University Press).

Wallace, H., Pollack, M.A. and Young, A.R. (2010) (eds) *Policy-Making in the European Union*, 6th edn (Oxford: Oxford University Press).

Wendt, A. (1992) 'Anarchy is what states make of it: the social construction of power politics', *International Organization*, 46(2): 391–425.

Werts, J. (2008) *The European Council* (London: John Harper).

Wessels, W. (1997) 'An Ever Closer Fusion. A Dynamic Macropolitical View on Integration Processes', *Journal of Common Market Studies*, 35(2): 267–99.

Wessels, W. (1998) 'Comitology: fusion in action. Politico-administrative trends in the EU system', *Journal of European Public Policy*, 5(2): 209–34.

Winter, S. (1999) 'New Directions for Implementation Research', *Policy Currents*, 8(4): 1–5.

Young, A.R. (2010) 'The European Policy Process in Comparative Perspective', in H. Wallace, M.A. Pollack and A.R. Young (eds), *Policy-Making in the European Union* (Oxford: Oxford University Press): 45–68.

Zürn, M. and Checkel, J.T. (2005) 'Getting socialized to build bridges: constructivism and rationalism, Europe and the nation-state', *International Organization*, 59(4): 1045–79.

Index